LETTER TO AN IMAGINARY FRIEND

LETTER TO AN IMAGINARY FRIEND

by Thomas McGrath

COPPER CANYON PRESS

The publication of this book was supported by grants
from the Eric Mathieu King Fund of the Academy
of American Poets, The Lannan Foundation, the
National Endowment for the Arts, and the Washington
State Arts Commission. Additional support was
received from David Bottoms, Elliott Bay Book Co.,
Mimi Gardner Gates, James Laughlin, David and Jan
Lee, William Merchant and Alice Pease, Carlyn and
George Steiner, and the many members who joined
the Friends of Copper Canyon Press campaign.

LIBRARY OF CONGRESS CATALOGING-IN-PUBLICATION DATA

McGrath, Thomas, 1916–1990
    Letter to an imaginary friend. Parts 1–4 / Thomas McGrath.
      p. cm.
    ISBN 1-55659-077-6 (CLOTH) / ISBN 978-1-55659-078-8 (PBK.)
    I. Title.
PS3525.A24234L4   1997
811'.54 — DC21   97-33929

COPPER CANYON PRESS
P.O BOX 271, PORT TOWNSEND, WASHINGTON 98368

This book is for Thomas McGrath Jr.:

And for all of us
Together
A little while
On the road through.

PREFACE

In 1953, at the height of the McCarthy Era, the House Committee on Un-American Activities began an investigation of "communist activities in the motion picture and educational fields in Los Angeles." Among those called to testify was a thirty-six-year-old Rhodes Scholar, poet and World War Two veteran, Thomas McGrath, then working as a teacher at Los Angeles State College. Taking the seat of dishonor at the American Inquisition, the poet studied the faces of his inquisitors, folded his hands in his lap, and stated in a strong clear voice, "As a poet I must refuse to cooperate with the committee on what I can only call æsthetic grounds. The view of life which we receive through the great works of art is a privileged one – it is a view of life according to probability or necessity, not subject to the chance and accident of our real world and therefore in a sense truer than the life we see lived all around us." He would also observe, "When I was notified to appear here, my first instinct was simply to refuse to answer Committee questions out of personal principle and on the grounds of the rights of man and let it go at that." He cited the First, Fourth, and Fifth Amendments to the Constitution, amendments routinely ignored by the Committee.

McGrath was blacklisted then, not exactly for his lifelong affiliation with socialist causes during the greatest expansion of what President Dwight Eisenhower termed, in a famous warning to the electorate, "the military-industrial complex," but rather because of his convictions about the very nature of poetry.

"Of course the Muse doesn't let one quit, the grand old bitch."

Five years later, McGrath wrote his friend E.P. Thompson, "Since the Committee got my teaching job, I've been working at several things, mostly very tiring and dull – and also bad paying. A very hard period. I wrote a long poem – about 150 pages – last year…" What he had written was Part One of what would, thirty years later, become the four-part *Letter to an Imaginary Friend*. He had begun his poem, inspired in part by having been blacklisted, and working as a casual laborer or semiskilled worker in furniture and ceramics. "Now, in the chill streets / I hear the hunting, the long thunder of money."

Letter to an Imaginary Friend is, above all else, a grand work of memory and recovery. "The work of the poem," he often said, "is to *create* a past in order to *rescue* the future that has been stolen from us." And if his political situation was a primary motivation, his struggle with Catholicism in particular and institutionalized religion in general nonetheless engaged him in serious explorations of native religions and iconography that eventually brought him to study cave art and its subsequent traditions, having been, he often said, "an atheist since age thirteen, and militantly antireligious."

In "A Note on Parts Three & Four" of *Letter*, he wrote, "There are some strange names early in Section I of Part Three. These are simply the names, according to medieval occultists, for first the powers of the cardinal directions (Cham is North, Amoyman South, etc.), then of 'the infernal kings of the north,' then (Azael, etc.) of the four elements, then of the great powers which I associate with the 'tetragrammaton' and the Kachina (of which more in a moment). These powers are ambiguous, and, from a Judeo-Christian-Catholic prejudice, demonic.

"The old Biblical myth," he points out, "gives Adam (and offspring) 'dominion' over Nature. But to have it, the pagan deities had to be demonized or destroyed. Then we had power over the world; it became 'dead nature' – so-and-so-many board feet, and so-and-so-much profit and loss. One project of the poem is to 'angelize' these (and other) demons. That means to return us to a view which all primitives, anyone who has spent time in the woods, or anyone simply in his/her right mind has always had: that Nature is just as alive as we are. Probably there is an equation there."

Commenting on his use of the Hopi Kachina doll as an emblem, he writes, "For the Hopi it is a 'God' – a deified spirit of great power. According to the Hopi we now live in *Tuwaqachi,* the Fourth World, but we will soon enter *Saquasohuh,* the Fifth World, which will be much better. This new world will be signaled by the appearance of a blue star. Kachinas are also doll figures which are made to symbolize spirit powers. The Blue Star Kachina will help these spirits to bring the new world into being. I see this as a revolutionary act to create a revolutionary society. All of us should help to make this Kachina. I think of the making of my poem as such a social-revolutionary action. In a small way, the poem *is* the Kachina."

It is no small irony that Thomas McGrath, alienated and sent into a kind of forced interior exile by a corrupt power structure in which the capitalist state is mirrored by institutionalized religion – and what is McCarthyism if not religious fervor applied to social policy? – should turn to an icon drawn from Native Americans, the first and perhaps greatest victims of the American institutionalization of greed. Like a good Taoist in search of "the power of virtue," he finds the greatest emblem of revolutionary power among the least politically influential. "Demons" and "angels" are emblems to an atheist, certainly not facts. If part of his work was to "angelicize" certain "demonic" practices, it was not only in the service of truth – and McGrath staked his life and his livelihood on his convictions – but in the service of ultimate communion. To humanize and contemporize the Kachina is to undo the "demonization of the Redskin," and to see with fresh eyes the vast North American landscape which our European founders viewed as "the Devil's country" and as "a dark continent populated by Savages." The myth of the nation, like the myth of Adam, sets us apart from Nature as well as from kinship with suffering humanity. The work of the poem, like that of all great poetry, is to expand consciousness.

The poem plays across the screen of the imagination structured like a movie, including flashbacks and flash-forwards, and at times certain confluences of time and place occur, the narrator sometimes speaking as an adult, sometimes as a child. At the end of Part Four, the little Lisbon of North Dakota and the city in Portugal where part of the poem was written become one place in the mind. Through juxtaposition and shifting scenes and narrative-within-narrative, McGrath allowed his vast erudition and unrivaled lyrical intensity to carry the poem. If it is a good idea to have on hand a reliable dictionary when enjoying *Letter to an Imaginary Friend,* that is only another reason among so many that make this an epic to live with over time. McGrath's wordplay, including a great fondness for the interlingual or intercultural pun, is just another expression of his irrepressible joy in the life and work at hand.

Born on a North Dakota farm in 1916, Thomas McGrath died in Minneapolis in 1990 without having seen the publication of a definitive edition of his epic. Special thanks are due to Dale Jacobson for his invaluable research on the manuscript, especially Parts One and Two, and for writing the afterword. Thanks are also due to Michael Wiegers for his close reading of the whole manuscript. No doubt the poet would delight in the circularity of our enterprise: Jacobson and I being old (younger) friends of the poet known to one another only through the work, and Wiegers representing to McGrath another new generation of readers. In its basic six-beat line, the poem circles back on us, continuing the poet's great round dance, continuing it out in ever-expanding circles.

– *Sam Hamill*

NOTE ON THE TEXT

Many errors exist in Parts One and Two *of Letter to an Imaginary Friend* in the Swallow editions. The first Swallow edition (1962) of Part One contains the same errors as the expanded 1970 edition, indicating no corrections by the author or the publisher. The 1985 edition of Parts Three and Four published by Copper Canyon Press exists mostly as it should as a result of close work between Sam Hamill and the author, although some small inconsistencies have been eliminated.

I depended upon three sources for corrections: for Part One, a hand-written draft, the only extant manuscript according to McGrath himself; for Part Two, two typed drafts, both containing (sometimes contradictory) corrections by the poet. Martin McGrath, the poet's brother, Abigail Potvin Jensen, his secretary, and I, all expended a significant effort to secure these sources along with other papers at the University of North Dakota. However, despite appeals from all of us, the University, suffering as Tom might say from being too far above the battle, refused to suspend difficult bureaucratic policies to facilitate my efforts. I recommend that papers relating to Tom McGrath be donated to the McGrath collection at North Dakota State University in Fargo, where I have already agreed to contribute what I hold.

This sort of task is a lot less mechanical than some might believe, though certainly tedious enough to accomplish carefully. It was an invaluable aid that McGrath considered me as close as a brother for two decades. I became familiar with his working methods and habits, his personality and thinking, his reading, and of course his poetry itself. The hand-written draft of Part One was composed hurriedly and sometimes the poet's intention would not become clear until several days or more of careful consideration, when clarity resulted from both deliberation and intuitive insight. Part One was particularly difficult because McGrath's handwriting was not always entirely decipherable. As well, since he was impatient with mechanical details and sometimes reckless with spelling and punctuation, there arose the question of what he actually intended. In such cases, as much as possible, I looked for consistencies where I was sure the evidence did in fact represent what he intended. I also consulted other poems or interviews where evidence might be found. Discrepancies in spelling or punctuation that were clearly not intended for poetic purposes, I converted to the convention, with careful consideration for his love of puns and japeries. There were a few occasions where McGrath had mentioned personally to me a change he wished he had made, and so I took direction from what he had said.

– Dale Jacobson

PART ONE

Whenever I see my Friend I speak to him;
but the expecter, the man with the ears,
is not he. They will complain too that you
are hard. O ye that would have the cocoanut
wrong side outwards, when next I weep
I will let you know.

      – *Thoreau*

In the moonlight,
The shadow of the bamboo
Is sweeping the great stairs;
But the dust is not stirred.

        – *Senzaki*

I

1.   – "From here it is necessary to ship all bodies east."
I am in Los Angeles, at 2714 Marsh Street,
Writing, rolling east with the earth, drifting toward Scorpio,
thinking,
Hoping toward laughter and indifference.
"They came through the passes,
         they crossed the dark mountains in a month of snow,
Finding the plain, the bitter water,
the iron rivers of the black North.
Horsemen,
Hunters of the hornless deer in the high plateaus of that country,
They traveled the cold year, died in the stone desert."

Aye, long ago. A long journey ago,
Most of it lost in the dark, in a ruck of tourists,
In the night of the compass, companioned by tame wolves, plagued
By theories, flies, visions, by the anthropophagi…

I do not know what end that journey was toward.
– But I am its end. I am where I have been and where
I am going. The journeying destination – at least that…
But far from the laughter.
So. Writing:
"The melt of the pig pointed to early spring.
The tossed bones augured an easy crossing.

North, said the mossy fur of the high pines.
West, said the colored stone at the sulphur pool."

2.   – And at the age of five ran away from home.
(I have never been back. Never left.) I was going perhaps
Toward the woods, toward a sound of water – called by what bird?
Leaving the ark-tight farm in its blue and mortgaged weather
To sail the want-all seas of my five dead summers
Past the dark ammonia-and-horse-piss smelling barn
And the barnyard dust, adrift in the turkey wind
Or pocked with the guinea-print and staggering script
Of the drunken-sailor ducks, a secret language; leaving
Also my skippering Irish father, landlocked Sinbad,
With his head in a song-bag and his feet stuck solid
On the quack-grass-roofed and rusting poop deck of the north forty,
In the alien corn: the feathery, bearded, and all-fathering wheat.

Leaving my mother, too, with her kindness and cookies,
The whispering, ginghamy, prayers – impossible pigeons –
Whickering into the camphor-and-cookie-crumb dark toward
God in the clothes closet.
                 Damp comforts.
                      Tears

Harder than nails.
A mint of loving laughter.

How could I leave them?
I took them with me, though I went alone
Into the Christmas dark of the woods and down
The whistling slope of the coulee, past the Indian graves
Alive and flickering with the gopher light.

3.   – Dry runs and practice journeys through the earthquake weather
Of the interior summer…

                                        the singing services
And ceremony cheerful as a harness bell.
– Bright flags and fictions of those hyacinthine hours
Stain and sustain me past the hell of this mumming time
Toward the high wake I would hold:

                              No ghost, but O ill and older
Than other autumns when I ran the calico lanes
Past sleepy summer, gone, and the late west light
Downfallen. Lost. Autumn of distant voices, half heard,
Calling.

                    Rain. Gunfire. Crows. Mist, far, woods.

Farther than winter birds in the most gaunt tree
Snapped in the frost, I was; or went. Was free, and haunted
By the reeling plunge of the high hawk down – down! O down
Where the curving rabbit lunged and was slapped with a sharp and killing
Heel.
There, in the still postsolstice dark, among
Rococo snow, the harp-shaped drifts and the ghost-marked trees of the season

I went all ways…
– Spring came; the first cold rainstorms, dropping
Their electric hardware in the bright-work of the snow.
Then, the leather seasons by, and my bundling times,
My eye sustained the cowbird and the crow,
Their feather terms…
                    Then horny Summer come…
                                        – And Autumn growing
In the west steep wrestling light and the rain-rung rheumy wind in the rag-headed woods…

❊   ❊   ❊   ❊   ❊

Way stations on the underground journey; the boy running, running…
– Search for Lough Derg, or the holy waters of the Cheyenne,
Or the calf-deep Maple. Running away
I had the pleasure of their company…

4.   Took them? They came –
        Past the barn, Cape Wrath, Oxford and Fifth and Main
        Laughing and mourning, snug in the two-seater buggy,
        Jouncing and bouncing on the gumbo roads
        Or slogging loblolly in the bottom lands –
        My seven-tongued family.
        How could I escape? Strapped on the truckle bars
        Of the bucking red-ball freights or riding the blinds cold
        Or sick and sea-sawed on the seven seas
        Or in metal and altitude, drilling the high blue

I fled.
I heard them laughing at the oarsmen's bench.
Conched in cowcatchers, they rambled at my side.
The seat of the buggy was wider than Texas
And slung to the axles were my rowdy cousins;
Riding the whippletrees: aunts, uncles, brothers,
Second cousins, great aunts, friends and neighbors
All holus-bolus, piss-proud, all sugar-and-shit,
A goddamned gallimaufry of ancestors.
The high passes?
Hunter of the hornless deer?

5.   A flickering of gopher light. The Indian graves…
       And then the river.
                            Companioned, and alone,
       Five, ten, or twenty, I followed the coulee hills
       Into the dreaming green of the river shade,
       The fish-stinking cow-dunged dark of the cattle crossing,
       The fox-barking, timber-wolf country, where…
       The cicada was sawing down the afternoon:
       Upstream a beaver was spanking Nature:
       The cows were wilder:
       Horses carnivorous.

       The kittycorner river cut through the buggy
       Through Dachau and Thaelmann
       Rolfe in Spain

Through the placid, woodchuck-coughing afternoon
Drifting
Past Greenwich, Baton Rouge, Sheldon, Rome
And past Red Hook and Mobile where the rivers mourn,
Old Thames, Missouri, Rio Hondo. Now
In far Los Angeles I hear
The Flying Dutchman in the dry river
Mourning. Mourning.
Ancestral night....

❋   ❋   ❋   ❋   ❋

Passages of the dark; streets with no known turning
Beyond the sleepy midnight and the metaphysical summer
Leading here. Here. Here, queerly here.
To the east slant light of the underground moon, and the rusty garden
Empty.
        Bounded by ghosts.
                        Empty except for footnotes
Of journeying far friends near.

                        Enter now,
O bird on the green branch of the dying tree, singing
Sing me toward home:
Toward the deep past and inalienable loss:
Toward the gone stranger carrying my name
In the possible future
                        – enter now:

Purlieus and stamping grounds of the hungering people
O enter

"They died in the stone desert
They crossed the dark mountains in the month of snow.
Finding the plain, the bitter water, the iron rivers of the black North."
Horns on the freeway. Footsteps of strangers,
Angelinos: visitations in the metropolitan night.

"Hunters of the hornless deer."

Ancestral baggage....

II

1.　Great God Almighty, but the troubles of the stinking street!
First Neighbor on strike since Come Monday, and Second
Neighbor on strike Come Tuesday.

　　　　　　　　　　　　　　　　　Eggs are dearer,

Bread has entered Marsh Street's realm of value,
And shuffling past Salsipuede Avenue
The age of education comes round the corner…

　　　I was born under an evil star in the black cloud of Lusath,
　　　Under the early sign of apocalyptic fire…
　　　I live in the distant present, endless indomitable potlatch
　　　Of journeying
　　　　　　　　　　　far
　　　　　　　　　　　　　　　hungering
　　　Ghosts;
　　　Amidst collapsing empires of irreversible
　　　Talk…Second Kingdoms and Ming Dynasties of ad hoc
　　　Exempla: kinked-up argument, a-temporal colloquies armed and dreamy,
　　　Unstable and wild as confederations of Sioux…

2.　And I hear the pad of feet to the union hall –
But that is New York (17th Street): Showboat Quinn
Goes by barefoot: fanfare of baseball bats –

They are whacking the seamen like mamba gourds down Hudson.
And elsewhere old Mister Peets is saying "Eeyah! He's the man!"–
Listening to Morrison blasting dead Huey Long
As the moon spins over Baton Rouge in the freezing Christmas,
And the waterworks crackle.

                          Plumber Peets cocks an ear,
As the pipes burst like shrapnel and the citizens, crazed,
Unshaven, their bladders bursting, bray at the moon.
At the moon and Peets, who sits at the radio, high
As a coon in a tree, near the rasping gas-fire, sucking
His sugar-tit pipe and his politics.

                             The Phony War
Sings in the streets.

              Jimmy plays football.

                          Warren,
Pinched and poor-favored as a parson's luck,
Carrying his future – that North Sea grave – like a mile
Of invisible water, comes by…

      Now, down in these flats, the imagined city dreams
      In its fiery cages…

              Cacodemons and Agathodemons

                            struggling in the pit,
And, in the heavens, the endless feuds and follies of the blazing far stars:
Ancestral vendettas.

                 Among whom I was born,
Among the flat fields, flat stores, and the bombed-flat burning towns
Under the sign of our degenerate fire…

Christ! but it's cold.

My garden bears in its tide the wreckage of summer flowers.

In the south forty the flax is flat with the rust…

3.   The bare feet pad in the street.

                     "Eayah!" says the plumber,

"Them cotton-pickin', possum-eatin', mammy-jammers *got* to go!"

His ear is cocked, while half of Baton Rouge

Pisses in the freezing street.

                     Peets is toasting his pinkies,

Sending his nine-foot wife for a jug of gin,

Listening.

           Will He win? Will O.K. Allen, will

Morrison win?

                  Anarcho-solipsist contraventions…

Under the hysteria of the tide-containing moon

The burghers rage. (They are hanging fresh sides of beef

in the frost-bound dachas of their morning-rooms,

Davening to Peets)…

And Quinn goes by in the street (Seventeenth) and my neighbors

Are striking on Marsh in that future where Warren is dead

And my brother dead…

     The flowers rust in my garden, pointing

Toward farthest Autumn.

The flax is flat

In the freezing heat.

And the plumber
("The folded arms of the workers," says Warren)
Pulls at his aural tether…

4.   Out of imperfect confusion, to argue a purer chaos…
I've lived, truly, in a Custer's Massacre of sad sacks
Who sang in my ear their histories and my own.
And out of these ghosts I bring these harvest dead
Into the light of speech…
Where now the citizens dream in a sleep of fire –
No more than a mountain breath, pulse-beat of rock –
Toward this distant present, in this nightjourney where all –

Borne beyond Libra
Southward
Borne toward the Gulf, the whole shooting match of these times
In the hiss and jostle of the Mississippi
The living and the dead
To the revolving graves and the glass pastures of the fined-down diamond-cutting Sea.

III

1.   Out of the whirring lamp-hung dusk my mother calls.
From the lank pastures of my sleep I turn and climb,
From the leathery dark where the bats work, from the coasting
High all-winter all-weather Christmas hills of my sleep.
And there is my grandfather chewing his goatee,
Prancing about like a horse. And the drone and whir from the fields
Where the thresher mourns and showers on the morning stillness
A bright fistful of whistles.

The water-monkey is late, the straw-monkey
Is late and the bundle-stiffs are late and my grandfather dances
In the yellowy kerosene smell of the morning lamps where my mother
Brightens a dish on her apron and feeds the stove,
Its iron, round, crackling mouth and throat full of bristling flame,
Gold in the five o'clock morning night.
Dances and raves. A worker has broken his wrist;
The machine is whistling its brass-tongued rage and the jackbooted weathers of autumn
Hiss and sing in the North.
The rains are coming, and the end of the world
Is coming.
                            My grandfather dances.
I am slowly fed into my B.V.D.s while the still-dark day
Assumes the structure of my nine-year world,
And the whistle hoots.

"You'll be the straw-monkey. Can ye do it boy?"
My grandfather capers about while I assemble my parts
And my mother fusses. Is the job too hard?
"Ach, woman, the chiselur's tall as a weed!
He's not to be spike-pitchin', a whistle-punk only –
A breeze of a job and he'll sit in the shade on his bum
The day long."
                    She pets me and cooks:
Bacon and eggs and the bitter, denatured coffee
Of man's estate. While my grandfather stamps and grumbles
And my brothers tumble from sleep into the kitchen,
Questioning. Owl-eyed and envious.

A kiss and a hug. A piece of pie in my pocket
For love and luck.
                              Then, in a jingle of trace chains,
The martingale's chatter and squeak of straps in their keepers,
I drove the big roan team through the gray of the chill morning,
My mother waving.
                    Goodbye.
And the kids staring, still sleepy,
Myself proud and scared and the echo of sleep still strong
In my veins. (The reins I'd looped round my hips so the fast-stepping team
Half pulled me, stiff-legged, and tacking about like a boat
In their dusty wake.)
                              Ahead my grandfather's buggy
Bounced down the coulee hill, up the opposite slope
Toward the threshing machine and its whistling brass commandments,
The barb-tongued golden barley and the tents of the biblical wheat,

Frontiers of sweat and legendary field
Of manhood.

Behind me my mother called. Something I could not hear.
The kids stood solemn.
                                        Still in the weather of childhood.
Waved.
                Throwing kisses.
                                        Waved my hand in return.
So long.
So long.
So long.

2.   Blind. Out of the labyrinthine sleep
        Of childhood I entered the brilliant alien arena
        Blind in the harsh light.
                                        Entered too soon, too young,
        Bobbing along on the lines, dragged by a team of roans,
        (Whose names *should* have been Poverty and Pride)
        Into the world of men at the age of nine.

        This was no ritual visit; no summer foray,
        Scouting party or cookout in the Big Horn country
        With the ridge-pole pine singing my honor and the streams full of fish and fancy,
        The light-fall valorous and God-creatures taller than tales
        To teach me camp-craft, to put a crimp in the nightmare,
        To fan my six gun.

Oh, I know that ten-sleep camp where the ticking Dechard rifle
Dozes by the banker's son, the half-real shooting gallery
Of the Dream Range where redskin and deer ride by
On an endless belt and the bear pop up, pop down,
In front of the painted scene of lake and mountain,
Where prizes are always given...
                                        Aloft on the shaking deck,
Half-blind and deafened in the roaring dust,
On the heaving back of the thresher,
My neck blistered by sun and the flying chaff, my clothes
Shot full of thistles and beards, a gospel itch,
Like a small St. Stephen, I turned the wheel of the blower
Loading the straw-rack.
The whistle snapped at my heels: in a keening blizzard
Of sand-burrs, barley-beards and beggar's-lice, in a red thunder
Where the wheat rust bellowed up in a stormy cloud
From the knife-flashing feeder,
I turned the wheel.
Far from Tom Swift, and farther
From Troop Nine, the cabin they built on the river.

3.   The rites of passage toward a stranger's country,
        The secret language foreign as a beard...

        I turned in machine-made circles: first from the screaming red
        Weather where the straw stack grew and the rattling thresher mourned;
        Then to the rocking engine where the flywheel flashed and labored

And the drivebelt waxed and waned, the splices clapped at its cross
Ebbing and flowing, slack or taut as the spikers
Dropped the bivouacked wheat in the feeder's revolving throat.

Feathered in steam like a great tormented beast
The engine roared and laughed, dreamed and complained,
And the petcocks dripped and sizzled; and under its fiery gut
Stalactites formed from the handhold's rheumy slobbers.
– Mane of sparks, metallic spike of its voice,
The mile-long bacony crackle of burning grease!
There the engineer sat, on the high drivers,
Aloof as a God. Filthy. A hunk of waste
Clutched in one gauntleted hand, in the other the oilcan
Beaked and long-necked as some exotic bird;
Wreathed in smoke, in the clatter of loose eccentrics.
And the water-monkey, back from the green quiet of the river
With a full tank, was rolling a brown quirly,
(A high school boy) hunkered in the dripping shade
Of the water tender, in the tall talk and acrid sweat
Of the circle of spitting stiffs whose cloud-topped bundle-racks
Waited their turns at the feeder.
And the fireman: goggled, shirtless, a flashing three-tined fork,
Its handle charred, stuck through the shiny metallic
Lip of the engine, into the flaming, smoky
Firebox of its heart.
Myself: straw-monkey. Jester at court.

So, dawn to dusk, dark to dark, hurried
From the booming furious brume of the thresher's back

To the antipodean panting engine. Caught in the first
Circle.

Was it hard? I don't know. It was terrifying.
The whistle snapped and I ran. The thresher moaned on its glut.
The Danaëan rain of the wheat rained down.
Hard? No. Everyone wanted to help me.
My father, riding the grain tanks from the field
To the town elevators, starting out in the chilly dawn
And home at the cold midnight, eating when time allowed,
Doing the work of a threshing hand and the chores of the farm to boot,
Harnessing the team I was too short to harness,
Helping me pick up a load when he got back from town
In the jolting musical empty grain tank.
                                    He had boils that summer,
His neck was circled with ruby light, I remember.
Poulticed with heated bottles.
My mother helped. I had cookies stuffed in my pocket,
Ginger…
Their crumbly sweetness.
                                    Worrying:
"Jim, is it too hard?
The boy's tired as a horse."
My grandfather too,
After the first week, when they found a man,
Came prancing and dancing, pulling his thin beard:
"Kate, let the boy be quitting.
It's hard, long hours. Let him quit."
My father came in the dark

(Where I'd gone into sleep, into the open flaming
Mouth of the dream, the whistle biting my ears,
The night vibrating,
In the fog of the red rust, steam, the rattle of concaves)
Came about midnight.
His last chore done, he led me into the bright
Kitchen. (The table was already set for breakfast;
The potatoes were sliced; the pie, crosscut; a cloth
Fenced out the flies.)
Then, his supper, we ate ice cream and cheese;
Sardines; crackers; tomatoes still wet with the night
Out of the garden; cucumbers crisp and salty
Cooled in the water trough; bacon and watermelon
Left over from supper.
"Tom, Old Timer," he'd say. "Ain't you had enough?
This workin' won't get you nowheres. Let the job go.
We got a man for her now."
But I couldn't. No way to quit.
My hand was stuck to the plough and I cried to stay.
(As at morning, with the sleep stuck in my eyes and my morning breakfast
Dead in my stomach I cried for the day to be gone.)

I couldn't quit. I came out of sleep at four
Dazed and dreaming and ate my food on the run,
And ran to the barn; the roan team knelt and dozed;
I clapped the harness on them and kicked them awake
And rode the off one, galloping, into the field
Where the engine slept in its heat.
The fireman grunted. He struck a match to his fork.

The crackling fireball, thrust to the metal heart,
Ignited the still dark day.

Sometimes, at night, after a long move to another farm,
Hours after the bundle-teams were gone and sleeping,
After we'd set the rig for the next day,
I rode the off horse home.
Midnight, maybe, the dogs of the strange farms
Barking behind me, the river shortcut rustling
With its dark and secret life and the deep pools warm.
(I swam there once in the dead of night while the team
Nuzzled the black water.)
Home then. Dead beat.

To quit was impossible once you had started.
All you could do was somehow learn the ropes.
No one could teach you.
When you were late the whistle
Blasted you into the kingly estate
Of the daylight man. Responsibility. The hot foundries
Of the will.
                    But when, your load up, you squatted
In the spitting circle of stiffs, in the hot shade
Under the sky-piled bundle-racks waiting their turn at the feeder,
Chewing on rose apples and bumming a smoke –
You were no man there.
A man to the engine's hunger, to the lash of the whistle,
But not to the tough young punks from Detroit or Chicago
Drifting the tide of the harvest the first time

And jealous of manhood.
                                        Not to the old stiffs,
Smoke shooters, their bindles weighted with dust
From Kansas to Calgary.
                                        Not to your uncle surely,
Boss of the rig who slapped you once when you swore,
Before the ritual was known or the language of men.

O great port of the Dream! Gate to the fearful country,
So near and magically far, what key will open?
Their alien smell, their talk, their foreign hungers,
And something awful, secret: I saw them, lost,
Borne on the fearful stream in a sinful valor
And longed to enter. To know. To burn in that fire.

4.   My father took me as far as he could that summer,
      Those midnights, mostly, back from his long haul.
      But mostly Cal, one of the bundle teamsters,
      My sun-blackened Virgil of the spitting circle,
      Led me from depth to depth.
                                        Toward the light
      I was too young to enter.
      He must have been about thirty. As thin as a post,
      As tough as whang-leather, with a brick-topped mulish face,
      A quiet talker. He read *The Industrial Worker,*
      Though I didn't know what the paper was at the time.
      The last of the real Wobs – that, too, I didn't know,

Couldn't.

                              Played a harmonica; sat after supper
In the lantern smell and late bat-whickering dusk,
Playing mumblety-peg and talked of wages and hours
At the bunkhouse door. On Sunday cleaned his gun,
A Colt .38 that he let me shoot at a hawk –
It jumped in my hand and my whole arm tingled with shock.

A quiet man with the smell of the road on him,
The smell of far places. Romantic as all of the stiffs
Were romantic to me and my cousins,
Stick-in-the-mud burgesses of boyhood's country.

What he tried to teach me was how to take my time,
Not to be impatient, not to shy at the fences,
Not to push on the reins, not to baulk nor pull leather.
Tried to teach me when to laugh and when to be serious,
When to laugh at the serious, be serious in my laughter,
To laugh at myself and be serious with myself.
He wanted me to grow without growing too fast for myself.
A good teacher, a brother.

5.   That was the year, too, of the labor troubles on the rigs –
      The first, or the last maybe. I heard the talk.
      It was dull. Then, one day – windy –
      We were threshing flax I remember, toward the end of the run –
      After quarter-time I think – the slant light falling

Into the blackened stubble that shut like a fan toward the headland –
The strike started then. Why *then* I don't know.
Cal spoke for the men and my uncle cursed him.
I remember that ugly sound, like some animal cry touching me
Deep and cold, and I ran toward them
And the fighting started.
My uncle punched him. I heard the breaking crunch
Of his teeth going and the blood leaped out of his mouth
Over his neck and shirt – I heard their gruntings and strainings
Like love at night or men working hard together,
And heard the meaty thumpings, like beating a grain sack
As my uncle punched his body – I remember the dust
Jumped from his shirt.
He fell in the blackened stubble
Rose
Was smashed in the face
Stumbled up
Fell
Rose
Lay on his side in the harsh long slanting sun
And the blood ran out of his mouth and onto his shoulder.

Then I heard the quiet and that I was crying –
They had shut down the engine.
                            The last of the bundle-teams
Was coming in at a gallop.
                                    Crying and cursing
Yelled at the crew: "Can't you jump the son-of-a-bitch!
Cal! Cal! Get up!"

But he didn't get up.

None of them moved.

Raging at my uncle I ran.

Got slapped,

Ran sobbing straight to the engine.

I don't know what I intended. To start the thing maybe,

To run her straight down the belt and into the feeder

Like a vast iron bundle.

I jammed the drive lever over, lashed back on the throttle,

And the drive belt popped and jumped and the thresher groaned,

The beaters grabbed at the air, the knives flashed,

And I wrestled the clutch.

                           Far away, I heard them

Yelling my name, but it didn't sound like my own,

And the clutch stuck. (Did I want it to stick?) I hammered it

And the fireman came on a run and grabbed me and held me

Sobbing and screaming and fighting, my hand clenched

On the whistle rope while it screamed down all of our noises –

Stampeding a couple of empties into the field –

A long, long blast, hoarse, with the falling, brazen

Melancholy of engines when the pressure's falling.

Quiet then. My uncle was cursing the Reds,

Ordering the rig to start, but no one started.

The men drifted away.

                       The water-monkey

Came in with his load.

                 Questioned.

He got no answer.

Cal's buddy and someone else got him up
On an empty rack and they started out for home,
Him lying on the flat rack-bed, bouncing.

Still crying, I picked up his hat that lay in the churned-up dust,
And left my rack and team and my uncle's threats,
And cut for home across the river quarter.

6.   Green permission…
                              Dusk of the brass whistle…
Gooseberry dark.
Green moonlight of willow.
Ironwood, basswood and the horny elm.
Juneberry; box elder; thick in the thorny brake
The black chokecherry, the high broken ash and the slick
White bark of poplar.
                              I called the king of the woods,
The wind-sprung oak.
                              I called the queen of ivy,
Maharani to his rut-bark duchies;
Summoned the foxgrape, the lank woodbine,
And the small flowers: the wood violets, the cold
Spears of the iris, the spikes of the ghostflower –
It was before the alphabet of trees
Or later.
                              Runeless I stood in the green rain
Of the leaves.

Waiting.

Nothing.

Echo of distant horns.

Then
Under the hush and whisper of the wood,
I heard the echoes of the little war.
A fox barked in the hills; and a red hawk boomed
Down on the darkening flats in a feathery splash of hunger.
Silence and waiting.

The rivery rustle

Of a hunting mink.

Upstream in the chuckling shallows

A beaver spanked the water where, in its time,
The dam would be where my brother, now in his diapers,
Would trap for the beaver's grandsons.

I could not

See in that green dark.

I went downstream

Below the crossing where I'd swum the midnight river
On my way home from a move.

I put my clothes,

Stinking with sweat and dusty (I thought:
How the dust had jumped from Cal's shirt!)

I put them on the broken stump.

I dived from the hummock where the cut-bank crumbled.

Under the river the silence was humming, singing:
Night-song.

                                        In the arrest and glaucous light
Delicate, snake-like, the waterweed waved and retracted.
The water sang. The blood in my ears whistled.
I roared up out of the river into the last of the sunlight.

Then: I heard the green singing of the leaves;
The water-mystery,
The night-deep and teasing terror on the lone river
Sang in my bones,
And under its eves and seas I broke my weeping,
In that deeper grieving,
The long, halting – the halt and the long hurry –
Toward the heaving, harsh, the green blurring of the salt mysterious sea.

7.   Later, climbing the coulee hills in the sandy dusk,
        After sundown in the long northern twilight,
        The night hawk circling where the ragamuffin crows
        Steered for the cloudy wood;
        In that dead calm, in that flat light,
        (The water darkening where the cattle stood to their knees)
        I heard the singing of the little clan.
        Comfort of crickets and a thrum of frogs.
        Sleep rustle of birds.

        In the dusk the bats hustled.
        The hawk wheeled and whirled on the tall perch of the air;
        Whirled, fell

Down a long cliff of light, sliding from day into dusk.
Something squealed in the brake.
The crickets were silent.
The cattle lifted their blank and unregardant
Gaze to the hills.
Then, up the long slope of air on his stony, unwavering wing
The hawk plunged upward into a shower of light.

The crickets sang. The frogs
Were weaving their tweeds in the river shallows.

Hawk swoop.
         Silence.
               Singing.
The formal calls of a round dance.
This riddling of the river-mystery I could not read.

Then, climbing the high pass of my loss, I tramped
Up the dark coulee.
         The farmyard dark was dappled
With yellowy ponds of light, where the lanterns hung.
It was quiet and empty.
         In the hot clutter
Of the kitchen my mother was weeping. "He wouldn't eat,"
She said, meaning Cal.
         She had a womanly notion
(Which she didn't really believe) that all man's troubles
Could be ended by eating – it was a gesture she made
To soothe the world.

My father had driven my uncle out of the yard
Because Cal was *our* man, and not to be mistreated
Any more than horses or dogs. He was also my father's friend.
I got some supper and took it out to the barn.
In the lemony pale light of a lantern, at the far end,
He lay in a stall. His partner sat in the straw
Beside him, whittling, not looking at me. I didn't ask
Where his gun was, that slept in an oily rag
In his suitcase.

                    I put the food beside him

As I'd done with sick dogs.

                    He was gone where my love

Nor my partisanship could reach him.

Outside the barn my father knelt in the dust
In the lantern light, fixing a harness. Wanting
Just to be around, I suppose, to try to show Cal
He couldn't desert him.

                    He held the tubular punch
With its spur-like rowel, punching a worn hame strap
And shook the bright copper rivets out of a box.
"Hard lines, Tom," he said. "Hard lines, Old Timer."
I sat in the lantern's circle, the world of men,
And heard Cal breathe in his stall.

                    An army of crickets

Rasped in my ear.

                    "Don't hate anybody,"

My father said.
I went toward the house through the dark.

That night the men all left.
                                        Along toward morning
I heard the rattle of Fords. They had left Cal there
In the bloody dust that day but they wouldn't work after that.

"The folded arms of the workers," I heard Warren saying,
Sometime in the future where Mister Peets lies dreaming
Of a universal voting-machine.
                                        And Showboat
Quinn goes by (New York, later), "The fuckin' proletariat
Is in love with its fuckin' chains. How do you put this fuckin'
Strike on a cost-plus basis?"

There were strikes on other rigs that day, most of them lost,
And, on the second night, a few barns burned.
After that a scattering of flat alky bottles,
Gasoline filled, were found, buried in bundles.

"The folded arms of the workers."
I see Sodaberg
Organizing the towboats.
                                        I see him on Brooklyn Bridge,
The fizzing dynamite fuse as it drops on the barges.
Then Mac with his mournful face comes round the corner
(New York) up from the blazing waterfront, preaching
His strikes.
                        And my neighbors are striking on Marsh Street
(L.A., and later).
                                        And the hawk falls.

A dream-borne singing troubles my still boy's sleep
In the high night where Cal had gone:

They came through
The high passes, they crossed the dark mountains
In a month of snow.
Finding the plain, the bitter water, the iron
Rivers of the black North…

Hunters

in the high plateaus of that country…

Climbing toward sleep…

But far

from the laughter.

IV

1. The immortal girls, the summer manifestoes,
    Startle the buzzard in the corpse-bearing tree.

    Explosion of daisies in the stricken field.
    The lilac is lifting its lavender toward Arcturus.

    Noon's incandescence, autonomy of night,
    Cracked open throttles on my resurrection bone,
    My moon-steered master, midnight fisherman,
    Bound for the Indies…

    Coiffeur of dream, oh bright improbable gold!
    The blond-haired women, crowned as with surplus light,
    Curls crisp as lettuce on their bellies' porch
    And slick and secret when the armpit yawns –
    Hair! dimension of heat!
                                        Lit by subliminal suns
    That shrink their dresses halfway up their thighs,
    It ripens outward.
                                        Furry as a peach
    It licks the hand that hungers at the knee;
    And where the back and buttocks sweetly mate
    Like queenly empires joined in natural peace
    (Equation of the palm! O sweet division!)
    Glints like shot silk. And where the pubis thrusts

Into my world to light me into dark
Is stiff and secret as a buried fence
Or bristles friendly as a welcome mat.

Yes: and those soft brunettes, their eyes like caves,
Their third eye winking in the knowing dark!
O ox-eyed honeys with the wine-dark hair,
Branches of midnight where all moon long I crowed,
Punching our tickets on the train toward dawn –
How black your hair!
                              Belly of smoky wheat,
Alabastrine buttocks, legs like a slow dream –
Oh as to a citizen of Jupiter's moons,
Your soft enormous breasts, over the bare horizon,
Loom, golden and dusky rose, tremendous planets
Pendulous…
Iris toward the nipple and the nipples pink, veiny
Shot with faint blue…
And your eyes, O magnificent black-haired women!
Invincibly glazed or wet as a pool-side stone,
Heavy with sleep; and your mouths wide and elastic,
And your lips, thickened with heat, which your tongue keeps wetting!
Ah, woman with your ass as thick as a pillow,
With your thighs like deadfalls and the black nest of your sex
Like a midnight-hungry quicksand where I drown!
Drown and am born. Upborne! Resurrected!
Startling the buzzard on my shoulder tree!
I've come through your black pass many's the sunny night!

And the brown-haired women, slim, with their lenten graces,
Or short and thickset and busy as a bear,
Their knees dimpled and their hips slung like a hammock,
Their bellies snug to my gut as a flesh muff;
And the redheads, electric, with their buttermilk skin
And the tickle inside the knee, and their burning bush,
With its wise unsleeping bird, more dark than their eyebrows –
Bucking like goats, quicker than minks, randy
As the wild strawberry roan: sunfishing by moonlight
They have ridden me into a stall where I sleep standing up.

2.   Sweet Jesus at morning the queenly women of our youth!
The monumental creatures of our summer lust!
Sweet fantastic darlings, as full of juice as plums,
Pneumatic and backless as a functional dream
Where are ye now?
Where were ye then, indeed?
Walking three-legged in the sexual haze,
Drifting toward the Lion on the bosomy hills of summer,
In the hunting light, the marmoreal bulge of the moon,
I wooed them barebacked in the saddling heat.

First was Inez, her face a loony fiction,
Her bottom like concrete and her wrestling arms;
Fay with breasts as hard as hand grenades
(Whose father's shotgun dozed behind the door),

Barefooted Rose, found in the bottomlands
(We layed the flax as flat as forty horses,
The bluebells showering); Amy with her long hair
Drawn in mock modesty between long legs;
And Sandy with her car, who would be driving and do it;
And June who would roll you as in a barrel downhill –
The Gælic torture; Gin with her snapping trap,
The heliotropic quim: locked in till daybreak;
Literary Esther, who could fox your copy,
And the double Gladys, one blond, one black.

O great kingdom of Fuck! And myself: plenipotentiary!
Under the Dog Star's blaze, in the high rooms of the moonlight,
In the doze and balance of the wide noon,
I hung my pennant from the top of the windy mast:
Jolly Roger sailing the want-not seas of the summers.
And under the coupling of the wheeling night
Muffled in flesh and clamped to the sweaty pelt
Of Blanche or Betty, threshing the green baroque
Stacks of the long hay – the burrs stuck in our crotch,
The dust thick in our throats so we sneezed in spasm –
Or flat on the floor, or the back seat of a car,
Or a groaning trestle table in the Methodist Church basement,
And far in the fields, and high in the hills, and hot
And quick in the roaring cars: by the bridge, by the river,
In Troop Nine's dank log cabin where the Cheyenne flows:
By light, by dark, up on the roof, in the cellar,
In the rattling belfry where the bats complained,
Or backed against trees, or against the squealing fences,

Or belly to belly with no place to lie down
In the light of the dreaming moon.

3.   Dog watch and silence.
                              In the high school yard, the dust
Settles; of vanished cars, the vast nocturnal migrations.
Under the moon,
Paler than flowers the condoms gleam on the lawn.
Delicate, blue,
Fragrance of lilacs drifts in the night air, purer,
Sweeter than moonlight.

The lilac points to Arcturus.
Points down the street to my grandfather's clapboard house,
To the gimcrack moldering porch where a beehive sleeps in the wall,
Toward his Irish keening.
"Ay-you, Tom. Avoid the occasion of sin.
You're a quick hand with a book. Pick up an education
And don't run around be the night!
                            Boy, it's a wide
Road runs down to hell and its clear coasting
And the skids are greased for the poor. Boy, be learning!"
And up to bed, past the squeaking third step, bearing
Through the whispering grandfather dust, in the bellowing night of my sex
My little learning (Gladys and Daisy) bearing
The golden apple of my discontent.

4.   The dust settles. Settles like time, the years
Swing round my head like birds. It is fall, now, evening,
The long and lonesome season.
The car bumps on the wagon road. In the lights
The dust is thick. The cattle hump and shuffle
The smell of the autumn river in the cold night air
Is wild and alien.
                                Out of the river pasture,
Out of the gone summer we drive the cattle.
They plod the road, blind in the carlight's dazzle,
Docile enough. The car bumps and complains.
Wally is driving. The car crawls in low gear
And the dash light gleams in the hair of my littlest brother.
"Where will you go?" he says. "Is it far to the town
Where they keep the college?"
                            He is five years old, maybe seven.
"What will you learn to know?"

I know it is warm in the car. The night stiffens
With black frost but the car is warm. What shall we learn
In the cold? In the cold country where the books are burning?
Across the classroom of the north forty
My father professes his love and labor.
In the black field, burnt now, where the flax's
Small breakers ran, the Wobblies' footprint is buried.
A cold moon hangs in the trees.

"I hate September," says Wally. "The damn blank lonesome fields –
What will you learn anyway?"

And Jack says, sleepy, leaning his furry head
Into my side:
"Is it far? Is it long?"

5.   And returned then, up the coulee hills from the river
Later than gopher light, with the colder and older moon
Riding my back like a buzzard.
                              Past the squeaking third
Step on the grandfather stair, past the dusty
Belfry and Daisy caught in the lilac,
Past barns where the country wenches were singing like cardinal sins –
And do they sing in the dust still?
                              Do their bones
Sing in the golden dust in the stallion summers?

O small girls with your wide knowledge, you led me
Into the continent of guilt and forgiving, where love is;
Through the small gate of your sex I go into my kingdom.
Teachers of men! O hot, greathearted women
The world turns still on the axis of your thighs!

V

1.   Love and hunger! – that is my whole story.
An education in the form of a night journey –
Congo of the heart…

               Dream voyage…

                          Safari

To the dark interior.
Chaffinch, miner's canary, O white mice
Of Sir Humphrey Davy be with me now!

Borne on the underground stream,
I entered the hornacle mine – trivium – quadrivium –
In the rattling Ford, through the black stopes of a dust storm
From Sheldon to Buffalo.

                     Stopped in that dead of night,
The midnight noon of nineteen-thirty-five,
Becalmed in a dark our headlights could not pierce
And my father gave me advice. Advice and ten dollars –
The money to last for a year, the advice for a lifetime.
I heard the wind howl in the night of the dust:
Somewhere a freight was poking a snout of sound
Through all that flying real estate.

And through the dark and the future I hear Showboat Quinn:
"What part in the fuckin' pageant of history did *you* play?"
Far horns.

The iron breath of the train.
A little treasury of Montana sifts in at the window.

What was he saying? What was my father saying?
He was wishing me luck, he was saying love in a language
That has no word for it, the language of fathers and sons.
He was saying that school would be hard, that times were
Hard, and that life was hard.
                              Country news.
                                        History
Blown past your headlights.

And the clanking boxcars banged on over the dead men,
Bearing the dead Communist – but that is all in the future –
And Cal is riding a reefer lined with the ice
Of an earlier summer.
                              Borne east-south-east as the night
Shakes all around me…
                                        Toward the high passes.
When the storm had lifted enough to see we went on.

2. How now, Poor Richard, with that ten-dollar pie in your pocket,
    In your cousin's fur-collared coat like a moulting scarecrow!

    Under the sign of Virgo I came to State College.
    At Fargo, North Dakota, where the Red River flows north,
    A far country.

                              "Where fatherhood was not honored,
Conception being attributed to the North
Wind, or the eating of beans, or the accidental
Swallowing of an insect."

                                      Still, they did not believe
That "snakes were incarnations of the dead"
Cast the bones of sheep for signs of the weather
Paint still lifes of the interiors of horses –
A most sensible people.

So come there with my scholarship and the notion
Of learning.
And the first man I met was some kind of dean.
O excellent title!
What did it mean? Did the tumbleweed
Blowing out of Saskatchewan know it?
A man, anyhow, thin as a rail and mean
As a cross-barred barbwire gate, with a flat face to him
Like Picasso's Vallauris plates; all piss and moment,
A pithy, pursy bastard, like a quidnunc espaliered
Against the ass of the North Wind.
He sat there like a chilly Lutheran Buddha,
All two dimensions of him – you could hear the storm
Boom up through his splined backside with a sound like a jug-blower's ceilidh.
Sat there and said that to go to his college
I must stay in such-and-such dorm, designed for freshmen,
Built by himself and some other learned doctors
And later to be presented to the college itself
When it was paid for.

And when he and his golden twins
Had been well paid for.
                              But I couldn't swing it,
Having no money to live like a proper student.

And sat there. Nestled on the cold col of his nose
(His astral hand, involved in taking the damper
Was caught in a till that was still five years in the future)
His pince nez, gemini of radar, tracking
Invisible flies, rode through a zodiac
Numbering all signs but my own.

Well, that is how it goes.
                              The bastard sat there
Like a man with a paper asshole, like a man
With his head under water, talking, talking.
                              At last his words
Said nothing but *money, money*. A conversation
We could not enter.

"Somebody should set fire to the son of a bitch,"
I hear Mac saying.
                              Seventeenth Street is jammed
With flags and seamen. May Day, '46.
"Somebody should tamp up on the hyperborean bugger!"
And my father says, "The dirty muzzler!"
                              And the flags toss
As we go out in a storm that's ten-years strong,
Where the freight cars rattle and the vigorous dead of the future

Ride in the reefers, preserved in invisible ice.
Dakota Montana

                                      blowing along on the wind

Those dusty slogans

                                              alive.

3.   God damn it to hell, the cargo man has to carry
And all the streets in the moon as slick as glass!

That's how I went to the country of Swedes, Minnesota,
To school there, in a college over in Moorhead,
A no-story structure of purest dream, a hornacle mine
Rampant.
                  By night those brick-built blonds
Turned up their pretty tails to scholastic gentry
That would be dreaming of their seminars
Through the cold classes where they learned to teach.

To teach by Christ! They hadn't learned to read,
To write, to think, to wipe their asses properly –
To teach!
                        And I was to learn to teach
Like it or not.
                      Thinking I wanted to learn
To think, I didn't like it.
                          So, was taught
To teach by teachers who could neither think nor teach –

Taught harum-scarum and arsy-varsy to teach!
Oh, they will teach you to worship Pallas Athena,
Those education departments!

                                    Anything unsexed
Sprung out of an empty head...

                              Anyway, that's how it was,
A surrogate college.

                              Still, I spent my time
In the library – a quack grass and sow thistle
Patch of books in a warm building with windows
Looking out on that same pageant of history
That Showboat Quinn contemned.

                              Perhaps I learned how to teach
Five minutes one day when my mind was wandering –
I grew to a teacher, later.

                              Meantime, I read.
I walked five miles to the college and then walked back
And lunched at noon on a five-cent bar of candy
They don't make any more.

                    Ambrosia.

                              Proust
Troubled my sleep, my tiger-lined room.

                              And Eliot
(What will the young take for guides in their chilly country!)
Was with me as I crossed the river, on my way to school,
Where the unemployed fished, the fish badly outnumbered,
At morning.

                              At evening as I came home,

The ravenous poor were doing side-leaps from hunger
At the river where one old gar was shaking the water with fright.
By then the winter rains had come. The streets were glassy
With ice. With their gray beards stiff in the angry wind,
Belly down on the burnished avenues,
The burghers sledded south like homing geese.

O season of the horizontal! The Marat,
The Anacharsis Cloots of the five seasons!
Anagogic leveler, commune of mystical ice!
Hallelujah! Everything dead on the level
For once!
                    In the didder and horripilation
Of mind and matter, the pants of the long blonds
Come down, the post office was raided and the postmaster general
Was found to be short ninety-million dead letters
In each of which was a gopher tail, and an ad
From Hercules Sandow, the prime god of that country,
And a splinter of the True Cross.

All for the American Dream!
The banks collapsed, the depositors
Were folded away like flowers in the night's cold book –
In a smell of tamped dynamite, in the light of the penny
Sales where the farmers, shotguns in their hands,
Were buying back land the Oglala Sioux
Had scalped them for!

In those days, in the icy galleries of noon,
When the belly-down poor, their noses flat on the roof
Of the stiffened river glared at the solitary gar;
When the mayor, taking his stand, walked all one day
Crossing the frictionless intersection of Hope and Truth:
Failed to arrive; when the journeying city fathers,
Flat on their navels as migratory fish
But howling their despair like banshees, slid down the amethyst street
Toward Wahpeton, and southward –
Oh, all was equal then!
Like cattle caught in a storm, our sterns to the polestar
We humped for warmth together.
                                    In those days, in the snow,
In the fiery cold of the library's brumal arêtes –
The boreal light of the public and published dark –
Climbing like Tenzing, I found, in the frost-furred bright
Kitchens and cirques (among the petrified bats
And stuffed condoms – all of the Second Empire)
And in the ice ranches of the maverick intellect
Deep underground – down there, I say,
Among man-eating horses and the antipodean bears
Who wear their assholes preludant like the open eye
Of a Dechard rifle (in the blind-storm, in the thick
Of the mine gas – and me with that damn dead bird,
Chaffinch, canary, or a white mouse maybe, stuck in my pocket
Where I'd hoped to find a chocolate bar)
                                    – O there

All odds were even.

                              The lion and the lamb
Lay down, sideways. Collapsed.
                                                    Fox and Wolfe

Supported each other. A book on dreams
Buttressed *The Crisis in Physics*. And Marx and Bakunin
At last at peace. It was the cold did it –
It stopped their peristalsis near the left ventricle of the moon.

4.   Circularity! That's half the curse of the times:
      It is to stop the circulation of circulating
      Libraries – that's the trouble. I did.
      Put everything down as flat as the skating fathers
      Going by on their beards.
                                    That spare silhouette
      Is hard to get a bead on: a low elevation –
      It's enough to make you look twice at the face of the dead.
      There's the equality of the Five Mile Shelf:
      And everyone equal.

      To shake like a dog in the cold
      Is not so bad when everyone else must do it –
      That's civilization prime, a bearable thing.
      But to dodge Cadillacs when your knees are cut off at your elbows…
      No. Put the books out, all flat on the table,
      Like the breakup of the Yukon – let the bloodhounds bay,
      Little Eliza will cross on the ice floe, her tail one snap
      Ahead of their judgment.

Cold winter, then! Maximum entropy
End of circularity, everyone flat in the streets,
Equal.

That's when I saw for the first time
Iron-jawed George, Jefferson with his flutes and farms
And radical Madison – all of them deader than mackerel.
Those dead don't budge.
No, in that polar light, all directions are North,
You must choose your stars there.

5.   So: I found my directions: by the blue moss
On the north side of a book, by the colored stone
In the eye of a blind professor, and steered ahead.

In the horizontal night, with everyone flat on his face
Pushed by the tides of the moon, sliding toward third
In the sempiternal anguish of suburban streets
Order! Sweet order!

In the busy leather of the old archives
Professor G. is weighing up the proof
That Bakunin wrote Marx.

South of the black ice
Where I crossed the river near the fishing poor
Toward the falls

Open water

The fish are eating the unemployed.

"An education now," Peets says. "Eeyah
It puts your mind in a practical order."
"Piss in your hand an' it gets wet," says Peets.
Order!
              Order everywhere!
South on the ice, belly down, the citizens tighten formation.
A man, standing up on his hind feet, can see for miles…
No one else standing to break his view.
Order!   Order!

How cold it is!

The blue eye of the moon is stuck full of bones.

VI

1.   Home, then, where the loss is: the rusty ports of the sun.

December's dog days, when the stalk of the gospel Light
Leans out of winter weaker than the moon –
They sang me home.
                        I came then, I remember,
In the downhill rattle of the ransomed Ford with the hustling wind
Filing the nighttime quiet and the dull scar of the road
With a white gentry of mixed sand and snow…
Past the night-shut dreaming farms, fixed in the bright enamel
Of the full-filled sentry moon.

                        In the high-piled, tight
Barns, the crystalline, white beards of the frost were growing –
Fierce acres of gone summer, now stunned in the shut-knife cold
Where once, summer-born, with breasts of oranges,
Ripe as the South, the Poontang Princesses
Received their subjects – honey-breath of the hay
Won from the humming coulees, coiled from between their thighs.
Locked in the old dark now.

                        In the white albums, the bare
Bone-farms of the moon, the homesteads gleamed and gloomed.
Coyotes…
                        The white night-hunting owl…
– Home then.

In the fox-prowling,
In the dog-barking, and daylight-seeming night.

2.   The house was thick with the cold wool of their sleep.
In the dark of the kitchen woodbox one cricket sang,
Gold ember of autumn, hung in the Christmasy night,
All metal and leather…

                                     Cal's lost country.

Then from the top-floor weather, downstairs as limber as rope
My brothers came: Jim, Joe, Martin – Jack as round as sleep,
His head as rough as a corncob – blinking like coons
In the hunter's light;

                             And my sister Kathy, my mother –
All sprung out of the dream-encompassing dark
Like need or terror.
Then, in the topaz pool of the lamp's warm solstice,
They dreamed me home.

                                Showed me the cloudy pebble,
Pointed to moss on the north of the steering pine,
Gave back my name…

                     Chipping the ice of distance from my tongue.

3.   Fiesta then; – the midnight supper
Bright ceremony of the voyager's return.

The cricket sang in the woodbox behind the stove
And the coffee clucked with its black voice.
Their heads nodding on the branch of sleep,
The kids nibbled their dream-cake.
I remember the pearl
Rounds of the sandwich onions (O asphodel
In Elysia!), and the thick and crumbly slabs of the homemade bread,
And the cat's-cradle of talk
As warm as wool, brighter than colored yarn.

Then I was home and it was time for sleep.
The kids went up to the dark.
My mother stopped me.
"It's the way the times are, Tom. Everyone's broke.
But next year the crops…next year, if there's rain…"
"Can't be bad times forever," my father said.
"Between them Washington goddamned politicians,
Bankers and debts – they turn a man anyway but loose.
Grasshoppers, rust and dust storms, mortgages and foreclosures,
But we'll make it, Old Timer. We'll make her yet."
"It's all right," I said. I knew I was home then –
Back and busted from another of my universities.

4.   Night now.

                               The breathing dark.

The icy room full of dream,

                  hung with my brothers'

Sleep.
                              Cold incantations of coyotes

Whine and shine on the bare
Hills.
                              In the dark glitter of the coulee draw
The moon is trapped in the ice.
                              Away to the north,
Stark in the pouring light, on a page of snow,
The black alphabet of a farm lies jumbled together
Under its blue spike of smoke.

The coulee is full of moonlight: it pours that water
South toward the river dark.
                                    I have come home
From the river. Come up the coulee, come past
The buckbrush breaks where the rabbits lurch and leap,
Where the hunting hawks of the summer make their kill,
Past the Indian graves and home.

How far was the river?
                        In that lunar glaze,
In a light as of bone suns I saw on the coulee hills
The long procession of my pawky selves:
My journeying small souls: helved, greaved, and garlanded
With the blue weather and the bronze all-favoring
Light of those first fine summers.
                                          Saw, behind,
The daffy caucus of gopher-hunters and swimmers:
Walking delegates to the ego's founding convention:

Runaways
     Shapes out of sleep
         Voyagers…
How far to the river?
       Perhaps I had never reached it…
Never came back; never left…

And now returned in the long cortege of myselves.

And now the wind lifts, and I hear the sift of the snow,
A breathing whisper, a steady seethe like the sea
In the shifting porches of pelagic night.

– Went toward a sound of water…
        Called by what bird?

At five I started walking toward my birth,
Working my way toward the water sound and the sound
Of the round song, the water-borne distant singing
Where man chants like a bird in the brilliant bony
Lightning of his tree.

The river is frozen, the moon is caught in the ice.

Returned, now. Home and alone and himselves and warm.
But returned.
     Alone.
       Alive, alive oh!

Night of the solstice now, when the long neck of the dark
Leans out of the sun, shadowing the north earth,
The precinct of the Goat.

                                     Far from the summer queens,
From the golden buttocks, from the high, thrusting thighs
Of last year's girls.
                    Far from my sleeping brothers.
In the middle of the journey, returned. Shipwrecked
In the snow of the north forty…

                           Drifting…

In Capricorn.
           Mac, the double Gladys, Cal, my hope
Swing round my sleep their constant zodiac.

It is far to the river, it is farther home.

The wind is sharpening its knife on the shakes of the roof

      Far

             Dark

                   Cold
             I am a journey toward a distant wound.

VII

1.   Nightmare, nightmare, struggle, despair and dream…

The narrow world and the Wain swing round my winter sleep…

Under the Scorpion's weight my garden flows
Into the dark of the year.
                        First Neighbor, lately
On strike, calls from his yard to Second Neighbor,
Raking the fallen leaves.
                        Calls, and I hear
The voice of my brother call through the river trees,
Through my nine dead seasons of loss and the frost-bound echoing dusk
Where the gat-toothed buzz saw burred, a whine and a whicker,
And the round of the oak stump smoked on the freezing ground.

The rust ports of the sun and no slice of moon in my pocket!
A cold winter that one, as long as absence is,
As white as hunger, a blizzard of lost identities,
When moss grew thick on the south sides of the farmers
And the quick felt of an old and abstract snow
Capped their Rolandic Fissures.
                        Winter under your hat!
A ten-year snowfall under the dome of your head!
You have to split plenty of kindling to warm up from that!

So, that winter, we got wood up from the river
While the migrant bourgeois of Moorhead slalomed south on their chins
And my auld acquaintance broke like a covey of quail
And rode the rods to Detroit or soonered westerly –
The Lares half-hitched to the buckjumping Ford –
In a cloud of bankers like Siberian wolves
Snapping at ninety-ninth mortgages tossed like brides in their wake.
Over the hills and far away
                                        westerly
To the golden apples of the Oregon.

That's how I saw my boyhood disappear
In a used-up Ford on Highway Number Ten
Toward Devil's Lake and land's end. Vanished. Gone
Toward the apple tree, the singing and the gold.
And my midnight riders gone, the sweet girls of my hunger,
Toward the broad rivers and the ripe and fruited vines,
Coals to Newcastle in the incontinent long winter
Whose cold made your balls ache when there was nothing to warm
But my burning and stallion need – that grand old religion
Of which I am the Pope.

So, entered the dimension of winter, zero of hope
And the only shelter the lee of a barbwire fence.

And far from the laughter.
Far from the high passes.

2.   Beginning and rebeginning, voyage and return and voyage…
     Past the last gate in the fence toward the white slate of the river,
     And past the Indian boneyard under its tight, bright blanket,
     And down the coulee and over the ford, now locked in its echo chamber –
     It spanged like gunshot under the caulks of the horseshoes,
     A ripping and fiery sound (the pure steel of the cold)
     That ricocheted from the hills and sifted snow from the branches,
     Unfurling one rusty crow, his sooty flag, to the air.

     Stump ranchers that winter, we felled the trees on the slopes,
     Scrub oak, elm, box elder, the flint stakes of the ash
     That snagged in the chokecherry slashes. In the crowded gooseberry brakes,
     Where the fox grape's bronze globes sag in the cloudy green of the summer,
     We knocked them down with a crosscut and snaked them out on a chain.

     All that winter, in the black cold, the buzz saw screamed and whistled,
     And the rhyming hills complained. In the noontime stillness,
     Thawing our frozen beans at the raw face of a fire,
     We heard the frost-bound tree boles booming like cannon,
     A wooden thunder, snapping the chains of the frost.

     Those were the last years of the Agrarian City
     City of swapped labor
     Communitas
     Circle of warmth and work
     Frontier's end and last wood-chopping bee
     The last collectivity stamping its feet in the cold.

So, with the moss on our backs and it snowing inside our skulls,
In a gale like a mile-high window of breaking glass
We snaked out the down ones, snatching the deadfalls clean
And fed them into the buzz saw.

                           The Frenchman's, it was.

A little guy, quick as a fart and no nicer,
Captain of our industry.

                         Had, for his company

The weedy sons of midnight enterprise:
Stump-jumpers and hog-callers from the downwind counties
The noonday mopus and the coffee-guzzling Swedes
Prairie mules
Moonfaced Irish from upcountry farms
Sandhill cranes
And lonesome deadbeats from a buckbrush parish.

So, worked together. Fed the wood to the saw
That had more gaps than teeth. Sweated, and froze
In the dead-still days, as clear as glass, with the biting
Acetylene of the cold cutting in through the daylight,
And the badman trees snapping out of the dusk
Their icy pistols.

                 So, worked, the peddler's pack of us

Hunched in the cold with the Frenchman raging around us,
A monsoon of fury, a wispy apocalypse, scolding,
Cursing and pleading, whipping us into a team,
And we warmed in each other's work, contestants of winter,
We sawed up the summer into stove-length rounds –
Chunks of pure sunlight made warmer by our work.

And did we burn?
We burned with a cold flame.
And did we freeze?
We froze in bunches of five.
And did we complain?
We did, we did, we did.

Sometimes at evening with the dusk sifting down through the trees
And the trees like a smudge on the white hills and the hills drifting
Into the hushed light, into the huge, the looming, holy
Night; – sometimes, then, in the pause and balance
Between dark and day, with the noise of our labor stilled,
And still in ourselves we felt our kinship, our commune
Against the cold.
              In that rich and friendly hour
When the hunting hawks whirred home, we stilled our talking
And silence sang our compline and vesper song.

It was good singing, that silence. From the riches of common work
The solidarity of forlorn men
Firm on our margin of poverty and cold:
Communitas
Holy City
Laughter at forty below
Round song
The chime of comradeship that comes once maybe
In the Winter of the Blue Snow.

That's how it was.

                                    Sometimes, going home in the evening,
We'd jump some pheasants and drop them out of the light –
The shotguns clapping and hollow in the empty world of the winter –
And their feathers blazed like jewels in the blank white fields.

Then, if there was plenty, we'd all eat together
At someone's house, and later play poker, for cigarettes or for nothing,
And I'd go home at the dark prime, the north flashing its teeth,
Or the moon white as a lamp in the blazing night.

3.   The moon fattens and fails. In the roaring wood fires
The winter burnt out. One day we stood in the blizzard
Blind as bats in the white rasp of the snow –
In the pure rage of the season one instant – the next,
(With never a slackening of wind or break in the storm)
White turned black and the perfect fury of dust
Slammed down a lid on the day.
                          Montana…
                              Saskatchewan

Blowing over our heads
Buried alive standing up…

                                Still walking around.

Holy Mother of Christ what a pisscutter Spring!
Oxymoronic winter! Anagoge of the snow,
A perfect Red Peril and Jukes of a season

With a muzzle velocity six times the speed of light –
In those days you could be fishing around in a pothole
Where a horse or a tractor had sprung a leak and submerged,
Up to your ass in the water, and the rain falling:
And the dust blowing down your throat like a fistful of glass –
And *that* not so bad, but pushing down on your hat
Were the vagrant farms of the north: Montana, Saskatchewan,
With the farmers still on them, merrily plowing away,
Six inches over your head…

And *that* not so bad, except for them singing.

So, spring didn't come. Didn't come for ten years…
A simple failure of light in the icebound, rusty
Ports of the sun.
                    But I would be sailing out.
Called by what bird? Toward what high pass, in the night,
In the bright blank of my future? Of that white chapter
What did I hope?

In the snowy evening, coming back from the hills
Or walking home after midnight under the tormenting moon
I lugged my brass grief, an unappeasable hunger,
Nameless.
                    Stood in the north forty,
With no tradition to warm me, demanding a name,
Needing a word for the Now…to nail its hide to the barn…
Needing to journey…

Exile begins early in my country
Though the commune of gentle woodchoppers be never so wide and warm.

In the language of water there is no word for fire.

So, carried my anguish around like a poem cast
In bronze:
                    Where verdigris grew like moss on a standing stone,
And sometimes I read its name in the flowing tree of the North,
The midnight river of boreal light.
                                        In the screel of snow
And the iron singing of the wheels of the gravel wagons
Where the WPA farmers worked on the roads
Sometimes I seemed to hear.
                    Immortal
Loneliness
                              Shapes of the dark
                                                    Cold
Partners.

This song the old moon sang me, coming home in the night.
And the icy tongues of the stars.

After Christmas.
              Drifting
Toward the Water Carrier…

– Sang me toward sleep.

And out on hills one coyote…

barking his lauds…

VIII

1.   "Expropriate the expropriators – that's Marx. But Plato's guardians
Might not eat off gold plate."

                                Hovey is speaking,
Muttering, low voiced, in the funky dark.
I hush him quiet, whispering, hearing
A papery rustle of onions, a surd trill
And a thudding and sighing collapse, the waltz of potatoes
As the pile slides. Then they tick in the sack.

"All property is theft. By stealing Prexy's potatoes,
Behold, I'm become a man of property."
I say nothing, fishing around in the dark
For the slippery onions that peel themselves in my grasp.
I feel the push of the wind on the low-slung roof,
The sound distant, like far trains, like the sea
Shoving its thunder inland.

"Stealing is better done without philosophy,"
I tell him. He mutters. Light leaps out of his hand
And the root cellar lifts around us its solid arms.
"Turnips," he says and points to a far corner.
"Third ingredient, the philosopher's stone, the magus
Of all stews. Get some."

                              The match goes out
And I fill the sack by feel in the darkness under

The earth; in the warm and vegetable dark
I mend my philosophy, stealing pieces of night
Out of the press of the long storm.

Outside, the wind still pushed its heavy freight
South. The cold laced at our throats. The night
Boomed down from the north. A hangdog moon
Was racing about in the clouds, and a rapid branch
Of music bloomed at the President's window, its flowers
Flapping loose in the gale.

We went, then, over the swell and swale
Of the campus backlots, past the dwellings of Greeks,
Their monogramed houses founded on light and their lawns
Crew cut. We passed the creek and came out
At the railroad siding.
                                        The raw edge of a fire
Rubbed at the windy dark. One old tramp in his hunger
Jungling up in the cold. Bummed us. We gave him
A part of what we had stolen, and made for Camp.

2.   Camp Depression!
                O smallest particular
In the chilly universality of want!
Pustulant diamond hung on the pure brow
Of our golden west!
                        O bobtailed quiddity,

Earnest of earnest compromise with the cold,
With the entropy of the failing system!
Now, under the northwest wind, in the first snow of the season,
We enter the ring of light.

                                      A string of cabooses,
Remnants of vanished trains, crouch in a square
Like the pioneers' covered wagons, a tight perimeter
Against the Comanche winter.

                                         Came with our stolen grub
Into the cooking stink and twitch of talk…

                                 – Crossed the high passes,
Came to the named pool, to the omen stone.

That's how I got there, finally, to Grand Forks
In North Dakota, to the University there,
And to Camp Depression, with a few potatoes and onions
Out of the President's cache.

                                    O impeccable faubourgs
Where, in the morning, you fought bedbugs for your shoes!

3.   Implacable need:

                                  the search for the blazed tree,
And the long and lonely hunt for the naming rune –
In that legendary journey so early and hard begun
Toward joy, toward the laughter, I was no longer alone
In that cantrip circle, in the bright chime of their talk
Among those pilgrim souls.

Wendell I see, wearing the dog on his back,
And Weston comes in with the snow, with the howling night,
And Sorensen, with his clenched face, and his hard
Opinions.
            And all the others.

                                        Shapes of the dark
Faces
Blown to windward
Blown past our headlights
Proofs
Of a lost, ebullient season.

Time has its tin ear, history drops at your gate its yellowing gazettes…
Offbeat functions, seasons too soon or too late
Begun.
                                    It was that sort of time. It was not
The Year of the Blue Snow.
But we couldn't have known it, plucked from the sweat of our sleep
In the north forty…blown out of spring toward
The steep of winter, the metaphysical cold.

We talked to keep warm (and made love, even, alas,
To keep warm). My vision of everything flat –
The ninety-nine-mile shelf of books, the sledding fathers
Touring south on their beards – in the smell of hunger,
In the small eye of a rifle six years unmade
The talk flickered like fires.
The gist of it was, it was a bad world and we were the boys to change it.
And it *was* a bad world; and we might have.

In that round song, Marx lifted his ruddy
Flag; and Bakunin danced (And the Technocrats
Were hatching their ergs…)
                                        A mile east, in the dark
The hunger marchers slept in the courthouse lobby
After its capture: where Webster and Boudreaux,
Bricklayer, watchmaker, Communists, hoped they were building
The new society, inside the shell of the old –
Where the cops came in in the dark and we fought down the stairs.

That was the talk of the states those years, that winter.
Conversations of east and west, palaver
Borne coast-to-coast on the midnight freights where Cal was riding
The icy red-balls.
                        Music under the dogged-down
Dead lights of the beached caboose.
Wild talk, and easy enough now to laugh.
That's not the point and never was the point.
What was real was the generosity, expectant hope,
The open and true desire to create the good.

Now, in another autumn, in our new dispensation
Of an ancient, man-chilling dark, the frost drops over
My garden's starry wreckage.
                                        Over my hope.
                                                        Over
The generous dead of my years.
                                        Now, in the chill streets
I hear the hunting, and the long thunder of money.

A queer parade goes past: Informers, shit-eaters, fetishists,
Punkin'-faced cretins, and the little deformed traders
In lunar nutmegs and submarine bibles.
And the parlor anarchist comes by, to hang in my ear
His tiny diseased pearls like the guano of meat-eating birds.

But *then* was a different country, though the children of light,
                                        gone out
To the dark people in the villages, did not come back…
But what was real, in all that unreal talk
Of ergs and of middle peasants (perhaps someone born
Between the Mississippi and the Rocky Mountains, the unmapped country)
Was the generous wish.
                        To talk of the People
Is to be a fool. But they were the *sign* of the People,
Those talkers.
                        Went underground about 1941 –
Nor hide nor hair of 'em since; not now, in the Year
Of the Dog, when each hunting hound has his son of a bitch.
Their voices got lost in the rattle of voting machines,
In the Las Vegas of the national politic…

4.   We go out in the stony midnight.
                        Meridian cold.
                                    The stars,
Pure vitriol, framed in the blank obsidian dark,
Like skaters' icy asterisks; smolder; and sing; and flame.

In the flickering light, auroral, of the North lifting its torch,
The stacks of the powerhouse fume and sigh...
                                        High up, streaking
The lower dark, the smoke whisks east in the slack of a cranky breeze.
A train mourns. Distant. A broken fifth of its spoor
Crowns the brow of the night with its wild mystique.
And under the hysteria of the time, its blind commitments,
Is the talk and electric whisper of the power
Loud in forgotten counties where the poor
Sharpen their harps and axes in the high shine of the dark.

That was our wintry idyll, our pastorale in the cold.
The train whistle for the journey, the smoking stacks for power,
And in every country the need and the will to change.
O landscape of romance, all iron and sentiment
Under the prose of snow!

Later, crossing the black yards of the campus,
We heard the dead cry out from the long marble of sleep –
The old heads of the past, adream in their stony niches,
Above their Latin Wisdom.
                              Being classical –
In the teeth of the northwest wind.
                                        The old dead, and the dead
Still walking around.

I saw all that as the moon spun down toward the Badlands
In the singing cold that only our blood could warm.
A dream surely. Sentimental with its

Concern for injustice (which no one admits can exist).

And some of them died of it, giving blood to the dream.

And some of them ran away; and are still running.

And it's all there, somewhere.

Under the hornacle mine...

In the tertiary deposits...

– Ten minutes before the invention of money...

IX

1.   _____ and the moon stuck in my pocket!
And all my infernal suns shining against the cold!

Now, what is harder to know than the simplest joy?
Under the lacing of anger and of lack,
In the rub of hunger, in the thick hug of the dark,
What brightness, sweetness, softness can we know?
What road to the honey tree?
                                 Sweetness falls,
A hawk from broad heaven sweet in his swift kill.
Softness grows on stone in the mossy watches
Its hardness keeps. And asleep in the shape of a cloud,
A brightness waits and leaps.
                                 Hawk, cloud, stone –
Pure marvel, here, this brightness, sweetness, softness.

The stars are shifting in the permanent sky…
Yellow Arcturus –
That star, my lifetime of light away, leans down the sleepy west,
Bright on the lifting lilac.
                               Our fellow of scars and wars
Drifting, old Earth, into the shine of the spring
Toward the stone-footed Ram and the Bull…

Marvel me no marvels: that lightness, softness, sweetness
Is no marvel.
                              Blood comes from a stone,
Night is the shining weather in which the blind go hunting,
But that all-purpose dark in which we seek our good,
Works from its bleak double, as night breaks into day
And the sleepy opposite wakes.
                              There is no marvel here
Where we get our blood from a stone, beating our hands at the wall.

No, but the pure joy, then; simple: got without effort.
Born without categories it puts the skids under
The blind eye of the moon – it jumps all fences.

It was she had it – Marian – a small slice of the sun
No bigger than the half of an orange – it was what the sun keeps warm by –
A rose, a flower of warmth in the heart of the abstract cold.
I was bound to lose it.

        The stars shift in the stony sky
        Arcturus
        Drifting…
        Boötes the Herdsman
                              chasing the Bear with his dogs.

A warmth, a sunlight, and an end of journeys –
That's what she seemed like, was;
Or the permanent sky, maybe,
                              myself drifting,

                                                                    or flame
Would light me north in the long collapse of Time
When Vega is polestar.

So the journey ended, or seemed to, in the sweet strength of her flesh,
That brightness…softness…
                                    in the fire-flower, in the fixed cone
Of light, I broke my fast, I woke my want.

The simplest joy!
                            And there is no way to say it!

Only that the birds in the boondocks hoisted my heart in their song.
Only that trees, only that the damn-all flowers
That work for no one, that wink their yellowy talk
Flag right, flag left, hallooing from field to field
Their breezy semaphores – only that the wind, the rain
Under my skin of names, the St. Elmo's fire,
The fur of my sensual animal, touched the quick of my ghost.

So, the birds in the boondocks sang.
                                    And the high-flying moon
Ground round on its bony axis.
                                    My newborn interior suns
Warmed all their hands in the single flash of a word;
In my four-alarm song, at the long wick of my joy.

Well, what's the use of talking? It wasn't like that.
And it was, enough. But to put the whole thing down plain,

It was the dancer's bulge in the thick of her calf.
It was a trick of the eye, a way of walking, of saying.
Or it was the shy sound of her talk or a knack for goodness.

None of these things, not one; no way says it.
Was it the flare and bulge of the charmed light as it eased around her,
Bright swarming of sun, like bees, nudging her hair?
It was. It was.
Was it the calloused first joint of her second finger,
Stigmatic short hand, got from the taking of notes?
It was. Christ yes it was.
Was it the young moon in the sign of the first woman
The quail-keeping girl, the girl with the red-eared hound?
It was. It was. It was.
And all thrown away?
It was.

2.   A spitfire oak of thunder, sky-high roots in a cloud,
Strikes down a branch of sound and the season splits like a grape.
The sooty elms, that all blanched winter long
Dragged their slow charcoal through the white brag of the snow
Now shift like smoke in the whelming rain.
                      A light, alive,
Alone:
                      A bright bird.
                      The yellow spike of a flower;
A shimmering haze of willows clots in the greeny light.

In that spring the rusty platitudes brightened
Old axioms of sun and night
The invisible selves under the skin of objects
Singing
Told me their secret numbers and the true count of their names.
So that I saw the snake split the long glove of his home
And go forth all new, man-killing, naked and moist,
Steaming in the cold morning, a smoky ooze through the grass;
And the gold-eyed pheasant leaped out from an ambush of light
Scattering the dew, and with the dew still on his wings,
Beating up tiny rainbows out of his coppery thunder.

       Sun like a gold swarm of bees; moon like a magical woman.
       These things I had once; things that she gave me.

3.   Love and hunger! – the secret is all there somewhere –
and the fiery dance of the stars in their journeying far houses.
And if hunger ended in the cantrip circle,
In the union of hungry men, in the blue ice of the reefer
Where Cal traveled…
Jawsmiths
Commune of mystical sweat.
If it ended there.

It was she built the fire in the heart of the winter night
And rang all the bells in the stiff church of the ice.
Miner's light:

Campfire:
Chipping hammer of purest flame, tunneling
The ultimate rock, the darkness that is as long as we are…

Seemed like no campfire,
But the permanent warmth, the absolute seed of the sun
I could sow in my personal blood-ranch…
But I am a farmer of bones.

❄   ❄   ❄   ❄   ❄

A season was ending.
                    White papers; architectural changes.
In Whitey's Circular Bar, in East Grand Forks,
We stood like the signal figures under the legend tree,
Drinking. With Sam and Dee. Who were talking of marriage.
Stood in the rain of music and silver under the illegal machines,
Where Alton pursued the mechanical capitalist,
Jacking the slot machine's arm down again and again.

"Marriage is the continuation of sex by other means."
(Sam was going away to drive airplanes for the government.
Someone sang in Norwegian, under the metallic laughter
Of machines and money.)
                    "Some people can be happy with a book by Donne
And a piece of Ass. It's lack of high thought keeps
My life poor."
                    (And went out in a chiming rain
Of jackpot silver.)

And crossed the black river one instant before the breakup.
And turned dreamward.

                                              One to the East and airplanes,
One, Marian the true North. One
To the West of Wish. Myself, South, toward speech.
And all to the wars and the whores and the wares and the ways of a rotten season.
And who could have guessed it?
The polestar stood to the North:
Fire was steady on the permanent sky.

4.   Then south to the University with the 500,000 pianos
Bought because Huey Long had written: "Get rid of them nags!"
(Horses for the young ladies' riding stable)
Because one of the horses had broken the neck of a possible voter.
To Baton Rouge, Louisiana, the University there.
Where they had bought football, pianos, horses and donnish Oxonians.
To start a culture farm, a little Athens-on-the-bayou.
And a good job too.

                                        And they all put in together and they got up
A tradition. They got hold of Donne, and before they had got done
They damn near had him.

                                     And they got hold of Agrarianism –
Salvation – forty acres and a mule – the Protestant Heaven,
Free Enterprise! Kind of intellectual ribbon-development –
But I was a peasant from Sauvequipeutville –
I wanted the City of Man.

And Cleanth Brooks would talk, at the Roosevelt Tavern,
Where we went to drink beer. And Katherine Anne Porter sometimes.
(They've probably changed all the names now.)
And down the street Alan Swallow was handsetting books
In an old garage. A wild man from Wyoming,
With no tradition.

                                        But it came in handy, later,
That tradition. The metaphysical poets
Of the Second Coming had it for God or Sense –
Had it in place of a backbone: and many's the scarecrow,
Many's the Raggedy Man it's propped up stiff as a corpse.

Then, Asia Street: where I roomed at the family Peets.
A bug mine, a collapsible chamber of horrors
Held together by tarpaper and white chauvinism.
There was Peets with his gin, his nine-foot wife, and his son
Who was big enough to be twins – and stupid enough for a dozen,
And the daughter, big as all three, with a backside for a face,
With a mouth of pure guttapercha, with a cast, with a fine
High shining of lunacy crossing her horsy eyes –
"Fuck or fight!" I can hear her yelling it now
And out of the room at the back the bed starts roaring,
The house is moaning and shaking, the dust snows down from the ceiling,
The old dog sneezes and pukes and Peets is cursing his wife:
"Teach your daughter some manners, you goddamn cow!
Tell her to close her door, and come back to this goddam bed!"

And Hopkins arrives with his latest girl and *they* start
Kicking the gong around; and the whole place shaking and roaring,

Like a plane about to take off; and the 'gators awake
Bellowing, under the house, and flee for the bayous
While the old dog screams at the moon –
Order! Tradition and Order!
And all the beds in the joint a-flap at both ends!

Then I would get up, maybe, leaving that sex foundry,
That stamping mill for the minting of unfixed forms,
And lug my chastity, my faithfulness, around the town.
Moon in the western dark and the blue permanent stars
Shifted a bit in the sky.
                                    Toward music, toward speech, drifting
The night.
High noon of darkness now and the loud magnolias lifting
Their ten-thousand-candlepower blooms.
                                    Proud flesh, these flowers,
Earth offering, inescapable
Emblems.
Offering of night birds too, and the traveling far stars
And the round dance of the seasons: inviolate
Torment.

Open the night's cold book.
                                    Salt for the quick.
Now from the farthest bar a music breaks and binds,
An icy necklace of bluest fire spills down the hour.
The river stirs and seethes, its steady working whispering
Into the ultimate South.
                                    Drifting

Toward Scorpio in the hangdog heat of the sullen season.
Toward the Gulf…
In the river-run hush and hurry of that great night water:
To the black lots and the god-mating beasts of the green man-farming sea.

5.   Living again on the outside – that's what it was.
– Outside of the Outside: drinking beer with a comrade,
A Negro guy, in a Negro bar – put into the kitchen
(Business being business, whether white or black).
And plenty of reason, God knows, two blocks away
From higher education.
                           Which was the Roosevelt Tavern,
Brooks, that sweet great man, K.A.P. etc.
(They've changed all the names now).
                                 And all of them stoned:
On Donne. Etc.
            And all of them sailing on the Good Ship Tradition…
For the thither ports of the moon.
                        Highflying days
I'll tell you right now!
                  And me with my three ideas
With my anarchist, peasant poverty, being told at last how bright
The bitter land was.
How the simple poor might lift a laud to the Lord.

That's how it was. Geeks, Cons and Lemon Men,
Guys with their intellects all ganted up out of the barbarian North

Tea sluggers and cathounds
The girl who, when I said that God had created
Male and female the Spanish Moss, wanted to see them in action:
People "with a groundless fear of high places."
O architectonic colloquy! O gothick Pile
Of talk! How, out of religion and poetry
And reverence for the land the good life comes.
Some with Myth, some with Visions out of
That book by Yeats would dance the seasons round
In a sweet concord.

                            But never the actual seasons –
Not the threshing floor of Fall nor the tall night of the Winter –
Woodcutting time – nor Spring with the chime and jingle
Of mended harness on real and farting horses,
Nor the snort of the tractor in the Summer fallow.
Not the true run of the seasons.

That year they set up machine guns down at the docks
To quarantine a seamen's strike.
                         And Warren went, by mistake,
Being new in the town, to the fink hall, looking
For the strike committee.
                               Got dumped. That was the year
They knocked off Carey, who edited the Gulf Pilot.
M_____ did it; who's now a great leader of men.

Serious talk, all of it. Serious people.
"The difference between lust and love is the difference between
Power and knowledge."

                          And Warren talks of
General strikes, Anarcho-Communist notions,
Picked up in Wobbly stewpots.
                          "Stick out your behind to the north
Wind and see which cheeks gets cold first," Peets says.
"Know thyself," he confides. "In the dark, a wise man
Can tell his ass from his elbow."

Palaver –
Tradition! Heigh-ho! Tradition!
Bobbery! Bobbery. Palaver –

DON'T GO BAREFOOT TO A SNAKE-STOMPING!
                          LOOSEN YOUR WIGS!

It's no use hooking them both on the same circuit –
The English and American traditions.
It won't take the play out of the loose eccentrics.
Cattlemen, sheepmen and outlaws, that's American tradition,
And few enough outlaws at that.
                          And it's no use
For the lonesome radicals to raise up the ghost of Tom Paine,
Los Muertos no hablan.
                          Them dead don't walk, either.
                          No, ghost-eaters, they'd like
To cuddle up to the bourgeois liberal tradition –

Go to bed to make love, not to keep warm!
I'll gentle my own horses.

Now come down from your mountain Master Don
     Gordon
All's dark down here.
       Asia Street.
          Marsh Street.
               My garden
Dreams in my window light.
          Somewhere – toward morning –
Is the true anguish and body of a man…
Buried in all that talk.
         Come down and find him.

❀   ❀   ❀   ❀   ❀

Stars in the night sky anyway, even though shifted.
To go out then, in the dark, leaving the talkers behind,
Tapping my stick of light on the smooth face of the road
To stir the snakes.
          They came up out of the inky swamps
To soak up heat from the blacktops in the long chill of the night,
Cottonmouths.
     Lay there like logs of wood,
        Sluggish, huddles of
Older darkness
     And out of the further night
The black rush and the voiceless hurrying call
Of the great beast of the river.
        Pushing south
Toward the long coilings of the labyrinthine Gulf.

Then home to Asia Street and the family Peets
The knocking-shop and threshing floor of love
Now roaring and shaking on the two o'clock jump.
A conversation of parts. Another tradition.
And someone is saying,
"Sex plus electrification equal socialism."

6.   First the talk, and after the talk the gunfire.
       After the hunt, with music, you walk back, avoiding the snakes,
       To the shaking loud house, your hireling momentary home,
       Through the crowding invisible snow and the quick ice of the times.
       Low temperatures there! Winter still in the streets –
       (Where Moorhead's migrant fathers, still belly-down on the roads,
       Their beards stiffer than boards, sledded past and around me,
       Heading toward deeper Souths).
                                        Winter of Winters:
       Forty below Mason-Dixon and the gauge still falling,
       The pressure rising, the middle sliding out toward the edges –
       Place where the blacker the man the brighter he burns;
       And the hotter the fire the colder.

       I left there then and hitched north in summer on the black roads through the swamps:
       Water hyacinths; and moss-fogged trees; and the soft thick rasp of snakes
       And flamingos on their thin stalks like passion aloft in a breeze,
       Heraldic emblems.

And on north then with the first of the dogfaces
(Who thought they were National Guardsmen) done with maneuvers
In Louisiana; heading for home in the North; and now
Rotten these many years.

                       North, past the turpentine
Camps of Arkansas; past the decayed, decaying
Limestone of the Ozarks.

                     North toward Bonne Terre –
(Missouri: the flat north; wooded: the chat heaps from the mines
Where they made cement) toward Marian and a kind of Red
Wedding.

                      Count of my name, number
Of my secret beast –
All true marriages are sacred and shake the King of the Year
Out of his sleepy past…

                     No – it was only
How to be happy.
(They've changed all the names; those systems are *long* forgotten,
But that's what it was.)

We lodged among madmen. The rain dripped through the roof
And my great toe turned to limestone – another story.
Later, by way of honeymoon, went to the nameless river,
Swam there.

        (Treeful of quarreling squirrels.)

                      Stayed there by the river,
In the half-life of a wet-wood fire, while the night
Seeped upward out of the ground.

                   Yet the light hung still

On the steep hill faces, in the long west sky; at tree top
It graced the birds' high houses.

It was then we heard the hounds and the sound of the hunt coming –
A far belling of dogs and a quick rustle of darkness,
And then all still.
                        The trees leaned up toward the light, the river
Dreamed on a stone.
                  Then, through the eldritch-tranced and dying light,
Like the quick of the falling dark, from a brake of willow,
A swift flicker of drawn-out speed, night's Presence leaped.
He splashed through the river shallows, a buck, running, while three
Low melancholy keenings came from the distant hounds.

Then came the long night-running by the river shallows:
Pursuit
Workings of darkness
The endless hunting.
Deer, their shapes like smoke, with their flaring eyes
Flowed out of the rising dark. Delicate, slight,
With the bitten-in red glare to her glance, and lightly stepping
The fox came, trotting easy for the length of the long running.
And the pigs came, bustling and scuffling in a storm of terror,
And the wildcats from the trees like fur on springs,
And the small thin things from the brush, and the stroller, the disdainful badger,
Rolling out of the dark – everything running, running –
The night running, the darkness alive with
Running and the terror of the long running.

The brush cracked like shot and the great shapes leaped,
Rode by like cloud, their eyes slashed long by speed,
In a great frieze of terror.
The great and the noble deer and the poor weak things of the dark
Running, running, the hills wild with their terror
The brush smashing and rustling and the shallows patterned with splashes –
Till the whole world seemed running in that long hunt.
And the tame cattle joined the running, came bellowing out of the brush
Their holy terror, their anguished disbelief that they were hunted;
The horses crashed by, screaming their hurt and hatred,
And the barnyard geese, and the very birds of the place –
And at the last a man – was it a man?
Came out of the willow brake, running without a sound
While the pealing keen of the hounds grew iron and round on the hills.
It passed us running, a thing of the purest night,
Soundless.
                    The terrible eyes begged no release.

Then the shadowy great figures, the long night running,
The night-long frieze like cloud or cloudy terror
Vanished beyond the river and the silence came.
Dead silence. No
Leaf fall or cricket-cry. Even the river
Stilled.

Then we smelled them – the fierce, sickening dog-smell,
The stench of their long pursuit.
                    And the huge forms come padding

Stinking, red-eyed out of the old dark.
We lay there by the small fire and they watched us,
Knowing, unhurried.

Then the hunt went on –
We heard it vanish past the farthest hill.
The night came back – the leaves were clashing
Their little leathery swords. A sleepy bird
Complained.
And, as the hunt grew still in the distant running
We made love there, hearing the farthering hounds.

7. The stars shift and maps are redrawn: of islands
Blown up at sea, of frontiers soft as chalk,
Of archipelagos adrift, blazing, and façades of cathedrals
Famous…
                    Redrawn in fire…
                                        As I went toward the North
Europe bled and burned. For each state line that I crossed
Nations were sold and collapsed.
                                        They died in the oily smoke
Of the high summer – the poor –
                                        died out in the country
Which before they'd never had money enough to see.

"Last year," said old Tom Brennan, "they made me dance to their tune.
Labor was scarce and they had me over a barrel.

This year I'll fire the bastards at the drop of a hat.
By God, I'll keep the roads black with 'em!"

And the roads *were* black with men. Toward Fresno, toward Dijon
Toward Terre Haute, Bonne Terre, toward Paris, toward Warsaw, toward
Medicine Hat the roads were alive.
                                    Refugees
International winter:
The long night-running toward another shore.

Yet, in the shifting light, love seemed enough:
By the wavering fire as the long hunt went by us.
And seemed enough as I hitchhiked north in the heavy summer
Through the Kansas wheat, toward the rust-red roaring harvest of the high North –
Enough to say *love:* and all those masterless men
To become their masters in the commune of mystical toil:
Round dance:
Lauds toward a newer sun.
But no one said love.
                            Toward Bonne Terre, toward Reno, Land's End –
Or if it was said no one heard in the long running.

Still, it *was* said. We said it, if no one heard it.
And, going north through the summer in what was the end of a life
(Though it seemed a beginning), the crazy jungles, the wild
People on the roads – *that* was my true country:
And still is so – the commune: of pure potential.

To be in love then was a desperate business.
Marvelous. It was to stand with a Dechard rifle
Against the charge of the Oglala Sioux.
It was a pledge to revolts that never come.
It guaranteed a future that could not exist.
And so many were in love then. Really in love. Curious –
Like a disease…

      The life of a dangerous time.

8. North to Maine, then.

          Past my home, with the ghosts
Loud in the house: loud by the river and all else fading, fading
As if to be ghosts.

         But it was myself was fading,
My number up, the summer falling away
Toward the crowding war and the gay and calling host of the dead
Who laughed all around me.

The road lead directly to the landscape of dream:
Birdsong and water-sound and the north coil of the rivers
Beyond height of land.

        And the long pines leaning down
Under Canadian winds.

       And the trapped lakes, lost
Under the green night and the steady whispering weight
Of the unsleeping trees.

Waterville, Maine, the coil of the Kennebec
The stars fixed forever in the winter ice.

It seemed so.
                    In the frozen purity of the long northern night,
Hearing the high pipes and the wild drumming, continuous,
Loud, of the Syrian (or Armenian) workers…
Alien song that was: a wintry hieroglyph
Hung in the ear of night like a freight-train whistle
Strange and familiar. Hearing that song the unfixed
World turned round and steadied. I heard again the old
Song, in that circle where solidarity and the obscene
Lie down like the lamb and the lion.

In the college I taught in, too: the familiar –
Hank, Bill, Jim – the second-order rebellion.
The cantrip circle where wish is king of the woods.

And beyond that to the Old China Hands of that province:
Christers from Little East Jesus Falls, from West Burlap,
From Unity, Chastity and Modest Bastardy, Maine;
And the faculty members, each of them riding fence
On some King Ranch of the intellect: Texas talkers,
With running irons in their soogans and an eye for the maverick dogie
Of a new thought: would slap their brands on fast
And next fall sell it upriver, to the slaughterhouse pens of the North.

The same old jazz: North Dakota with pine trees
And the coiling rivers. Hunger alive in the compounds

Where the workers sang, the Wish prowling the streets
Where the jobless demonstrated under the icons
Of Its insurrectionary Name.
Potential – our love seemed to insure it…

9.   Stars in the black ice, fixed, and the shining figures
Swing through their formal houses. The long pond spangs and crackles
Under our flashing skates – a zodiac of my loves
Rings round the drowning stars…
                  Periphery, periphery –
                  How shall we say that brightness trapped in the black ice?

Item:
The one with the beard was Hank, who was proving something
With starfish he cut up in his own apartment
And the place stank of them. Also of hot-buttered rum.

Item:
The aimless Finn, the organizer frozen to death on a freight –
Somewhere beyond Bangor – "whose name I cannot remember."

            Periphery   periphery

Item:
Mrs. Mintz with her watery, no-color eyes,
Like those of some unclassified bird and her hoarse croak.
Had lost her voice selling bread which she lugged through the streets –

The great black loaves of the rye as hard as stones
In the bright cold.
                              Had a suitor,
A junkman from Concord who sold scrap iron to Japan,
Who coveted her mortgaged house.
                                        He came one day, bearing
The gift of a chicken and demanding a straight answer
To his modest proposal.
                              She said no.
                                        Thereupon
He divided the chicken in half and went on his way. Proper
Bostonian.

We had an apartment in that same mortgaged house:
Chandelier like a landslide on the Glass Mountain,
A great brass bed that seemed to be hung with bells.
All winter long, in the apocalyptic night –
The wolves howling at the edge of the pines, the Armenians singing,
Hank explaining his starfish, the wars sharpening their knives,
And Mrs. Mintz, like a mad saint, proffering bread in the streets –
All the wild dark, invincibly riding toward sleep,
We sang our love like a four-alarm fire. We rode past
Auroral midnights like Lapland majesty.

Then, spring. The shifting light altered
The shapes of the hills. The hollows ponded with sifting
Sun and the small lakes filled with the tall, fallen, meridian
Blue.

And in fence corners where, in the rainy autumn
I found the secret fruit, the winy, wind-downed cold
Apples – green shoots! now, of the hyacinth.
Daffodil, pickerelweed in the ponds, in the sedgy shallows;
And coppery crowds of the willow clouding the river's edge.

And all new! New as the black snake under
The winter house of his skin!
And the first true warmth in the blue thunder, the light.

These things I had once. This brightness, softness, sweetness
She gave me once to my keeping.
Piece of the true sun.

❀   ❀   ❀   ❀   ❀

Then the bird sang down his loud and ignorant note
And the stars were shifted in their fiery towns:
Arcturus:
Trapped in the lilac:
And I went south, by the coiling Kennebec River
(While the still stones sang, and the trees – and that free idiot bird –
Of the joys of the season)
Went with password forgotten – and the moon stuck in my pocket!
Toward War and the City;
Toward cold change and the anonymity of number:
Downriver, downriver,
Toward the bone-cold, wrestling coils of the salt, dumb-foundering sea.

X

1.   "Put me down, God," Preacher Noone says. "Put me down.
Here am I, 10,000 miles up and I'm flyin' blind;
Got no wings, got no airplane, got no passport – I say to you, God,
Put me down, Sir."

The stormy midnight. A scatter of stars scuds north
Under the rip-tooth clouds.

                          The little lost towns go by,
Towns of the dark people: a depot, a beer joint, a small
Fistful of lights flung east as the red-ball train goes past.

So we went north, taking a trip toward a war,
A long picnic, a sleep-out three years long, a regular pisscutter,
Went through the town of Buffalo, where once, with my father,
We stopped in the eye of a dust storm and I heard
The rattling freight go by.

                         Went through there now –
Whistling fistful of light blown east toward the morning,
Toward what was becoming our Past – ten miles north of home
And eight years into that older and colder dark
I once was strange to.

("This train ain't bound for glory," says Preacher Noone. "This train
Ain't bound for glory. Put me down God, please Sir.")

History:

       blown past the headlights to windward.

2.   West to Seattle and a cold camp.

                        Got our ship in that harbor,
And the first sailing we did was to circle around for a day
Like an old dog nosing the place he intends to lie down.
Correcting the compass, that was, so we wouldn't sail toward the wrong war.
North, then on the Inside Passage, like a dream of rebirth:
Ocean river between islands, between islands and mountains,
Between waterfalls on the mountains and the cold, exiling sea,
Her green estrangement.

                  Unhurried, out of the night,
The old, great, constellations, the soul-boats and ships of the heroes,
The fiery cities and signatures of the dead – burning –
Sailed up out of the North.

                 And the North itself was blazing,
A cold and prophetic light.

               By night: that ghost of warmth;
And the days gray as the Host in a pale mizzle of rain,
Transitional.

          There the piled salmon shoaled at stream-mouth,
And the dreamy, fishing bear hoisted the old, melancholy,
Great, hairy, disguising, joke of his head.
He stroked the sea with his enormous paw.
Silver and red the dull light gleamed on the bloodied salmon!

Holding the fish like a flag, he turned us his hooded stare,
Uncaring, alien, wild.
                              The ship sailed past
That massive indifference, into the lagging, transitional, wilderness
Light.

3.   And all toward the wars and the whores and the wares and the ways of a rotten season…
       Anchorage, Alaska, a little nugget of dung
       Hung in the eye of legend, in the quick-summer ice of gold braid.
       There the little war was going forward on schedule:
       The citizens, sharpening their knives, were six jumps ahead of the soldiers –
       They were already living in nineteen ninety. The whores
       Were working three rooms at once – for the dressing, the undressing, and the business,
       And the whorehouse lines, past the General's house, went round the block and past
       The Athabascan, the Great Slave, past White Horse, Winnipeg,
       Past Kalamazoo and Boston, toward Independence Hall,
       Where the last yardbird was easing his fly in the cold light
       Of the north and towering stars.
                                        There's patriotism for you –
       In the black light of the louring midnight sun!

       Somehow the Army, those reluctant civilians, sleepwalking
       In the bronzy dream of their elders, that khaki expensive night,
       Got past the whores and the open doors and the forming fours
       And past the true ice of Cook Inlet and the ugly frozen river,
       And supply sergeants: offering their tropic equipment.
       And took ship again at Seward.

("I give you up, God," says Parson
Noone. "I give you up, Sir. You got me cornered
With a williwaw roaring around my ass and my pants down –
Doctrinal matters blown past at ninety an hour –
I do hereby give you up, Sir, truly.")

Cold Bay, Adak, Sitka, Indifference Bay
The brown mountains, smoky, lifted out of the sea
Burning.
Kulaga. Semisoposhnoi. Dutch Harbor
Where the bombed ships lay rusting like dirty cardboard
Tramped flat in the icy water, and the rats fought at the rat-guards –
Their bodies brown as the brown mountains under their mottling fur –
Fought and fell in the freezing urine-colored sea.

Then down the Chain in a five-year fog, in a ninety-mile wind.
Below decks the crackers (no one went overseas
Except Southerners and myself) were cleaning their rifles:
Enfields that hadn't been cleaned since nineteen fourteen,
The bolts rusted tight as a safe.
But now and again they fired them,
The ricochets rattling around in those iron kitchens
Like angry popcorn.

So: we came to my island:
Called Fireplace, then, in the comfortable code of the admen
Who could send out a flight of children – and shoot them down the guns
Of that fiery island Kiska – yes: and call those dead ones home –
Under the name of Rinso White.

It is hard

To die for an adman –

Oh Adman Kadman!

Got to Amchitka then, under a yellow alert,
The two planes of the place orbiting, the water gun-colored
In a smoky drizzle of rain.
A miserable, choked-up harbor
So shallow that landing craft went aground and those Misplaced Persons,
Drowned or just too pooped out in the landing, bobbed round
In the mankilling-cold surf: among the orange crates and oil drums
And the sealed filing cases of the people who'd bought the war.
Climbed ashore there, too tired to be scared when the usual Charlie
Came beating his eggs or washing his clothes in the skies
We had never longed for.

But there was no war that day.
And we climbed the long hill, through the mud, toward a bed in the snow.

4.   Everything externalized; everything on the outside;
Nowhere the loved thing, or the known thing.
In the night of the army, the true sleepwalkers' country
All are masked familiars at the deaths of strangers –
It was the strangeness moved us.

In the cold blur of the rain
The bombers call: "Fireplace, Fireplace, do you read me,
Fireplace?"
Call and come in: great truckloads of the dead,

And the crazy medics, with needles stuck in their arms,
Come down to greet them.

In that country, under the suntan statutes of the place,
All death is by accident; and all life is also.
"War is the continuation of life by other means,"
Saith the Preacher (Noone). "It's like walking naked
Through the mating grounds of the Buzz Saw in His native habitat,
It's *one side or a leg off.*"

                                   It isn't like that.
No. In the war, if you didn't die, someone
Did your dying for you. It's there the guilt comes –
Nothing chosen and real: only the bombers loading
Reluctant bodies that someone else must shoot at –
Distracting.

                         It was *that* set the poets all wrong.
So that they went off to the war – in their insured opinions –
And (properly bitter) wrote like the minor versers
Of 1916: The one about getting equipment,
The one about firing for score, the one about
The Christian and/or Jew buried "abroad," the one
About the corpse in the green house.

                                   – All of it proper, of course,
A good "oppositional" poetry, as if it were made to order.

(Ho! John Thomas! What a sad state you're in now!
Your balls as cold as the brass monkey's, and around your neck
An old zodiac of bombers: falling down with their dead!)

Perhaps it was balls they lacked, the careful poets –
Or a proper respect for the dead, being brutalized
By too much writing for the *Sewanee Review* and Co.
(Come down now, Don Gordon, there's the body of a man here no one
Is prepared to bury.)
                                        (No one prepared for John
Thomas: a woman behind every tree and the last tree
At Kodiak, a couple of years toward Christmas.)

But no one comes down; only that corpse hung round
My neck by the circling bomber – a stiff in the cloud-high pastures
Of the lacklight, strange, permanent, feckless, enshrouding skies,
Prowling:
Fixed like the Hunter:
Fixed like the Bear:
In the cold house of the black starless North.

He did my dying for me.
                                        To each his own place

According to his need:
According to his ability:
The dead:
In their crowded cities, the living
In their isolation.

5.   The armed children at their terrible play, John Thomas!
        Into the gun-colored urine-smelling day, heroic,

The bombers go. The sad sacks and the weird sods,
And the gay deceivers: cranked up into the loud sky
At the end of the immaculate chain of money.
                                        The grieving day
Comes with its rains and ruins and across the bay and the drained
Downs where the fighter strip is, the guns go and the colored
Tracers mew and mow, for practice.
The planes loft up. The gunman children
(The radarscope on the voting machine for firepower)
Like leaves in the cold heaven, flung forth in their bombers.

So the day comes.
                                And down to the hornacle mine
Under the arch of the tracers to dig for the færy gold.
In those days (wakening under the cold comforter-snow,
Or awash above freezing water in our dug-down pyramidal tents,
Then wading into the fierce day, like mad frogs,
Amphibious); In those days (the wind
Exploding the tents out of the eight-foot caves
Where, against the williwaws, we'd dug them in –
The whole thing blown inside out: the tent, the men,
The glowing, red-hot stove with its stolen high-octane fuel:
Blown into the empty lunar lots and the wide acres of the high North,
Its lonely houses); In those Aleut days
(The dry-bones poets fussing over who owned the dead,
And the dead-ones in their high coffins singing around my ears –
Those windy bones) – From those days it's Cassidy I remember:
Who worked on the high steel in blue Manhattan
And built the topmost towers.

                              Now, on our island,
He was the shit-burner. He closed the slit-trench latrines
With a fiery oath.

                                    When they had built permanent structures
And underlaid them with the halves of gasoline drums,
He took the drums out on the tundra in the full sight of God
And burned them clean.

                              Stinking, blackened, smelling
Like Ajax Ajakes, he brought home every night
(Into the swamped pyramidal, where, over two feet of water,
Drifting like Noah on the shifting Apocalypse
Of the speech of Preacher Noone, I read by the ginkgo light)
Brough home mortality, its small quotidian smell.

That was a hero come home! (The bombers swinging
Around his neck, the gunners blessing his craft
For dropping their load in comfort!) Him, who on the high and windy
Sky of Manhattan had written his name in steel, sing now,
Oh poets!

But that's a hard man to get a line on.
Simple as a knife, with no more pretension than bread,
He worked his war like a bad job in hard times
When you couldn't afford to quit. He'd had bad jobs before
And had outworn them.

                              Now, in a howl of sleet,
Or under the constant rain and the stinking flag of his guild,
He stood in his fire and burned the iron pots clean.

6.   "What a goddamned second-hand war!" says Harry Merer.
We are passing the fighter-strip boneyard in an eighty-mile wind
With the horizontal rain going by us like buckshot.
The wrecked P40s glisten in the storm, their skins rattling
Under the slatting gusts.
"Like a goddamn Brooklyn junkyard,"
He says; and goes past the wreckage to the sand-bagged crash-tent
And Bob Kinkner and Charlie Wallant, and the long
Boredom.
                The war there was not one that could have been fought.
The Japs could have bought the island for two bottles of *sake*.
Still, it went on.
Cassidy stood in the wind, burning,
And we fought the weather: the fog solid around us
In a sixty-mile-an-hour gale, the sleet like gunshot
That ripped through the tent walls…

So, another day rusts out in the windy light.

❀   ❀   ❀   ❀   ❀

Toward quarter-time in the afternoon, the sky breaks:
Its floors shifting and the tall walls falling off seaward;
A brief lifting: Like night's wake shied off by a rafter-raising
Gust of surreal noon.
                In that metaphysical space
(As between lover and lover, between Longfellow and Night
The planes race out, race in: Our own bombers and Jap

Fighters – the latter a little early, since the weather blows from their way –
All hurrying out and home).

                               The planes come in
From Adak, from Umnak – from as far as Cold Harbor the planes
Come out of the door of the weather and home at my window like bees.

(The mail has come in: people still know how to write.)

Then comes the counting of the sexual cost,
The great Vulvar Shift and the Gemination of Cunt:
(The machine-gun's colored sperm is arching over the harbor
In a Blindman's Fourth of July, where no man may speak,
And the hunting Hands – Oh Jesus Jason John Thomas –
In the high Oh Jerusalem fleece of the incoming fog,
Golden: in new-come sun: up to their balls in the sky):
Shot down at ten thousand miles by the blast of a Dear John.

Then the bombers:
Blown home on the squall line:
A jump behind buckshot:
Bad news:
At the end of the girls', fathers', shotguns'
Twelve-gauge prejudice:
Blown out of the unkempt counties of the west unfriendly sky.
Those dead come home to the medics, frantic-McGantic,
Dropped down the mailslot of the early night
(The mantic frail-quail and the fright-wigs, and the simple
Big-ass birds)…
                    Burning…

Like Cassidy –

Burning: burning:

Then the calm evening – the one calm evening we all remembered:
And the dead planes come in, dropping like flung stones,
Like falling slow stars, burning, onto the flat preachments
Of the metalled runway's hot gospel – a whirring blur of light
As of summer sparklers, and a huff and a puff of flame
Like a dream of Emma Goldman – the undropped bombs raining
Around our ears, the iron dung of those birds – and the dead
screaming
In their blazing cages.

We ran like rabbits down the dead flat road of their light
To snatch them home to the cold from the fiery cities of air,
Their sky-high blazing foxholes and the smoldering houses
Of the zodiac of the dead.
The medics came down
With their nine-foot flutes, and the joy-pumps stuck in their arms,
To bind them home.
We pulled them out of their rig,
Screaming, and gave them over to the mercy of the medical arm.

Then, in that one clear evening, the planes burned!
Fighters and bombers: P40s and 38s, B24s, 26s
Burning! Burning!
And the ammo burning, exploding, shot in the eye of heaven
The salmon-leaping tracers arching their backs to those stars –
Visible, newly, but shifted – and the whole for-once-bright evening

(Old-fashioned Fourth of July) under the changed constellations
Strange, in the high North.

_____ carried them out.
And the meat-wagons took them away.

                                        Blue, green, yellow,
Their peculiar gear was burning across the night,
Those Roman Candles.

        There is a corpse in the snow…
        "It's dead, bury it," says the Captain.
        There is a blue fox come into the chow line.
        "Bless it," says Preacher Noone. "It's hungry; it's holy."
        There's a madman lives in my tent, got a two-foot knife. "Shoot it,"
        The Captain says, "It's alive; it fouls up my Morning Report."

7.   Then, Night.
        Night, first of the high, great fog: blown down
        From the vast Siberias and freezing unknown lands
        Of the fierce bear and blue shy fox.
                                        Blown past our sleep
        In the ninety-mile wind, a shifting of space itself.

        Night of the Army then: its paper snow: proper:
        And its fog of number: cold: and its graceless mossy
        Sleep, like wine in a stone ear.
                                        Night, too,

Of khaki: in the wet, cold dark, a claustrophobia
Of rancid clothing: implacable oppression of unchosen things,
A uniform irritation – though god knows
We dressed like bums, like pirates, in rainclothing
Stolen from the Navy's house, its many mansions.
Still, heavy, heavy, was the wear of that alien skin.
Cold cave, rough womb, from which we could not be born,
It filed the dream to a vision of sharp light,
Some bright and burning beach and ourselves naked upon it –
The wild need to undress home to the Self.
A romanticism of light…

But now the dark comes down cold, like a wet beast
Dropped on the dreaming floor of a farther and other night,
Terrible.
                              Over the tundra the guns of the lost people,
The impatient ones, the midnight suicides,
Salute the war they have immoderately lost.

Fireworks in the rain! And the dark circus…
Now the night-crawlers and the water-walkers appear:
Those who go home by sea to the ten-foot line;
And then the ingenious: swallowers of razor blades,
Truck drivers with ten feet of hose, the inventors
Who have found something high enough or strong enough to hang on;
And the shy loonies who can fall off cliffs.

Oh night! Night! In the nine hundred countries of the endless war
How cold you come: and sane! John dear, dear

Thermotropic anonymous letters that explode at blood heat
And will blow you ass-ways just because you are warm…)
Part of the Engineer's great dream: a war without bandages.

It was through all this altruism that Cassidy moved,
Cloudy, in the oil and smoke of burning excrement,
In his fiery cloacal mask.
                                        Was run over, one day,
By an off-reservation aircraft.
                                        Nowhere, now, on the high
Steel will he mark on the sky that umber scratch
Where the arcing rivet ends.
                                        Gathered away
Toward the unknown stars, in the general drift toward Aries:
In the blanketing dark:
Salmony deadfall of the fishing Bear:
Outward:
His speed increasing to the speed of light and his mass infinite –
PUT THAT MAN DOWN, GOD!

❊   ❊   ❊   ❊   ❊

                    Later…
And home then, the war ending…
The port: drifted two hundred miles to the south, the stars
Shifting in the permanent sky…
                                        Put me down

Sir.

XI

1.   Dream and despair; the journey around a wound…
Circularity again, with nothing laid true in a straight line
Nor square with the sailor star nor the fence of the north forty
But turning, turning…
               Dakota, New York, Europe, Dakota again,
Los Angeles Frisco Dakota New York, Los Angeles
Turning and turning…
               Outbound on the far night journey
As some long-chained animal, loosed, would pace his imagined cage
Turning, turning, I turned
Around the dead center of some unnamable loss:
Nowhere and nowhere…
               Like a man in the dark, searching
A vast wall for a door, through which he dreams his escape:
But he's on the outside…
               Or, like a man going round
And round some fogbound lake, trying to find a crossing
(The buried lake of the past in which he must drown)
Turning; turning and turning –
But never the direct voyage, the short journey toward the endless wound.

2.   They were fighting: soldiers, sailors, marines, civilians
As we came down the gangplank, or spilled out the door of a bar,

Fighting four sided, the whistles blowing, the cops and the MPs coming.
I tried to run; and the nightstick slugged me, and sang me home.

Then began the war that Patchen had foreseen:
"When the cops were there in sufficient numbers, they all blew their whistles together.
The fighting stopped, and everyone changed clothes –
(The civilians got off the worst because everyone wanted their duds)
Then the whistles were blown again, and the war ended:
There were five seconds of silence…
Everyone swapped sides, in accord with his clothing…
And the whistles blew once more and the fighting started again…"

New York then: picketing the Franco ship,
Walking around in circles in the end of an older war.
And Showboat Quinn, barefoot on 17th Street
In the early cold autumn, across from the CYO
(Where the local boys shot up the Puerto Rican newcomers) saying:
"What part of the fuckin' local pageant are *you?*"
Saying: "Money talks these days; stop whisperin' there in the dark;
Get out in the stream and *sing!*"

And up the street, in Mac's pad, where he lay, great-chested,
Stuffed with the borrowed air of the pneumo shots,
The lads came: the activists, the hotshots and the live-o's
From the NMU, the ILA, the Teamsters and Electrical Workers
To pace up and down and curse.
                                        Turning and turning

Fighting mainly each other.
                                        Turning round, turning round

The massive and central grief, the great secret loss of the war:
The cantrip and singing circle dreaming against the cold.

❋　❋　❋　❋　❋

And home then in the first black frost of the fierce and peaceful season –
High shine of the north drifting toward willful Scorpio
In the waste of October light…
To a houseful of ghosts and a wild autumnal singing
Of the spilled seed and the lost hosts of the dead.
The rusty ports of the sun…
                                    Turned, and returned, and alone,
And the moon in my pocket as thin as a lousy dime.

In the north forty, the tractor has eaten the horse.
You can't hear the crying for the sound of the counting of money.

3.　We lay in the east room, Marian and I, in the cold October light,
Light of a hurrying moon blown past the few thin mare's-tail clouds.
Downstairs my mother was singing her rosary over my brother's bones.
Under the North Sea somewhere the fishes were eating my friend,
And far in the woods-dark, on the coulee hills, toward the distant river,
Under the disturbing moon a coyote barked toward the Prime.

She, asking:
"Are you going then?"
"I don't know."

"Will you be gone long?"
"I don't know."
"Will you be back?"
"I don't
Know."

4.   Country full of strangers in their queer costumes…
And a hurrying fury clapperclawing their lack…
Bandits…murderers in medals holding hands in the catch-as-can dark
With the carking, harked-back-to, marked-down virgins of the stark little towns
Where, once, their paper histories dropped on the thin lawns
And rocking porches of the dead-eye dons and the homegrown dream-daddies
Now stiff with their war-won monies.
                       Bandits…gypsies –
Under the humped cloth of war…
                     Those sad children…
Older than headlines, under their khaki print.

And mad for money, those guys: for the lost prewar
Landlocked virgin and the homespun moss of her historical North
Forty.
        Aiee!
               Great God in a basket!
                         Those famous men
All green with their green-backed hope!

Country of strangers…

                Myself strange, under the corroding moon,

And the cold charity of the first, thin, early, snow.

5.   Snow fell slight, pale filings of the icy sky, sifting

Fast into bare brown woods we went past in the thinned-out, downfallen day,

Turning on the high hinge of the winter-come night.

                            Some light still

Splintered on the height of the hueless corn…

                       _____ went through there –

And the pheasant leaped! Leaped out toward his death

In the feathery color of thunder!

                        Under the gun's black clap

Fell.

Enamel feathers; eye more round than his blood,

More jeweled, that stretched out neck with its ring of moonlight…

Red and Sorenson walk up out of the deepening gloom,

Through the leathery clatter of the thin corn that is shaking its winter rattles,

Still wearing their uniforms, talking of Saipan: of Marathon.

Red puts out his hand. "Too thin," he says

Feeling the bird's crop. "Farmers picked their corn

Too close this year. He's too thin. Leave him lay."

And that fall the bandits went hunting –

Still in their uniforms, but getting too thick for 'em –

And shot up everything that could run fly or crawl.
Cleaned out the deer as slick as a whistle,
Bucks, does, the half-grown fawns and the yearlings –
Killed them with everything from buckshot to Schmeissers and Tommy guns;
Blew holes in them bigger than their own hard heads;
Hacked off a haunch and let them lay.
                                                            That fall
Those gypsies in uniform drank all the wine of the province,
Down to the last corn-squeezins:
Ate all the food:
Screwed everything that could walk:
And ran off around breakup, just before spring work started,
Complaining of obscure hungers.

And myself, Tom Fool, ran with them: in a journey around my hat:
The cantrip circle dispersed:
Nothing to hold to:
No center there and no center in myself.
Leaving Marian, though we didn't know that till later,
Turning and turning.

Some ran toward money, and some toward hunger, and all were lost.
You have seen the bones in bank vaults, or in glass cases over the bars
Among the foreign money, where Custer once fought
And the great golden nude slumbered above the whiskey.
Do those bones live? Do they sing still in the whirling
Dust on the grandfather stair where first my loves were singing?

They sing still; and are still; in the grandfather dark.

6.   It was that dark I entered, blown toward no certain shore,
     Turning and turning.
                              Past the Indian graves and the river,
     Past the north forty, past Dakota, New York, Villefranche,
     Past love, past work, past any plan, past hope,
     Past sex, past whiskey, past defeat, past
     The bottom of the interior night and that antipodean great beast
     (Whose charity is to devour), past common sense
     And solidarity –
     Oh journey – Oh journeys – around the unnamable years
     And circumvention of joy…

     And come at last to the condominium of monsters:
     Ulan Bator of the Outside:
     Fantastic godowns and submerged kraals
     Of the underground man.
     And swam there in the sea-light of alcohol and unspeakable loss,
     In that parade of freaks:

                    A bandage comes by wearing a man
                    A walking eye with a cunt grown on its pupil
                    The Porcupine Man with his hide stuck full of syringes
                    The Lady Built Backwards
                    Geeks, ploot, quim, loogans and hooples,
                    Liz's and queens and
                    Pathics with the rough trade of the quarter,
                    The benny-workers and the Monday-men,
                    Wino chenangos,
                    Lumpers, humpers, and keester-bumpers,

The Monkey with the Man on his Back,
High-graders, God-hoppers, mission-stiffs, marks and sharpies,
Punks and meatheads *Apackapus Americanus*
Drifters, queers, losers; the underground men
Hung on the pukey weather of the skid row street.
And continual wind of money, that blows the birds through the clocks,
That plucks a cold harp inside the bellies of horses;
In those days: a blizzard of continual bones
Under the stony sky of the counting heart.
In those days – blood of the dead freezing in blind eyes.
House of smoke, hour bitter as knives,
And the avalanche, cooling its fevers, on the second floor of your tomb.

Nightmare, nightmare; despair; dream; and despair.

7.   It was down there,
Past the milestones of my tombs and the singing bones of my true loves
I come there:
Drifting:
In the high march and dead set of the night,
On the most direct road to my death –
Most careless there –
I come into the Old Dominion, the true, breathing, holy Dark.
There, old bird on the branch of the lost midnight,
The Dark closed and clothed me, and the pushed, furious beast
That burned and bit in my side lay down to sleep.
Hushed at last.

Then I saw the bones go singing –
Like stars or fireflies –
And came to the laughter:
The Holy Joke of myself in that blizzard of dark and light:
To Laughter:
Laughter of light and dark and the Holy Joke of the real world,
And the great open secret that we all know and forget.
Samadhi. Satori.

Then the great night and its canting monsters turned holy around me.
Laughably holy.
And that lank gentleman, the æsthete snake, came by to bite me,
And the littlest scared mad dog of a crazy world,
And I gave them my heel to kiss –
In my sudden pride:
In my ridiculous love:
In my wholeness and holiness:
In solidarity and indifference:
In the wild, indifferent joy which is man's true estate.

Love and hunger: solidarity and indifference –
So I ended my journey to the enduring wound,
In the holy and laughing night with the stars drifting
Indifferent;
And myself indifferently drifting
Past the randy Goat and the Water Carrier,
Past Easter, and the high Feast of the Fools,
In the thin rain of the time.

XII

1.   All changed; the world turned holy; and nothing changed:
There being nothing to change or needing change; and everything
Still to change and be changed…

Now…
           Past Solstice…
                        The infrequent rain
Of a cold, unseasonal season…
                         My neglected, arrogant garden
Lifts in the night its indifferent gold and green:
Fuchsia with its Greek fighters and Dutch girls;
And the freckled small tunnels of Foxglove which the bee drifts;
Yellow Iris, bronze Day Lily, Lupine, Larkspur, Linaria
Bend in the chill, thin rain: infrequent: past Easter and the Feast
Of Fools.
          Night now:
                        First Neighbor's dog
Frets at the ghost of a moon.
                        Mourning like a lost ship
A diesel hoots and harks in the railroad yards, past the river;
And the dead come home, riding the blinds, at last
Crossing the dark mountains after the months of snow.

2.   Strange season now, nothing but wars and the sound of money
And the hills alive with crazy men and deserters…
_____ and past Capistrano, where the road cuts down to the ocean,
Past oil fields where the pumps like herds of great insects,
Prayerful, bow and daven:

                                    We head south, to the Border,
To export the Revolution, taking Mac into Mexico.

After the Immigration ordered his self-deportation.
1955 that was: on a cold afternoon:
Autumn dropping its metal in the blue wound of the weather
And the papers full of news from the scientists
Who were dreaming of wars without blood, of blowing us clean out of history
Without even the need for a Band-Aid.
                          Past Pedro
Where Mac had been organizer: past the strikes, past the Thirties,
Past the Baltimore Soviet, past the Bremen where Mac
Had cut down the Nazi flag –

For the exile it is always ten-degrees colder beyond the border.
Southward, to Ensenada,
To the cold sea and the confusion of foreign speech
I took him.
"Goodbye, Tom Fool," he says
Last of my fathers.

3.   "When the fix is equal, justice must prevail"…
        Blue violence of the eye, that lends its shape to the world,
        Fixes no proper image for the times.
        The Committee comes by with its masked performers
        To fire you out of your job, but that's expected.
        Money breeds in the dark – expected.
        Weeping and loss – expected.
        _____ What was hard to imagine were the do-it-yourself kits
        With four nails and a hammer and patented folding cross,
        And all the poets, green in the brown hills, running…

        I needed a word for the Now, to nail its hide to the barn…
        There is one of Lubner's paintings – people among the rocks,
        Refugees, a Madonna with a curious witless smile,
        A mystery.
                        Also a great gentle horse, and a man with an odd
        Figured shirt and several women in black,
        And there ought to be (but there isn't) a birdcage with, in it –
        What?
        A tame star, perhaps?

        Working in the animal foundry, I puzzle toward it.
        Schwartz is burning the horns of an ibex, perhaps –
        Product of his dark fancy – and I daydream through the sound
        Of the wood saw and the drift of the golden poisonous dust:
        And see Mac standing – Mac or Cal – with Maggie his wife
        And a scatter of Mexican kids by the ocean's cold confusion –
        An image of exile.

I turn away then
Unforgetting
Seeing a little piece of the old true unregenerate dark
Extruded into the afternoon classical light –
A little Contra-Terrene matter among the pure shit of the poets –
The world's inescapable evil that we must eat and sing.

And turn away then
From the shop, from the sea,
Toward the desert of the world, the wild garden,
With my politics: to be with the victims and fighters.
Turn North, toward the dry river, to journey in sunlight
Beyond the sea's conventions and the winter's iron and ice.

4.   Blesséd, blesséd
                    Oh blesséd
Blesséd be changing day and night and the old far-ranging
Starry signs of the loved, continual, surprising seasons;
Blesséd be dark and light, blesséd be freezing and burning,
Blesséd be the gold fur of the He-sun and the moon's-down shine of the great,
Bold, changing, Woman queening the wild night sky;
Blesséd be the metric green confusion of the crowding, cold, estranging, and inconstant sea;
Blesséd be the stay-at-home land, the rocking mountains under the loose loud sky;
Blesséd be speech and silence;
Blesséd be the blood hung like a bell in my body's branching tree;
Blesséd be dung and honey;

Blesséd be the strong key of my sex in her womb, by cock and by cunt blesséd
The electric bird of desire, trapped in the locked-room mysteries of country charm;
Blesséd be my writing hand and arm and the black lands of my secret heart.

Blesséd be the birds of the high forest hung on a wing of song;
Blesséd be the long sin of the snake and his fangs blesséd;
Blesséd be the fishing bear in his shine and fury;
Blesséd be flower and weed: shoot, spike, rhizome, raceme, sepal, and petal;
The blued-out wildlings; metallic, green marsh-hiders shy; high-climbers, low-rooters.
Beast, bird, tree, stone, star: blesséd, blesséd.

And blesséd be friends and comrades:
Blesséd be Rolfe in his dark house and the hearts of friends.
Blesséd, by the loud continuous: Naomi.
Blesséd on their mountains under the enshrouding shine of the spent stars' light:
                                                Don and Charlie:
With their wives, children, heirs, and assigns.
Blesséd, blesséd
In the wastelots and the burning cities of man's estate,
Fishers by still streams, hunters on the hard hills, singers, dreamers, and makers:
Blesséd be all friends
With their wives, husbands, lovers, sons, daughters, heirs, and assigns
Forever.

Blesséd be the fighters:
The unknown angry man at the end of the idiot-stick with his dream of freedom;
Jawsmiths and soapboxers, gandy dancers setting the high iron
Toward the ultimate Medicine Hat: blesséd, blesséd.
Blesséd the agitator: whose touch makes the dead walk;

Blesséd the organizer: who discovers the strength of wounds;
Blesséd all fighters.

Blesséd be my loves: in the wreckage of morning light,
In the high moon-farms, in the horny hot nights of the dry, gone summers,
In the heat of lust and thunder of noon sheets –
Blesséd be flesh and voice, blesséd forever;
Blesséd thy belly and legs;
Blesséd be thy woman's warmth in this human winter.

Blesséd, blesséd
                              Oh blesséd
Blesséd be Marian,
All ways the honey flesh of this girl with light on her shoulder
Oh blesséd, blesséd!

And blesséd now be all children:
Hunters come through the space warp, waking
Into their unmade world under the sign of our outlaw fire;
Blesséd their hopes and confusions;
Blesséd their deeps and darks
Their friends and lovers, heirs, and assigns forever.

And blesséd, blesséd, blesséd, blesséd
Be my wife and love, and her body's being:
Green song of the double-meaning sea;
Tree of my dreamless bird, unsleeping quarry of seamless
Light; feathery river of the sensual continent, unseasonal rain

Under the riven sky of my dry thunderstruck night-side heart
Unending lightning....

                                   Oh blesséd!

And blesséd myself and myselves...
Turning homeward...

                         under the waking shapes of the rain....
Blesséd.

5.   Now, toward midnight, the rain ends.
        The flowers bow and whisper and hush;

                                   the clouds break
        And the great blazing constellations rush up out of the dark
        To hang in the flaming North.....
        Arcturus, the Bear, the Hunter
        Burning.....

        Now, though the Furies come, my furious Beast,
        I have heard the Laughter,
        And I go forward from catastrophe to disaster
        Indifferent: singing:
        My great ghosts and the zodiac of my dead
        Swing round my dream.

        Star-shine steady over this house where I sit writing this down –
        2714 Marsh Street –

                                   Drifting toward Gemini...

Night, pure crystal,

        coils in my ear like

                song...

– Los Angeles, 1955

PART TWO

Everything or nothing! All of us or none.
    – *Bertolt Brecht*

…luck, chance, and talent are of no avail,
and the man who wishes to wrest something
from Destiny must venture into that per-
ilous margin-country where the norms of
Society count for nothing and the demands
and guarantees of the group are no longer
valid. He must travel to where the police
have no sway, to the limits of physical resis-
tance and the far point of physical and moral
suffering. Once in this unpredictable border-
land a man may vanish, never to return; or
he may acquire for himself, from among the
immense repertory of unexploited forces
which surrounds any well-regulated society,
some personal provision of power; and
when this happens an otherwise inflexible
social order may be cancelled in favour
of the man who has risked everything…
Society as a whole teaches its members
that their only hope of salvation, within
the established order, lies in an absurd and
despairing attempt to get free of that order.
    – *Claude Levi-Strauss*

Don't give your right name! No, no, no!
    – *Fats Waller*

I

1. _____ coils in my ear like song…
                                        the dawn wind riding
Out of the black sea, knocks at my shutters. Cockcrow.
Before cockcrow: the iron poet striding over
This village where the horses sleep on the roofs, where now a lone
Rooster rasps the beak of his song on the crumbling tiles.

Skyros.
        In the false light before sunup.
I wait while the breeze,
Or a ghost, calls at the shutters.
                                    Beyond the window the wild
Salt north forty of wind and water, the loud, galloping
White-maned mustangs of the cold ungovernable sea…

Honeysuckle, lavender, oleander, osiers, olive trees, acanthus –
All leafsplit, seedshaken, buckling under the drive
Of the living orient red wind
                                constant abrasive
North Dakota
            is everywhere.
                            This town where Theseus sleeps on his hill –
Dead like Crazy Horse.
                    This poverty.
                                This dialectic of money –

Dakota is everywhere.
                    A condition.
                              And I am only a device of memory
To call forth into this Present the flowering dead and the living
To enter the labyrinth and blaze the trail for the enduring journey
Toward the round dance and commune of light…
                                        to dive through the night of rock
(In which the statues of heroes sleep) beyond history to Origin
To build that Legend where all journeys are one
                                    where Identity
Exists
        where speech becomes song…

                        ❊   ❊   ❊   ❊   ❊

                    First bird sound now…
This morning Lambrakis overthrew the government in ghost-ridden Athens
Having that power of the dead out of which all life proceeds…
Genya smiles in her sleep. The arch of her foot is darkened
With the salt of the ancient sea and the oil of a bad century…
The light sharpens.
                The wind lifts.
                            The iron poet
Strides out of the night and the instant world begins
Outside this window.
                    World where the rebels fall under
The Socratic tricycles of NATO gangsters, are plugged in the heart
By intercontinental ballistic musical moments mechanical
Pianos loaded with the short-fuse scrap iron of Missouri waltzes, guided

Missiles of presidential rocking chairs timed to explode on contact…
Texas fraternal barbecues: "Bring your own nigger or be one."

(And, of a mountain of wild thyme, its thunderous honey.)

❊   ❊   ❊   ❊   ❊

The sea builds instantaneous lace which rots in full motion –
One-second halflife – just beyond this window.
                              Full light.
Cicadas.
        A donkey brays on the citadel.
                              The world,
                                    perfect
And terrible.
        Sun in Gemini.
                    New moon at summer solstice
Perfect.

❊   ❊   ❊   ❊   ❊

        All changed and nothing changed and all to be changed.
I want the enduring rock, but the rock shifts, the wind
Lifts, Hell's always handy, you may enter the labyrinth anywhere
Beyond the window.
              Where now the first fisherman goes out:
To the mother sea, to mine for the small fish and the big –
The hours and minutes of her circular heart – to dig in the turquoise
Galleries of her tides and diamond-studded lobsters with their eyes of anthracite…

Where his partner, the Hanged Man,

                                  strangled in nets of poverty…

                                                     last night…

Last night. This morning. The rock and the wind.

                                    North Dakota *is*

Everywhere.

2.   "_____ seems like it was right here somewhere…

                                      place where you git out –
Hey there, resurrection man! ghost haunter, crazy damn poet,
What you do now kid?"

                  (Voices from sleep, from death, from
The demoniacal dream called living.)

                              – I'm here to bring you
Into the light of speech, the insurrectionary powwow
Of the dynamite men and the doomsday spielers, to sing you
Home from the night.

                Night of America.

                      Gather you
At my million-watt spiritlamp, to lead you forward forever, to conquer
The past and the future…

                    ❊   ❊   ❊   ❊   ❊

                 "Well just a doggoned minute now,
Whilst I gits my possibles sack, my soogans, my –"

             – Heavy,
Heavy the weight of these choice souls on my sun-barked shoulder, heavy
The dark of the deep rock of the past, the coded legend
In the discontinuous strata where every voice exists –
Simultaneous recall: stone where the living flower leaps
From the angry bones of Precambrian dead.
                         Heavy the weight
Of Jim, of Jack, of my father, of Cal, of Lambrakis, Grimau,
Hiroshima, Cuba, Jackson…
                 heavy the weight of my dead
And the terrible weight of the living.

❀   ❀   ❀   ❀   ❀

              "It's dark down here, man –
This slippery black – can't keep my footin' – like climbin'
A greased pole, man –"
             And always, as I go forward,
And older I hear behind me, intolerable, the ghostlight footsteps –
Jimmy perhaps; or Jack; my father; Cal; Mac maybe –
The dead and the living – and to turn back toward them – that loved past –
Would be to offer my body to the loud crows and the crass
Lewd jackals of time and money, the academy of dream-scalpers, the mad
Congressional Committees on Fame, to be put on a crisscross for not wearing
The alien smell of the death they love
                   – they'd cram my bonnet
With a Presidential sonnet: they'd find my corpse worth stuffing
With the strontium 90 of tame praise, the First Lady to flay me
For mounting in the glass house of an official anthology…

                                        catafalques
Of bourgeois sensibility
                    – Box A to Box Z…
                                        And my body to suffer
(As my soul) dismemberment…
                        transmemberment…
                                        my head
                                            singing
                                                go down
The dark river…
                    necessary –
                        not to turn back.

                    ❋   ❋   ❋   ❋   ❋

"_____ and seems like it was right here someplace – place you git out…"
"Stick beans in your nose and you cain't smell honey." (Peets talking)
"Ain't no grab irons a man can lay hand to. *I tell you it's* DARK
DOWN HERE, MAN!
                    slippery dark
                            can't see
                                I tell you it's hell – "

We must walk up out of this dark using what charms we have.
Hell's everywhere, this only seems like hell, take my hand,
It is only required to open your eyes –
                                    see
                                        there's

The land as it was
                    these poor
                              the Indian graveyard
                                        the coulee
The quaking aspens Genya and I planted last spring
At the old farmhouse.
                    Unchanged and changed.
                                        I tell you millions
Are moving.
               Pentagon marchers!
                              Prague May Day locomotives
With flowers in their teeth!
                         And now the red ball is hammering in –
Spot an empty! Grab an armful of rods!
                              I'll take you
In the final direction…
               Only:
                    open your eyes…
But it's hard, hard, man.
                    I'm standing *here,* naked
As a studhorse in a rhubarb patch
                         waiting
                              waiting
                                   and here –
Around me
          trouble built for small boys and crazy men!
For my purpose (as I keep saying) is nothing less
Than the interpositioning of a fence of ghosts (living and dead)

Between the atomic sewing machines of bourgeois ideology
(Net where we strangle) and the Naked Man of the Round Dance…
"To perform instantaneous insurrectionary lobotomies for removing
The man-eating spinning wheels from the heads of our native capitalists."
To elaborate the iconic dynamite of the authentic class struggle
In other words to change the world
                                        – Nothing less.
                                                    It's hard and I'm
Scared…

                        ❋   ❋   ❋   ❋   ❋

        The beginning is right here:
                            ON THIS PAGE.
Outside the window are all the materials.
                                    But I am waiting
For the colored stone…
                            for the ghosts to come out of the night…
And now the village sleeps.
                    A heavy static,
                                golden
Like the honey of lovesick buzz saws clots in the steepy light
And the tall and aureate oak of the august noon-high sun
Crumbles.
            That pollen.
                    Seeding the air…
                                The cicadas (tzinzaras)
Are machining the sunlight in their chattering mills
                                        kind of Morse code

With a terrible signal-to-noise ratio – is it information
Comes through all that clatter or a mere random conformity
To a known Code?
                    Minimax
                            bobbery
                                    palaver
                                            – you can reduce shortfall
Only so much – finally…
                        it is necessary to act.
                                            Even
When the information is incomplete…
                                    – That's all right:
I'll cut for sign – and don't leave the gate open
                                            I'll
Catch my own snipes.
                    The village is *not* asleep, it is only
Siesta…

        A poor fisherman hanged in a net
Puts all heaven in a sweat…
                            The ratio of signal
To noise improves. I read you loud and clear. Over.

"– get out in the stream and *sing*.
                            It's a branch assignment,
                                            a job
For the revolutionary fraction in the Amalgamated Union of False Magicians,
Kind of boring, from within…"
                            Insurrectionary

ancestral voices…

                                         – coming now –

Ghosts wreathed with invincible wampum –

                            "Hey buddy

What you doing there in the dark?"

                      – How should I know?

                                  What I'm doing

Ain't nobody

        nowhere

           never

              done before.

II

1.   Fictional breakfasts, feasts of illusionary light!

                           "Poo ine

O dromos sto horyo where is the lonesome road
To the village where is it the hydroæroplano leaves
For Buenos Aires?"

           I'll cut for sign…

                   mark of the blazed tree

Where I left the note and the colored stone in the hopeful intervals
Between cyclones and waterspouts, while the firing squads
Were taking a five-minute break…

                "was right here, someplace…
_____ place where I left it…"

          Patience.

             I am the light. I'm

Wearing my blazer…

        Begun before Easter in the holy sign
Of the Fish.

     Dakota.

       The farm house…

             – but before that…

             ❋   ❋   ❋   ❋   ❋

Ten years – doing time in detention camps of the spirit,
Grounded in Twin Plague Harbor with comrades Flotsam & Jetsam:

Wreckage of sunken boats becalmed in the Horse Latitudes
Windless soul's doldrums LosAngeles AsiaMinor of the intellect
Exile.

     I arrived in the form of a dream, the dream-formed
Journey begun in love and hunger, Dakota, the Old
Dominion of darkness…
                  from labor
                        ignitable books
                                unsettled
Terms of a murderous century
                    dynamite
                        the eternal bourgeois
Verities of poverty and money _____ to voyage forth toward the light…

Got there by way of War and His cousin Personal Misery.
And of that journey and time and the records thereof kept
As of books written   logs   tallies   maps   manifestoes
As of resolutions past or not passed in aforementioned intervals
Between stampedes   shipwrecks   logjams   battles with hostiles
Catatonic inventions   hellsfire   attacks of personal and spurious
Revelation –
       Tokens:
             stone
                  marked tree
                        immortal
Blazonings…

2.   Windless city built on decaying granite, loose ends
Without end or beginning and nothing to tie to, city downhill
From the high mania of our nineteenth century destiny – what's loose
Rolls there, what's square slides, anything not tied down
Flies in…
          kind of petrified shitstorm.
                        Retractable
Swimming pools.
            Cancer farms.
                Whale dung
At the bottom of the American night refugees tourists elastic
Watches…

          Vertical city shaped like an inverse hell:
At three feet above tide mark, at hunger line, are the lachrymose
Cities of the plain weeping in the sulphurous smog; Anaheim:
South Gate (smell of decaying dreams in the dead air)
San Pedro Land's End…
                   – where the color of labor is dark –
(Though sweat's all one color) around Barrio No Tengo
Among the Nogotnicks of the Metaphysical Mattress Factory, where the money is made.

And the second level: among the sons of the petty Bs –
The first monkey on the back of South Gate, labor – at the ten
Thousand a year line (though still in the smog's sweet stench)
The Johnny Come Earlies of the middling class:
                      morality
                        fink-size

Automatic rosaries with live Christs on them and cross-shaped purloined
Two-car swimming pools full of holy water…
                                    From here God goes
Uphill.
          Level to level.
                          Instant escalation of money – up!
To Cadillac country.

                    Here, in the hush of the long green,
The leather priests of the hieratic dollar enclave to bless
The lush-working washing machines of the Protestant Ethic ecumenical
Laundries: to steam the blood from the bills – O see O see how
Labor His Sublime Negation streams in the firmament!
Don't does all here; whatever is mean is clean.

And to sweep their mountaintops clear of coyotes and currency climbers
They have karate-smokers and judo-hypes, the junkies of pain,
Cooking up small boys' fantasies of mental muscles, distilling
A magic of gouged eyes, secret holds, charm
Of the high school girls' demi-virginity and secret weapon
Of the pudenda pachucas (takes a short-hair type
For a long-hair joke) power queers; socially-acceptable sadists –
Will tear your arm off for a nickel and sell it back for a dime.

And these but the stammering simulacra of the Rand Corpse wise men –
Scientists who have lost the good of the intellect, mechanico-humanoids
Antiseptically manufactured by the Faustian homunculus process.
And how they dream in their gelded towers these demi-men!
(Singing of overkill, kriegspiel, singing of blindfold chess –

Sort of ainaleckshul rasslin matches to sharpen their fantasies
Like a scout knife.)
                              Necrophiles.
                                   Money protectors…
– They dream of a future founded on fire, on a planned coincidence
Of time and sulphur…
                              Heraclitean eschatology…

And over it all, god's face,
                                   or perhaps a baboon's ass
In the shape of an ICBM beams toward another war.
One is to labor, two is to rob, three is to kill.
Executive
          legislative
                    judiciary…
                              – muggery, buggery, and thuggery
All Los Angeles
               America
                    is divided into three parts.

                    ❋   ❋   ❋   ❋   ❋

"If you can't screw 'em – join 'em," Peets says. "They come here
Answerin' the *Call*."
                    And it may be.
                                   The distant horn sounding…

They heard it first perhaps in the faded, dreaming polemical
Grandfather cadence: how this one caught the old bear

Belted for winter swimming the cold lake; how the last deer,
Antlers in mossy felt, shot down in the aspen scantlings
Fell: as the final take of the long march west; how the light failed
While the flights of wild geese crossed on their high arch of darkness
Calling.

    The land failed them; or else they failed the land.

And turned westward their canvas-covered argosies
Freighted with dreams: the Daniel Boones of the last myth
Toward free land and free labor, the commune and round dance
Journeying…

    But a myth's not as good as a mile.

          Came to the echoing
Horns of Disneyland, faintly blowing; to the jockeys of nightmare
The dream-scalpers and the installment purchase blue-blood banks
Of the Never-Never Plan.

      The dream had ended but they didn't know it –
Rootless at Hollywood and Vine slumbering in rented shoes.
And still *there!*

    – chained to the chariots of Scythian kings…

Times change.

   The wind shifts.

      There are countries with no
Immediate future worth having.

       This is the windless
City.

  Dead air.

Dynamite, dynamite

dynamite…

ll stand there –

er"…

oet.)

"

np.)

–

e underground moon

hese wide loose acres

ed lost

City…

Many nights, ghosting these shores in the shifting moonshine,
I read the weather-signs of the spirit and the spoor of the sour times:
The citizens wrapped like mummies in their coats of poisoned sleep,
The dreamers, crazed, in their thousands, nailed to a tree of wine,
And written on the bold brow of the filthy unbending sky,
And sung among imperfect strangers, chanted in studio back lots,
Among three-way Annies and gay caballeros at home on all ranges,
Or shouted in top-secret factories where they make inflatable breasts,
Sung by the glove-faced masters of money with the sex of knives,
By the million grandmothers drying like cod, like anti-cod, like blind
Robins in the smoky terraces of Pasadena, rung out
On the gold-plated telephones in bankers' graves at Forest Lawn,
In the unbalanced books of sleep where the natives dream on credit –
Sung out in every language, alive in the sky as fire,
Is the Word:
      the little word:
           the word of their love:
                to die.

❄   ❄   ❄   ❄   ❄

"Traveler under the street lamp, I am farther from home than you."
Not so, old poet, Dreamy Don Gordon. No farther than I was:
Among the gigantico-necrosaurs, who misread size
For vitality, wheeling dervishes mistaking speed for movement –
These records put down between flash floods and forest fires:
(My duty to keep the tally book: me: ring-tailed roarer
And blue blazer – I'm wearing my blazer) this sacred page
The burning bush and rune stone emblem of Plague Harbor

Necessary document
                     laughter out of the dark
                                this sign
Of a time when the wood was in love with fire, the fire with water…

Not all of it like that either, no place being perfect in death.
Myself there to make a winter count and to mine my bread.
And others like me:
                     mavericks in lonesome canyons, singing
Into the desert…
                 Bone-laced shining silence faced us…
– But sang there!
                 "Making a little coffee against the cold" –
(Alvaro showed me.)
                   Inventing again the commune and round
Song gathering the Crazy Horse Resistance and Marsh St. Irregulars,
Building the Ramshackle Socialist Victory Party (RSVP)
And Union of Poets.
              Bad times.
                   The Revolution
Decaying as fast as the American Dream – whose isotope lead
Bloomed in the nightsticks of the company cops.
                                   And we offered our bodies:
On the Endless Picket Line of the Last of the Live-O Americans
For the Rosenbergs, murdered by Truman and Ironhead Eisenhower –
For all the lost strikes sold out by the labor fakers
Of Business Unionism Reuther Meany Social Plutocracy;
For Communists jailed or on the run in the violent darkness;
For the Negro sold again and again in slave trade Washington –

And lent them our bodies there, giving our blood to that other
Dream…
        It still lives somewhere…
                        accept these tokens…

Lived there.
           And every morning down to the hornacle mine,
To the vast dream foundries and mythical money godowns
Of the city of death. (And always with Comrades Flotsam and Jetsam!)
Reading the wish to die in translatable shirts of autochthons,
Blacklisted by trade unions we once had suffered to build,
Shot down under a bust of Plato by HUAC and AAUP.

Outlaws
      system beaters
                  we held to the hard road
(While Establishment Poets, like bats, in caves with color TV
Slept upside down in clusters: a ripe-fruited scrambling of assholes).
But it's a hard system to beat: working under the hat
On the half-pay offered to outlaws by the fellow-travelers of money:

And time runs fast on a poor man's watch.
                         Marsh St. eroded.
Dry wells…
           But I still remember the flowers and Cisco singing
Alive
      and the flowering names of that commune of laughter and light
Those I have named and the others – flowers of a bitter season –

They'll know who I mean…

And I worked there.

I went to work in the dark.

I made poems out of wreckage, terror, poverty, love.
Survived.

But times end.

My wife was looking uphill
Toward the Gadget Tree (was last seen crossing over the smog line
Approaching an outpost of sports cars).

We came at last to a house
With more windows than money: and written over the door –
(In fire I think) – NO DREAMS IN THIS HOUSE!

But my dream begins
Three dreams to the left…

✳   ✳   ✳   ✳   ✳

Well – money talks. It's hard
To say "love" loud enough in all that mechanical clamor
And perhaps the commune must fail in the filth of the American night –
Fail for a time…

But all time is redeemed by the single man –
Who remembers and resurrects.

And I remember.

I keep
The winter count.

And will remember and hold you always although
Fortuna, her heavy wheel, go over these hearts and houses.

Marsh Street…

        blowing into the universe…

                winds rising

                    change.

4.   Twice, now, I've gone back there, like a part-time ghost
To the wrecked houses and the blasted courts of the dream
Where the freeway is pushing through.

                Snake country now.

                  Rats-run –

Bearable, bearable –
Winos retreat and the midnight newfound lands –
Bearable, perfectly bearable –
Of hungering rich lovers under the troubling moon
Their condominium;

        bowery close; momentary

             kingdom –

Wild country of love that exists before the concrete
Is poured:

     squatters there.

         That's all

O.K. with me.

             ❁   ❁   ❁   ❁   ❁

First time I went back there – about an age ago come Monday –
I went hunting flowers: flowering bushes, flowering shrubs, flowering
Years-grown-over gardens: what was transportable.

What was transportable had been taken long away.
Among the detritus, rockslides, confessions, emotional moraines –
Along the dream plazas and the alleys of the gone moon –
Some stragglers and wildlings: poppy, sorrel, night-blooming
Nothing.
            And found finally my own garden – where it had been –
A pissed-upon landscape now, full of joy riding
Beer cans and condoms all love's used up these days
Empty wine bottles wrappers for synthetic bread.

❋   ❋   ❋   ❋   ❋

Larkspur, lupine, lavender, lantana, linaria, lovage.
And the foxglove's furry thimble and the tiny chime of fuchsia
All gone.
            The children's rooms have a roof of Nothing
And walls of the four wild winds.
                              And, in the rooms of the night,
The true foundation and threshing floor of love,
Are the scars of the rocking bed, and, on certain nights, the moon.
Unending landscape…
            dry…
                blind robins…

❋   ❋   ❋   ❋   ❋

Blind Robins, Blind Robins – Fisherman, do you take Blind Robins
In the stony trough of the dry Los Angeles river?
No charmed run of alewives or swarming of holy mackerel

From the pentecostal cloud chambers of the sex-charged sea, no
Leaping salmon on the light-embroidered ladders of eternal redemption?
Damnation of blind robins…

                  bacalao…

                        dried cod, is that,

Is that all you take on your dead-rod green-fishing Jonah,
Poor boy, mad clean crazy lad I pulled once from this river in spate it is not
Bearable.

                  ❋   ❋   ❋   ❋   ❋

Well, wait, then.
        Observe.
                Sky-writing pigeons, their
Blue unanswerable documents of flight, their
Unearthly attachments.
              Observe:
                    these last poor flowers,
                              their light-shot promises,
That immortality, green-signature of their blood…

Now, instantly, the concrete comes: the freeway leaps over the dead
River and this once now twice-green moment into the astonished
Suburbs of the imaginary city petrified
Megalopolitan grief   homesteads of lost angels   anguish…

On this day nothing rises from the dead, the river
Dying, the dry flowers going under the mechanic stone…
                          Sirs!

Archæologists! what will you find at that level of ancient light?
Poverty destroyed sweet hearts and houses once before Progress His Engines
Put down a final roof on the wild kitchens of that older
Order.

      These lovers long are fled into the storm.
The river is dry.

         It is finally.

            Completely.

Bearable.

5.   _____ All funeral wreaths must wilt around my neck
In time.

      From that place they ship all bodies east.
And eastward I went

         turning

           crossing the dark mountains
In the months of snow

         turning

           Los Angeles, San Fran, New York
And return.

      Sustained only by a thin gruel of moonlight
And the knowledge that all was perfection outside my prison of skin.

And perfect there also, although it seemed for a time
That the villain mathematics had sown in the dreaming soul's dark
A sick fancy of number: but there's no number higher
Than One.

All number drowns and dances
                              in still light
                                        the great
Aleph of Satori…
              New York, then…
                              granite island, mighty
Rock where the spirit gleams and groans in the prison stone:
Held there in black entrapments: soul's Harlems: the steamy
Enchantments of lack and luck: the lonely crucifixions
In the ten thousand endless streets of the megalopolitan dark…

And did you come there in summer, tobogganing in the slow sheets
Of earliest love; come there to work your secret name
On the frozen time of a wall; and did you come there riding
The tall and handsome horse whose name's Catastrophe?
I came there
          I loved
                  I rebelled with others
                                        I shed my blood
With theirs and we bled a dream alive in the cold streets.
And returned there: after the wars and the years: and colder those iron
Plateaus, and older that dream, and the rapid walls are rusting:
Immortal slogans
                fading
                        that we wrote in fire out of need…
Out of need and the generous wish – for love and hunger's the whole
Burden of song…

And went down there – after years and wars and whores
And loaves and fishes: the double-dyed miracles pulled off by Generals
Motors and Moonshine (those gents' act: to starve you while stuffed
With the jawbreaker candy of continual war: the silent American:
Mounted
        automated members of the Hellfire Club
                        Zombies).
And the talking walls had forgotten our names, down at the Front,
Where the seamen fought and the longshoremen struck the great ships
In the War of the Poor.
          And the NMU has moved to the deep South
(Below Fourteenth) and built them a kind of a Moorish whorehouse
For a union hall. And the lads who built that union are gone.
Dead. Deep-sixed. Read out of the books. Expelled. Members
Of the Ninety-Nine Year Club…
            "Business unionism!" says Showboat
(Quinn). "It certainly do hit the spot with the bosses!
Backdoor charters and sweetheart contracts – sell out the workers
And become a by-god proletarian statesman like Sweet Walter.
Takes a liberal kind of a stiff to make labor-fakin' a *pure* art."
Had swallowed the anchor, that one.
             And many thousands gone
Who were once the conscience and pride of the cold streets of the workers;
Dissolved in numbers is that second Aleph, the Order of Militants,
And the workers defenseless: corralled in the death camps of money
Stoned in a rented dream frozen into a mask
Of false consciousness…
       lip-zipped
           the eyes padlocked the ears

Fully transistorized
                    – living a life not their own.
Lost…

Still, in the still streets, sometimes, I see them moving –
Sleepwalkers in nightmare, drifting the battlefields of a war
They don't even know is happening –
                                        O blessed at the end of a nightstick,
Put to bed in the dark in a painting by Jackson Rauschenberg,
Machined to fit the print in a rack 'n' gawk jukebox, stomped
By a runaway herd of Genet faggots, shot full of holes
By the bounty hunters of Mad Avenue, brains drawn off
By the oak-borers of Ivy League schools' mistletoe masters.
Everything's been Los Angelized…
                                Alone, now, in the street,
What sign, what blazed tree, what burning lightning of the radical Word
Shall write their names on the wall break down that mind-framed dark?

Northern lights in winter; in summer the eccentric stairs
The firefly climbs…
                    But where is the steering star
                                                where is
The Plow? the Wheel?

                    Made this song in a bad time…
No revolutionary song now, no revolutionary
Party
        sell out
                false consciousness

yet I *will*

Sing

    for these poor

         for the victory still to come

RSVP

Stone city…

        And the dumbstruck dim wonders

(Crow voice, hoar head, pig mug)

Citizens of Want County as the Bowery spreads its diseases –

Contemporaries…

          An age of darkness has entered that stone

In a few years between wars.   The past holds,

Like a sad dream trapped in granite: what foot can slip free what trail

Blaze in that night-rock where the starry travelers search?

I hear them knock at the far doors of the night I see

Through the haze of marble those shadowy forms…

                  comrades…

                      I'll sing you

Out of the prison stone, I'll pick the lock of your night…

But lonesome song, for a fact.   History's been put into deepfreeze

In libraries and museums…

          those limestone bowers its prisons…

But still the wind blows and the stone shakes in the night

Sometimes…

       a shrill singing wakes in the granite matrix:

Music of bone flutes, a skeleton harp the wind

Thumbs and fondles...

                skull-trumpets...

                                voices under the ice...

The song I hear them singing is the Miseries and the Terrors of New York...

The misery of morning when the moneyclock turns loose its five loud lions
(The lion of the landlord, the lion of bread, the lion of a lone girl
Dying in Cheyenne, and the twin lions of loss and age).
Terror of morning late dreams like clouds stuffed
With eagles of scrap iron: sagging over the slow fires
Of anxious beds: those peat bogs that once held hands with the lightning.

The misery of six o'clock and the nightshift oozing like ghosts
Sidereal ectoplasm through hellholes in pavements: a scandal
Of blind birds swelling the clogged sleeve of the dead-lighted
Dayside...

            a host burning

                    a nation of smoke...

Terror of the time clock mechanical salaams low-pressure systems
Blowing out of the nightbound heart's high Saharas,
A muezzin of blood blazing in a cage built out of doves...
Terror of the noonday bullhorn pulling its string of sound
Out of the lunch box: time where the tides rage off Hatteras
And the drowned locomotives roll like dream monsters slow in the grip
Of the clashing vast deep: and their bells chime: and the whistle rust
Lights submarine tunnels toward dead harbors, sounding far stations
Closed forever...

                retired at sea

their circular shoes

Still

       Terror of the quitting hour, the air full of skinning knives
And the damp buffalo falling through the scaly tenement walls.
Thin-fit lives: tamped matrimonial gunpowder, ancestral pistols.

And the terrors and miseries of the arc of darkness extending past midnight:
Charismatic lightning of alcohol dead in its chapel of glass,
The harping dream song in the round ditches of revolving roads
Silent. The last ship sinking on the sea of a wounded brow –
All terror and misery present now in the loud and dying
Parish past midnight – a thousand fast mustangs freezing in jukebox
Ice, the little shelters built out of temporal wine
Blowing away in the wind the night-bound death wranglers
Stumbling into the day
                wait.
            For the angel.
                Wait.

In New York at five past money, they cut the cord of his sleep.
In New York at ten past money they mortgaged the road of his tongue,
Slipped past the great church of song and planted a century of silence
On the round hearts' hill where the clocktower the cock and the moon
Sang.
    At a quarter past money in New York a star of ashes
Falls in Harlem and on Avenue C strychnine condenses
In the secret cloisters of the artichoke.
             At half-past money in New York

They seed the clouds of his sleep with explosive carbon of psalms,
Mottoes, prayers in FORTRAN, credit cards.

>   At a quarter to money
In New York the universal blood pump is stuffed full of stock quotations:
And at Money all time is money.

>   False consciousness.

>   Bobbery.

Meanwhile, of course

>   – wait for the angel…

>   Meanwhile of course…

6.   Wait. Wait. The long waiting like the long running:
In the cold. In la noche oscura darknight of Kelvin. Of Godot.

On the avenue of C, which Christ led into this slaughterhouse,
A wintry dynamite of absentee landlords, misplaced herrenheit,
Explodes the campesinos into the East River ice.
Tall walls fall.

>   Slow.

>   Aristocratic

Exfoliation.

>   But *that's* the work of ice, not wind…

And came down there in a bad time – if there's any other
Time on that lost way.

>   Time when the moon is full

Of abandoned beds, fissioned by sexual centigrade, lofted
Out of the black apostle streets where the C note sings.

Waited there on the cold plain with Charlie and Mimi
For the wind to shift, granite to wear, our stony history
Turn a bright page: waited for nightmare to open…
(All those years in detention camps of the spririt, waiting!)
Meanwhile, of course, smuggling a few guns to the distant
And distancing counties – the ones reached only by laser and Lazarus –
To the truly outside Johns.
                              Meanwhile occasional *de*rail
Of the soft express: the one turned round at the Finland Station
By the plastic professors, by two-car agitators and labor-fakers
Who were bundling Lenin back into Switzerland.
                                        But all that
With dreamy dynamite: the slow fuse made from my blood
And jism.
          I waited that year for the light to turn
Blue.
      For the dream.
                  – 'cause I'm a fast dreamer, a dream
                                        champ.

"– Times I been there myself (Mac speaking). You got to play it
By ass, like a country whore in a ten-dollar house. There's some
Couldn't pump piss from a ten-gallon hat with a sandpoint.
                                        I *been*
On *that* corner.
            Been give up for left, lost *and* dead;

Been busted, disgusted and not to be trusted; been struck by lightning
Hellsfire and congress; seduced by playgirls: half-female and half-
Playtex; signed petitions: ALL POWER TO THE PEOPLES'
NEUROSIS; found some dark glasses and become a humanist;
Holden five kings – man had six bullets. It don't
Hump me none to stand in this cold. I was born *here*…
Seegaseega."

       Seegaseega.
            Take it easy
You've got the moon in your pocket and the dark fur of the night
To warm.
       And a charm of pot croons in a far safe
Where Dorothy sings.
          Where Genya will come.
              (But later.)
                  While the rifles –
Bill Epton's, are oiled but sleeping in Harlem's frost and fire…

But, hard.
       Granite matrix of false consciousness.
              No kite
Nor lyre to fly over the fatal deep of the lost
Farfallen city.
       Dead anticyclones.
          Anti-historical
Highs and hang-ups slumber in the tranced inhuman stone…

– and Charlie kept me alive there:

Humboldt:

the warm current.

– Making a little coffee against the cold – it was Alvaro
Taught us all.

And daily he went out in the New York night

(To the hornacle mine) with Mimi.

Each dark they wrote the names.

(Lent him my blazer sometimes: to see in the spider-colored
I-spy light.)

In those days the revolution had come down

To a voting machine in East Asshole Georgia, an off-color
Jerk or joke in the Let-My-People au Go Go night
Court club.

And the Catholic liberals taking instruction

From the stiff theses of a Bald Twin while El Roy Bones
Is preparing his nation's house: i.e. to yell *Motherfucker*
In the Mies van der Rohe jakes of the ancient Anglo-Saxon death.

And I'm for it, of course, you can't put down the dead nor the grave
And bravely living.

And some of my best friends are dead.

And black.

And dead for unfashionable things the bourgeois just don't dig:
Be they white *or* black.

But I mean black's not *all* black, you come *right* down to

It.

NOTHING's all *that* perfect.

At the congress of the colorblind

I put up the communist banner my father signed and sang:
LABOR IN A BLACK SKIN CAN'T BE FREE WHILE WHITE SKIN LABOR IS IN CHAINS!
Or, otherwise:
"Everything or nothing – all of us or none:
We better all be swingin' when the wagon come."

❄   ❄   ❄   ❄   ❄

Wait for the Angel.
              SAQUASOHUH:
                            the blue star
Far off, but coming.
                  Invisible yet.
                       Announcing the Fifth
World
      (Hopi prophecy)
                  world we shall enter soon:
When the Blue Star Kachina, its manifested spirit,
Shall dance the *kisonvi* for the first time.
                       In still light
Wait.

"But it's cold here!"
              Hush.
                  I'll take you as far as the river;
But no one may dream home the Revolution today though we offer
Our daily blood, nor form from the hurt black need
The all-color red world of the poor, nor in the soviet

Of students transform this night; nor alcohol compound
Manifestoes; nor pot set straight a sleepy rifle's dream.

Still we must try.

SAQUASOHUH

Far off: the blue

Star.

The Fifth World. Coming.

Now, try:

Necessary, first, the Blue Star Kachina to dance the *kisonvi*;
Necessary that the *kópavi* at the crown of the head must be
Kept open always.

Loosen your wigs.

I go to the far

Country

to the sacred butte and the empty land

I'll make

The Kachina…

7. Alcohol is the labyrinth, ganja the curved arrow, but labor
   Is the low high-road to our common heaven

(make the Kachina).

Time to return to the grand labor of the resurrection man the
Blue blazer…

Windless Los Angeles built on decaying granite
And windy Manhattan entombed in its granite sleep these impotent
Contradictions…
                    What holds nothing and what imprisons
All ways:
                    locked-room mysteries of tradition or history blown
In the cold and bone-choked wind to the farthest ends of the night.

It was time then to be going from that place to another.
Lunacy of cities, idiocy of the villages – turned away
Toward a marriage of rock and wind, toward stony lonesome,
                                                    the high
Country.
        To do a little coyote.
                        To make the Kachina…

Goin' to Dakota to throw the hooleyann…
                            "Beyond Chicago
The true snow begins"
                    Fitzgerald said it.
                                    Went there
Sixty years into the wrong century, carrying
The Medicine Bundle.
                (It was Genya showed me.)
                                    To make
The Kachina…

                    ❄   ❄   ❄   ❄   ❄

Far.
    Dark.
        Cold.
            (I am a journey toward a distant
And perfect wound)
                – got there in the blazing winter night
(January showing its teeth like a black wolf in the north,
And the blank farm buildings fenced with ancient sleep)
                                    – to the stark
And empty boyhood house where the journey first began…
– to search there, in the weather-making highs, in the continental sleep
For the lost sign, blazed tree, for the hidden place
The century went wrong: to find in the Wobbly footprint Cal's
Country…
        – and sat there
            in those first nights:
                        waiting
(Genya, the ransom of cities, and all my past, sleeping
And the ghosts loud round my light).
                    Waiting.
                        Southbound, the coulee
Carries its freight of moonlight toward the fox-brightened river breaks.
All time condenses here. Dakota is everywhere. The world
Is always outside this window: Now: a blaze of January
Heat: the coyote: the cicadas of Skyrian snow – all *here*
Now or later.
        (The poem is merely what happens
                        now
On this page…)

Night here.

The breathing dark.

Cave of sleep.

I enter.

Descending is ascending.

Go down

Past the stone decades and the bitter states of the anguished and enchanted salt
Toward my dead.

A static of hatching crystals ticks in the rock
Like a clock of ice.

The dead swim through the night-stone, homing
Into my side.

Come now

my darlings

my dear ones

begin

The difficult rising.

I'll help you.

Slip your foot free of the stone –

I'll take you as far as the river.

Sing now.

We'll make the Kachina.

III

1.   Begun before Easter…
                     the snow rasps on the porch, the cicadas
Rust in the long sealight
               – and the poem going on forever
Forever
        – coyote calling his last late-winter song
In Skyros's caroling heat   Dakota   high   lonesome
Twilight.
        The owl circling…
               – over the windfall trees…

❊   ❊   ❊   ❊   ❊

Out of imperfect confusion to argue a purer chaos…
Bare-handed   start there: and my hands are
Barer than most at best: and after ten years on the blacklist
Barest. Embarrassed and bare-assed, like my master: go into the woods:
With an ax. High thinking and low chopping keeps baby's
Ass warm.
        Bad case of the Gotta-No-Gots.
Start *there,* then.

❊   ❊   ❊   ❊   ❊

So, next day, go out:
Sunny midweek morning no more than forty below;
Take the double-bit ax, the crosscut and bucksaw and go
(Trailing an oily stink in the stun-breath cold – kerosene:
To work the rust off the blades).
                              Enter the ancient woodlot
My grandfather planned and planted and prayed from the virgin soil.

Stand alone there, at the first tree: and strike!
Old cock of Nowhere crowing: alive in the winter light!

Tree of rusty stone: it kicks out sparks like flint –
Like wintry fireflies in the deadfall gloom they arc down, dying!
Elzevir edition meteors, pigwidgeon-planets, dandyprats –
Almost I heard them sizzle, burning out in the snow!

And now a great hush: the universe halts: holding its breath
For the death of those infant worlds and the great shout of this my labor
Done for love only.
                    Halts for a moment.
                                        Then the great bush
Of the silence unfurls in a fury of snow cursed out of a towering
Ash tree by a lout of a blasphemous jay.
                                        He knows
My name.
        All of 'em.
                    And the little world awakes, scolding:
"The bronco's back on the range! The lunatic's in the trees,

Chopping wood for the purest hell of it, wouldn't you know!"
And the crows come by to stone me, and the jay is filing his tongue
Like the deaf man tuning a buzz saw, and around in the ark-fat farms
They turn up their thermostats…

                   And one blow does all this,
One man cutting wood for fun, for the blaze of his own work!

In joy.
     That does it.
                   Rockefeller revolves like a goose on a spit
In his whited sepulcher
                  a Texaco station goes down with all hands
Off Venezuela…
          This ax, comrades, has blasphemed against fuel oil…

              ❊   ❊   ❊   ❊   ❊

First crack out of the box and the tree takes a bite of my ax!
Check that.
        Fact. There's a dent in the bit.
                  The cheek
Sinister.
     Examine:
                – a stone grown under the hide of the tree!
From the long-gone summer cyclone that laid these deadfalls down:
This marriage of wood and stone, the tree taking into its system
This outer and alien order.
             I lift my ax and go on.

All through the brilliant morning the woods rang.

                                                 But slower –

Toward noon.

                      My muscles like wet newspapers – and ones moreover

Containing archaic disasters and the deaths of long lost friends…

The cold

           pure crystal.

                               The dead calm air like glass. And a chiming

Of thin and distant voices from the milesaway red-roofed farms

Carrying perfect over the bonewhite blazing, the blank blinding

Perfection of the empty fields.

                          Train sounds. Far.

                                    And near

My animals-in-law, the red squirrels, their furry coal

Aglow in the flocculent cloud-shifting drifts of the newdown petalperfect

Platonic snow.

                    Across the feedlot my cousin's cattle –

The high-haunched Holsteins and ground-gripper Herefords drop their dung

And the steam, like the crooked smoke   the god's love, rises

Shining.

         High passing through.

                          The great wheel of the winds

Still.

     Blue

          eye of weather

                    Sun

                  Smile.

Cottonwood. Ash. Oak. Chokecherry. Box Elder. Elm:
Trees of the wind-down deadfalls I mined that sovereign day
For the circular light of their dusty hearts, the ringed roads
Where the riding lust of the highwayman's sun in summers by
(Lifelightyears away) buried his august and aureate warmth.

Cottonwood. Box Elder. Chokecherry. Elm. Ash. Oak –
And not like that other winter we got wood up from the river:
The cantrip and singing circle, last commune and round song,
The bunched cooperative labor of poor stiffs in the cold.
All dead now: that kind of working. Only
The trees the same: cottonwood; chokecherry; elm; ash;
Oak and box elder.
                    Every man on his own.
                                        It's here
Someplace
            all went wrong.
                            For work alone is play
Or slavery.
            Went wrong somewhere.
                                    I'll find it for you – I'll blaze
That tree…
            Cottonwood, chokecherry, box elder, oak, ash, elm…
I rip them out of the drifts and clap them flat on the block.

❊   ❊   ❊   ❊   ❊

Working alone is play

             is a way back

                 (maybe)

To something lost…

             I enter the world of the dead, the stormdowned

Deadfalls: I mine for my darling these stovelengths of buried light this

Ancestral warmth…

             And home in the early dusk. The cold

Steel-sharp and still.

             Full moon pale in the deadfall.

                  First stars

Burn:

     The winter dark is setting its clock toward spring its

Blazing integers of ancient light:

               smolder and sing.

And the feathery gears and pinions of the continental highs and lows

Mesh; turn; wind.

             The helix of terrestrial winds

Drifts and shifts: slow: a new season works forward…

History is the labyrinth, Art is the curved arrow, but Labor

Is the gunstraight line to our common heaven.

                  (Play or slavery…)

You expect?

       Nothing.

         Hope?

         Nothing.

           What do you want?

Nothing.

     All's well.

          Inside the prison of skin…

Now into the woods in the starry dusk goes the hustling winter
Crow: the dark's collateral and raucous eclipse of light – one bar
Of late-winter-early night: late, late he goes home.

Glass   falls   now   winds   rising

              change

2.   Working alone is play or slavery.

             And working with others?
Slavery or play.

       Or the holy round song of labor danced
Out of love and need. World outside the invention of surplus
Value.

     Prewar and westerly, that.

           But once upon a distant time…

            ❈   ❈   ❈   ❈   ❈

"Doublebarreled shitepoke sheepcroakes, swillbelly like a poison pup!"
Packy O'Sullivan down from the wilds of the Irish Bronx
Speaking.

     Of the hemisemidemifascist leadman, the pipeshop plague.
"Corkonian motherjumper – steal slop from a blind sow:

He would. Put him in rubber boots and kick his royal
Ass so hard that he'd bounce so high they'd have to shoot him
To stave off starvation!"
                                        Ah! Uses of anti-aircraft
In Federal Drydock & Shipyard. O
                                        in the merry months of war!

(Kearney New Jersey.)
                         Now out, like a weasel downhole he rushes,
Like a Bantu beater rousting a thicket for a pride of lions,
To a jackstraw deadfall and lumberjack's dread of a logjam:
The stacked unwelded pipes' blind cuckoos' nest.
– Leaps (as at insult) with a chain-fall, to quarry there
(Out of confusion) the ghost-gray galvo and the dung-dark iron.

Comes in. Swinging on the chain-fall chainsend his pick of the heap
Some Dead-Sea-monster-shape unarticulated: built up, like pride,
In the (almost) infinitely reticulated blueprint mind.
(Got to be mind somewhere if you're building a ship.) He drags
It: to the wheel of the welding table; lifts his catch
And turns the wheel.
                         I hit an arc, building a loop,
And bead the joint with bubbling, steely, vitriolic ovals
In Palmer Method.
                         Under my mask the fierce destroying light
Softens is softened.
                         I look out of my Platonic cave into
Hellsfire: electrico-magnetico-mechanico-metallico seventh

Circle. But soft.
                    Turning the wheel in the ancient way.

And over and around me the cacodemons are building arches
Of purest noise.
                    Ancestral loup-garou and banshee assholes
(With attendant cluricaunes, deevs, afreets, dwergers, bogies –
Each hell-hurrying at the top of his stick to create the Domdaniel
And instant Malebolge, the Broad Church of Blast). *Now Hear This:*
Here: first the spitting arc under the poisonous
Smoke I build: at the end of my line the welding machine
Barks   whines   groans: the chain-fall is rattling and grinding
Like judgment day on a dental farm: and the demon benders
Squeeze out of their Torquemada-machines the bass moans
Of the ten-inch pipe.
                    Ah, Dy, bach – there's organ music
Would last a Welsh choir till Maundy Thursday or Hell-come-Sunday.

A little nightmusic now: add in the anti-boss cursing,
And rehearsed squeals from the whoring cunts in the wild world of the yard –
And a distant keen of money from the cost-plus counting machines.
Morgan's Allgotnick's Bank.
                    They rinse out exhausted condoms:
A double sawbuck!
               Or Johnny come early:
                              a fast five.

"After the war we'll get them," Packy says.
                    He dives

Into the iron bosque to bring me another knickknack.
The other helpers swarm into it. Pipes are swinging
As the chain-falls move on their rails in.

                              Moment of peace.
The welders stand and stretch, their masks lifted, palefaced.
Then the iron comes onto the stands; the helpers turn to the wheels;
The welders, like horses in flytime, jerk their heads and the masks
Drop. Now demon-dark they sit at the wheeled turntables,
Strike their arcs and light spurts out of their hands.

                                        "After
The war we'll shake the bosses' tree till the money rains
Like crab apples. Faith, we'll put them under the ground."
After the war.
              Faith.
                  Left wing of the IRA
That one.
        Still dreaming of dynamite.
                              I nod my head,
The mask falls.
                Our little smokes rise into roaring heaven.

Graveyard shift in the pipe-welding shop at Federal Ship.
Halfway through is the lunch break.
                              The machines die.
                                        A stunned
Uneasy silence falls on the vast infernal yards.
One by one on the ways the arcs of the deck-top welders

Sputter out. The burners' fires and furies are quenched.
The guns of the riveters hush their yammer.
                                        Peace is growing.
Like a midnight mysterious flower, its tendrils enter the beams
And bones.
            But only a moment: this is the waking hour
For the cost-plus featherbedders who come forth from their dewy bowers,
The camouflaged tax-endowed nests where they sleep the long shifts through.
The hour of the numbers-man and the bookie, the hour of the cost-plus
Whore (if you're padding a payroll and have two men for one job
You might as well have some women as well). Eagerly they come
(Like dollar-a-year merchant-patriots to the Washington swill-barrel
Where the blood-money contracts are made)   come out now to offer
Their all-American service: a little three o'clock jump
For the heroical war-workers weary. Historical commerce.

The peace ends.
            The machines roar into life.
                                        The malignant
Arcs of the welders sizzle across the darkness.
                                        The yard
Groans and curses and shakes, tormented, as if to tear loose
From the anchoring stone and mount toward heaven on its anguished song.

❊   ❊   ❊   ❊   ❊

They are sending me down to the ways where I don't want to go.
                                        But I go.
Under the ghost-walking gantries sky-hung leaning out

Of the high dark.

                    Past the rolling-mill's raven and red fire.
Past the housing riggers trolling the winch lines down out of darkness
And talking a load of steel away into the night.
A conversation of learned hands.

                         I walk under
The signs and signatures of lawful fire – great constellations
Flare and burn and hiss where the black hulks rise:
Galaxies flash and fall. Zodiacs of angry forms
Fill and fail, form and reform, shine and flame out.

Now a thin drizzle softens the light.

                              The welders
In cloudy aureoles, the burners in auras and saints' halos
Move.

          Dangerous rain.

                         On bad nights the air
Thickens with falling metal: dropped tools, rivets, men:
A general Fall, everything descending.

                              I go into the ship.
Descend.

          Lower.

               And lower.

                    Down to the inner bottoms.

                                             Now

I am inside the whale.

               Voices sound.

                    Far.

A world away.

                    But I am umbilical: tied to a war

By electric cable, by a blower to breathe out the poisonous fumes

From the iron I weld.

                        In this strange cave with branching tunnels

(A claustrophobe's hell) the ship's lowest intestine (diseased:

With odd growths of pipe and wire, gobs and gobbets

Monstrous, necrotic) I crawl; hearing, sometimes (not knowing

Whether far or near) some worm and comrade in a brother shaft

Working along in the dark like me.

                          (And some to die there,

And they to bring cutting torches to burn you clear of the ship.)

Worked there (waiting for light and the new day, end

Of the long night shift) and at every turning:

                                  immortal

Blazonings:

      Kilroy was here.

                    Or Clem's mark:

                            the inspector

Had been there before me.

                  In his sign I went on.

And so into the dark on that blazed trail

Night long.

                And not so lonely with the fellow worker gone

Into the dark ahead.

              Finally: another morning.

                   ❄   ❄   ❄   ❄   ❄

Morning when the eagle screams: payday. End of the long
Nightweek.
                    By the curbside dog-wagons the workers stand and wait
Till the pay office opens. The welders, easy to spot, swilling
Their quarts of milk to damp the burn in their bowels.

                                                  (It's poison –
Welding-smoke of galvanized iron puts fire in your belly, O
Poets!)
                The office opens.
                                  We sweat the line
                                              count it
And run.

Strange world of the early morning the night shift
Enters…
            Mysterious
                            because we come in from the opposite side
Of time.
                In the newcome sun the island over the river
Is translated fresh from the darkness and born again in our glance
Out of another dimension where all night long it swam
Discrete, tenuous, the parts drifting away from each other
Like a drowned ship on the seafloor breaking apart…
And the dayside men come drugged, their heads milky with poison
Of sleep while their veins are throbbing still: the mechanical pianos
Of dreams, their heavy music…
                              darkening…
                                        And we to them

Distant perhaps: the daze of the work still on us and the gray
Of the nightside world…

O tanist, twin, O ancient

Brightness: accept us: strangers: come home out of the dark!

❋   ❋   ❋   ❋   ❋

At Paddy-the-Pig's then stand and drink the payday cup.
Where the last flyblown freelunch like the haunch of a hairy mammoth
In time's cold aspic sickens: but holds from a gentler day
The antique welcome.

"Slan leat!" says Packy.

Peers out

Of his internal Siberia (that's brightened by the eyes of wolves
Only). "Down all bosses! After the war we'll get them!"

Ay. But war got us first. Got the working class
By its own fat ass: screwed by the metal whore of gadgets,
Bought off and fobbed off by Mad Avenue sou-soul fashioner's
Bobbery and palaver of false consciousness: doing the sacramental
Till-death-do-us-part on the Never-Never Plan of Death-by-Installment,
In the Holy Layaway Order of Resurrection: meditating
On the four last things: as: psychiatristsportscarswimmingpoolstatus.
Mercenary eschatology!

Here's blaze surely

Where we went down the wrong trail hellbent. And a long way home
– Father in heaven and if not where and if not why not?
– Let in a little air! Can't breathe for the galvo!

Still, hard to blame them.
                                They came to it pluperfectpisspoor;
The Gottanogotnicks from Barrio No Tengo and the raunchy and rancid
Haywire-and-gunnysack shanties of a cold and hungry time:
Out of the iron Thirties and into the Garden of War profiteers.
Once it was: *All of us or no one!* Now it's *I'll get mine!*
People who were never warm before napalm, who learned to eat
By biting spikes, who were bedless before strontium 90
Hollowed their bones: the first war victims…
                                        – in cost-plush cars.

Bought up.
        Corrupted:
                        their dream was that the war should
Go on forever.
               And it hasn't stopped yet: one war or another…
And the guilt comes there:
                      sold to the stony generals
Their sons go forth to die for dad's merrie Oldsmobile:
(Kind of Layaway Plan)
                   to die in a great blaze.
Of money.
        Blaze they went wrong by.
                        And here's the first
Sellout from which the country is a quarter-century sick.

               ❂   ❂   ❂   ❂   ❂

Bugles!
     Parade!
          The mad generals are coming.
                    They are leading a captive,
A twoheaded falloutmade monster, disarmed and de-armed by napalm,
Orphaned by Navy, unhoused by Air Force, tortured by Army –
In closest collaboration with syphilitic fascists and quislings
From the boy's own home country – (which the generals cannot
Pronounce).
          And after the enemy passes the patriots come:
Bespectacled professorial mass murders all ivy grown:
The gentle swingers and makers of minds from Mad Ave:
A farmer carrying a pet pig: a pop artist
Palpitant on a field argent (escutcheon of a home-grown
Brass-ass millionairess: money from arms)
                  Hats off!
A labor statesman in Brooks Brothers harness, with Cadillac, passes
(The light a nimbus on the ring in his nose):
                      and now the workers –
(Blood to the elbows) out of the arms plants to cheer a mortal
Victory.
     And afterwards came the rest.
                A nation in chains
Called freedom.
        A nation of murders – O say, can you see
Yourself among them?
        You?

Hypocrite

      lecteur

           patriot

❊   ❊   ❊   ❊   ❊

But Packy's not among them anyway: crossed to another quarter
One morning we left the ways where we launched the great ships;
(The holes in the whistles alone weighed seventeen pounds)
                                turned
To the whys and wherefores and whores and hang-ups of that other war
Where fascism seemed deadlier and easier to fight – but wasn't.
– Never came back, that one.
                  But most of that time I remember
Kilroy – immortal spelunker! Man I never met
(Or joke perhaps – ghost-joke: ubiquitous as god His Name
On every wall later) who in the dark night
Of the innerbottoms cramped hell crawling worked always ahead
To scrawl his fame in a rebel joke or slogan, to point
To the work that had to be done.
                  Where's Kilroy now?
                     Turned
From one dark to another or lost in the war's fast shuffle?
In the underground lightning of a deadman's bones I see him
Writing his slogans still on the closed door of the world.
We see them sometimes yet…
            And that too
                is a blaze…

3.   Megalomaniacalpseudomniestheticalisticalistical!
Lobster for breakfast! McJoseph: Of the Cadillac of many colors!
War-built millionaire and all-round retired Revolutionaire:
Too far left for this world and not right for the next.

Man with four projects and the first: never to die.
Second: to fabricate a glass heart: in case his own
Softened – what? – into mere mortality.
                      Third: to build
A little something to go with the first man to the moon –
(Middle initial V: for Vicarious). Finally: four:
To set up a small savoir-faire-farm in the wilds west
Of Beverly Hells: in Brentwood: to become culture-faker-in-chief
To Lost Angels to gar a crasis of replication on all
Fronts.
        Had arranged with god about point one and bought
Factories (didn't trust god) for points three and four and got –
God – another god – only knows how – a Brentwood newspaper.
The Weekly Nuisance.
                Throwaway.
                        Carried the price of beans
At all supermarkets: pictures of the mayor's daughter: homey
Jazz to flutter shopkeepers and keep the ads flattering in.
The idea was to turn this garbagewrapper into
A glorious garland of gallant invention and hip prose foundry,
To spread a rich compost of culture in Hell-Beyond-Beverly –
Where on Sunday the kiddy-car lawn mowers are roaring like lions in suburbia!

Puerperous parturient publisher! All-Begetting Renaissance Man!
(And a good man enough, though a little forgetful at times
That he dealt with mortals: a god's weakness perhaps: or absent-
Mindedness induced by a rare virus *spondulix sempervirens* –
Had been bitten by money as a small boy and carried the marks
On his soul, poor man.

                        Gave rise to strange behavior, sometimes:
As, instance: to go forth finned with a bloody big
Can of oxygen on his back to the great green mother
Sea: a parting of waters; to drop down the blue
Fathoms, salt; to sink in the tide's groin, cold;
To come to some drowned sea-cave or the littered table of the sea's
Underside; to sit there, mopish like a sad case of the sulks:
Counting his money.

                      Wheeze and thump of his mask.

                                      Curious

Fish.

    Still, a good man for all that, the Metawampum Kid,
Wheeze.

        Thump. Thump. Money under the sea.

And myself to edit that paper having come by blacklist degrees
To the bottom: dropped out of the labor market as unsafe
To a government at wars i.e. the cold, the Korean, the Pretend
(Against Russia) the Holy (against Satanic citizens the likes of
Myself).

        And so came there to the capital of Paranoia
Brentwood.

        To the savage citizens – the last of the '49ers –

Who had come by to beat gold out of the rocks:
To pan for the wily megabuck from downgrade uphill film stars
Their zodiacal houses and constellated-many-mansions secure
On the fast decaying granite of L.A.'s collapsible hills.

But the declination of film stars never approaches the smog line.
And the citizens camping in their hip-kitsch shops among their mouldering
Go-to-hell-or-Paris ballgowns gay and their gimcrack quack
Art (their pisspots fur-lined and fey and their handworked French
Ticklers) got small smell of that money: only the spoor
To make them squall like wolves on a winter night, ravenous.

So they saw me as a claim jumper or bold bandido
Come with my willow wand to dowse for astral gold.
To cross the village square was to tread the thin crust
Of the petty-B inferno hate-hot.
                              One middling class
ESPer and my body would swing for the carrion crow
On the ornate fake Nineties' lamppost: seditious scribe pro-
Thanatory perilous!

              And J.J. McJoseph my jingolo johnny gave
Me – as coconspirators and penance for sins – helpers:
Two (three would have been enough and one too many).
Primero: Coca (a demi-liz para-alcoholic) and Mister
Twister (O Prester John!) the master pressman (consultant
To the three kings of Azusa and Cucamongas royal Raz) –
Debile meathead and absquatulant horse's ass!
                              Ten times

Around the corner and over the wall: quasi-resident
Of the loud funny farms. Fat flatulent and phthisic.

                                              And Coca

The perfect bitch to lead him a dog's life.

                                    (And *her* ploy

To sink the paper and buy it up cheap with the help of her pressman
Whom she pressed often on the muezzin-screaming leather of the editorial couch.

So she screwed them both at once: the printer in his sanctum pandemonium
And McJoseph (J.J.) at long distance: he having answered the call
Of culture in upper Italy. (And J.J. helping her out
By nonpayment of press runs to drive down the twistering prices
Of Mister T.

              O Trinity Unholy!

                            O Kilroy where

Art thou!)

              So Friday all sleepless dark we put to bed
Our Cosmic Courier.

                        Nightlong.

                                    Last on the list of Mister
Eponymous Twister as deadbeat rep and walking delegate
Of transcontinental conman and carpetbagger J.J. McJoe.

I might be out at the stone, the presses thumping around me.
(And the office sofa thumping Cacophonous as she got in her licks:
Beast with two backs in the darkmans.)

                                    Then silence.

                                    Trouble.

                                        Himself
Charging into the light.
                    "Outa that!" (To the make-up man.)
"This sheet comes last till your high-building bastardboss pays up!"
(And McJoseph of the many-colored Cadillac, gobbling his pasta in Florence,
Scheming to drive down the print cost, nibbling his caveat:
Master of pure thought: or at least the electronic equivalent.)
"Take that crap off the stone!"
                              One hour to go and now
Must wait for morning: for Mister T.'s high to blow over.
He goes out kneading his baby-bottom face: after the Cacajam
He slaps cologne on his jowls
                    – liniments of satisfied desire.

Thump.
        Wheezethump. Wheezethump.
                              Thumpathump.
The pelagic banker.
              The coupling she-crook.
                              Patriot and whore.
Money at the bottom of the sea…
                    Thump.
                              Wheezethump.
                                        Cacathump.

Nothing to do then but go out into the dark
Neon night of the soul, hillbilly the honky-tonks and cheap
Ginmills of Santa Monica's Skid-Road-by-the-Sea.
Talk with the whores and the night cabdrivers; talk with Lo

(Bill Smoke by name) the poor Indian. Apache
And Cherrycow (Chiricaua) at that.
                                        Shipwrecked on this strange
Coast a war ago. Lost, here: like the others;
Doing his time.
                    And so we wait for morning and the light.

And then back to the printshop where time, hangover, and avarice
Have had their way with Mister Twister.
                                        The forms are locked up;
The presses roll.
                Thump.
                        Wheezethump.
                                        Money: sea-changed.

And so till the last day and parting of ways with J.J.
McJ.
        He'd had me prisoner while he was in Italy: myself
Saving his bacon from Coca and Twister. Then, returned
McJ, and no gratitude in that quarter (but time will wound
All heels).
                So on the last day stood at the open
Rear door of the shop watching the Pacific: ("Damn best
View of any printshop in the world," testifies Twister).
There, under a gray sky, dandiacal:
The sea:
            its cuffs of lace
                                its infinitely extensible blue
Coffins, cold.

Thump.
                        And out of that colorless heaven
Some poor mad whore falls a whirling praying
Ten stories.
             Thump.
                    To give us our Daily News:
Written in blood all over my pants: too late for the press.

Thump.
        O poor beat bitch.
                          Thump. Thump.
Wheeze-thump, money-thump, press-thump, fucka-thump, heart-thump, god-thump
Megathump, warthump, metathump.
                                Dig the graves.
                                        Thump.
Thump thump thump thump thump thump.
Thump.
        Thump thump thump thump thump.
Thump thump.
             Thump thump thump thump.
Thump thump thump.
                   Thump thump thump.
Thump thump thump thump.
                        Thump thump.
Thump thump thump thump thump.
                              Thump.
THUMP THUMP THUMP THUMP THUMP THUMP —
THUMP THUMP THUMP THUMP THUMP THUMP
Thump.

Thump.

    Thump.

        The sound of the ax in the tree…

4.   Play or slavery. It's there surely in labor: the place
We went wrong. One place anyway. Put a blaze
Here.

    Sixty percent for war and murder and the rest
Not worth the doing.

        But it gets done.

            Half the national product
Is guilt.

    And all in the trap of the midnight slot machine
Of a politics with smokeless gunpower: for a criminal nation
Of the rich and the mighty within the nation, for a compromised country
Half-dead at the bottom and rotten ripe on top.

But then (begun before Easter) in the axbright late winter cold
I cut wood.

    Trees exploding around me…

           secret dynamite
Smuggled into their systems by the black Aquarian frosts.
I cut wood.

    Dreaming of this.

        This page…

And in spring broke new soil and Genya planted a garden:
That green enchantment, sprung from her loving hand, I sang then: how
The vegetables please us with their modes and virtues.

The demure heart

Of the lettuce inside its circular court, baroque ear
Of quiet under its rustling house of lace, pleases
Us.
    And the bold strength of the celery, its green Hispanic
¡Shout! its exclamatory confetti.

And the analogue that is Onion:

Ptolemaic astronomy and tearful allegory, the Platonic circles
Of His inexhaustible soul!

O and the straightforwardness

In the labyrinth of Cabbage, the infallible rectitude of Homegrown

Mushroom

Under its cone of silence like a papal hat –

All these

Please us.
    And the syllabus of the corn,

that wampum,

its golden

Roads leading out of the wigwams of its silky and youthful smoke;
The nobility of the dill cool in its silences and cathedrals;
Tomatoes' five-alarm fires in their musky barrios, peas
Asleep in their cartridge clips,

beetsblood,

colonies of the imperial

Cauliflower, and the buddha-like seeds of the pepper
Turning their prayerwheels in the green gloom of their caves.

All these we praise: they please us all ways: these smallest virtues.
All these earth-given:
                          and the heaven-hung fruit also…
                                                        As instance
Banana which continually makes angelic ears out of sour
Purses, or the winy abacus of the holy grape on its cross
Of alcohol, or the peach with its fur like a young girl's –
All these we praise: the winter in the flesh of the apple, and the sun
Domesticated under the orange's rind.
                          We praise
By the skin of our teeth, persimmon, and pawpaw's constant
Affair with gravity, and the proletariat of the pomegranate
Inside its leathery city.
                          And let us praise all these
As they please us: skin, flesh, flower, and the flowering
Bones of their seeds: from which come orchards: bees: honey:
Flowers, love's language, love, heart's ease, poems, praise.

                     ❋   ❋   ❋   ❋   ❋

But that was later.
                          What was *then* was only the work and the waiting:
To find the first blaze:
                          to begin the lonesome labor
Of the resurrection man:
                          to elaborate my legend:
                                                        to make
The Kachina…

Great clocks of the highs and lows tick out
The white weather
               – and the windy angels of the compass points
Blow and blare under the night sky's blazing nocturnal
Powers and adornments…
                  Here I stop. I begin with identity
And seek the Wilderness Trace and the true road of the spirit.
I start alone with labor and a place.
               Not much
                  But at least

That.

IV

1.   Love and hunger: all is done in these signs or never
Done.

      Or done wrong.

            Blazes.

                (Left or right.)

And when work goes wrong, love goes wrong.

                         And the other way also.

So:

    praise the green thing

              in the hand

                  in the eye

                      in the

Earth!

    Perfect.

        And: the queenly women of our youth,
Middle age, old age, and the grand princesses
Of death

    if any such be

           it clearly behooves us to praise

Most highly.

    Here, then:

        Hear!

          I begin

with
Jenny.

❋ ❋ ❋ ❋ ❋

Moon in Virgo.
Autumn over the land,
Its smoky light, its…
hawkhover
crowhover
its lonely distances
Taut with migrant birds and bodiless calls far – farther
Than noon will own or night
cloaked all in mystery of farewell.

Morning stirring in the haymow must: sour blankets,
Worn bindles and half-patched soogans of working bundlestiffs
Stir:
Morning in the swamp!
I kick myself awake
And dress while around me the men curse for the end of the world.

And it *is* ending (half-past-'29) but we don't know it
And wake without light.
Twenty-odd of us – and very odd,
Some.
One of the last of the migrant worker crews
On one of the last steam threshing rigs.
Antediluvian

Monsters, all.

         Rouse to the new day in the fragrant

Barnloft soft haybeds: wise heads, gray;

And gay cheechakos from Chicago-town; and cranky Wobblies;

Scissorbills and homeguards and grassgreen wizards from the playing fields

Of the Big Ten: and decompressed bank clerks and bounty jumpers

Jew and Gentile; and the odd Communist now and then

To season the host.

         Stick your head through the haymow door –

Ah!

   A soft and backing wind: the Orient red

East. And dull sky for the first faint light and no sun yet.

4:30. Time to be moving.

        Into the barnfloor dark

I drop down the dusty Jacob's ladder, feeling by foot,

The fathomless fusty deep and the sleepy animal night

Where the horses fart, doze, stomp: teams of the early

Crewmen: straw-monkey, water-monkey (myself) and the grain haulers.

They snort and shift, asleep on their feet.

           I go, carefully,

Down the dung-steamy ammonia-sharp eye-smarting aisle

Deadcenter: wary of kickers, light sleepers and vengeful wakers.

A sleep of animals!

      Almost I can enter:

           where all is green,

Where the miles are shorter, the winters warmer, but barbed fences

Higher, sharper, than for me:

where the devil is man or a wolf;
Where color drains from the flower in the smiling charm of the universal
Green; and the beautiful is the edible…
                              the dreams furry, far-ranging
Straightforward fore-and-four-footed only; their boots, barn-battering,
Dream-burnished: O rutilant ruminant ruminative right beasts!
– Running the moon-long marches and meadows of the free range
Or racing their shadows in the hot noon or tree-shaded in the high
Afternoon heat: or at streams in the cool evening coming
To rake with their burning hooves their sunbright and cloud-formed images
Magnificent…
                and nuzzle their deeper selves in the lucent flow…
Muzzle velvet, mane of moonlight and lightning, tail
Of smoke and aching speed; and neck of hunger and thunder!
                                                    So
Themselves see themselves.
                    I too.
                              But, in the world
Of work and need that sacred image fails.
                              Here,
Fallen, they feed and fast and harrow the man-marred small acres
Dull; and dulled.
                Alas, wild hearts, we have you now:
– Old plugs
        hayburners
                crowbait
                    bonesack
                              – Hail!

Morning chores.
                I fire up the lantern
                              the hairy mysterious
Legend beasts leap full-formed out of the gold of the light!
All rational.

               I go to the box stall where wary Ringo
Sleeps with three eyes open and a mutiny under his heart
The size of his native Montana. Bronc. Half-mustang half-
Hellion. At fourteen years he's as old as I and ought to be
Wise – wiser. A rebel. I treat him with all respect,
Puffing the padded saddle onto his skinny back.
I lead him into the corral and mount. Docile. I wait –
Then nine buck-jumps to limber his joints and mine
And out the corkscrew lane at a gut-jolt gallop he goes!

No halt for the hillslope – he hurls himself runaway down
Taking great gulps of space in break-my-neck lunges: teaching me
Prayer: a prayer for tight cinches, for his crazy and eagle eye
To spot the leg-snapping gopher holes in his downhill flight.

Shouting, singing, praying – the hills shake to our sound.
O holy marvelous morning! Ecstatic plunge into fullest
Being! Blazing down to what end? None! To none!
But straight through the strait gate and into reality prime!

After the insane downslope dash he drops to a jog,
Lazy. Blows like a hairy whale. Nips at my leg –
Since he hasn't succeeded in killing me, we can be friends.

South toward the river in the brightening morning through the hill-held silence

– Or south toward the morning:
                              the heaven-high riverhills held at their tips
The green fur of the unfarmed sun in their tree-trap fingers
While we rode through the chilly lingering dusk of the coulee floor.
Such risings there!
                    The lorn jackrabbit kiting away
Husked from his buckbrush break; and out of their thin tents of grass
Partridge: smoking away on wings of wind and wet:
The dew collecting the vented light like vapor trails in their wake!
And the early snake
                dry creek
                        carries his sand
South with us: cold trailblazer: road in the high grass.

Southward all of us.
                Then the river.
                            The ancient song
Of cold stone and water.
                    Winds mouthing the trees
                                    sigh…
And sacred silence
                panic
                    structure of blood and change
Still mystery
            spills and holds.
                    Here, then.

The horses are hidden in thickets.

                                             Charge in like a brush-popper,
Stampede them out of the river trees and hooraw them home!
And in good time: the sky is building a fence of lightning
Over the hills; a door in the weather opens; light dies;
Wind and water burst out of the high house of the clouds –
The dust on my clothes still dry and I'm soaked to the skin!
Home, then: headlong
                         under the buckshot rain.

2.   Paradisiacal morning! for the boy in a man's clothes!

                                              Heavenly
Rain-recess from the light-long labor in the harvest fields –
Pie-from-the-sky!

                      Shivering, I stable Ringo and run
For the lank unpainted house: its windows yellowly lit
In the second-come night of the rain-black morning's stormy show.
Enter headlong.
                    From the wood range the dark violence
Of oratorical coffee!
                And eggs crackling heraldic
Voices in a hell of burnt bacon!
                   A Robinson Crusoe
Raft of toast in the warming-oven!
                     An alarm of onions
In the mansion of fried potatoes!

                         Apple pie!
                                Cookies!
                                        Chow-chow!
And the cool cucumber stoned in his salt-and-vinegar broth!

At the head of the table: Parsons, the farmer we work for, owly
And sour with his twenty-four apostles around him, seeing his provender
Devoured by these locusts in blue jeans: No work today
Rain says.
            And Parsons sees us, hundred-headed, eating
The roots of his house.
                        Dolorous dour.
                                        His gloom condenses
In the cellars of salt. Thickens. The stuff won't pour.

                                        But O then:
Jenny!
        Entering, the light swarms around her!
                                        The rain
Ceases and the sun leaps out of the trap of wind and cloud!
And she enters: under the full sail of her breasts and body
Magical.
            A poor Jane of a Sand Hill crane, maybe but
Jenny of the light blond hair
                                of the musical breasts
Of laughter warmer than sunlight and song like a moon-crazed bird!

What human Heisenberg principle made her possible who
Can say?

Came out of a Sand Hill farm that was blowing south
By acre and home-forty each time the north wind raised.
Flower of poverty and ignorance – but a flower!

                                         Each petal perfect.
And ripe. Or ripening outward as flowers and fruit ripen –
A woman with the sun in her belly and her own interior summer
Always at prime
                and the yellowy winds of the summer solstice
Ripening her hair.
                  Woman like a Renaissance palace
                                          grand plazas
Her ass, each part: or matchless mares of her buttocks perfectly
Matched: not either was faster
                        sculptured steeds in the vast
Apartments where the moon kept shop
                              little more than the size of your palm…

And this young queen was the hired girl, come in to serve us
In that holy morning.
                  Perhaps she was seventeen – she seemed
Old; to my almost-fourteen and woman-loverless years –
And wise.
          Eve there.
              Far.
                  Ancient.
                      Knowing.
                            A mystery:
– Of what?
              Why what but first-off the mystery of holy Woman

And the mystery of her Mysterious East directly south of her belly
Button – all more mysterious from the spanceled and furious need
Of thirty celibate stiffs – and stiff we were when she brought us
The hearty heartening egg in its nest of chastened bacon.

And sweet she was also: her queenly coming-and-going –
Little canoe on the dark lake of the morning – brought us
The honey and lightning of a world outside our own brutal
Male thunder and mind-dulling labor.
                                    She came like a guide –
Some Indian princess: singing, exotic, prophetic…
                                            occult
News –
        word of the high passes, the dark crossings
Over the bitter mountains in the months of snow…
                                            – but the Word:
Blazes…
        in the masculine darkness funky…
                                    Sacagawea
Female kachina…
                    girl with a gift for making your pants
Too small in front.
                    Fine and superfine hung over our heads:
The bread and honey she brought us and the pure wine of her life!

❉   ❉   ❉   ❉   ❉

And afterward the day of unwork opens: magical morning,
The rain-soaked earth steaming under a blowtorch sun.

Too wet for threshing!
                              The dice-doctors and demon dealers
Drop the blanket, unseal the packs, make devil-deft passes –
Invite the multitude to a convocation of money.
                                                    Ada
From Decatur is there – and her tiny cousin: Little Joe
From Kokomo – and every defunctive and nadasymmetrical flush.

Meanwhile others are sousing their shirts in the nightblack iron
Enormous washpot that broods like a cancerous phoenix over
The moody backyard fire.
                              And the liars are lying and the lyres
Telling truth: auguries spelled out in the mantic entrails
Of traveling harmonicas' musical threshing floors.
                                                    O and the odd
Mildman mending his socks in the wash of enduring sun!

Now come the subtle apothecaries of the catch-as-catch-can concoctions:
Fabricators of Blast Head, Skinny and Forty Rod
(Will kill you at forty rods or stun you at half-a-mile)
Descanting and decanting the enchanted smoke of unjugged moonshine –
Milky dynamite of oily spoiled corn: coiled
Snake in the bog of a Mason jar: by coonlight lugged into
The twentieth century: that longest unfulfilled inside strait
Flush in history.
                              And the master-whittlers: carvers of fans,
Creators of piny Granadas from the lace of lazy wood!
And wooing in the watertrough-shade-Workers'-University: the spadehanded
Fellow-worker-comrade-professor expressing Marx!

And mumblety-
Peg! Like a gypsy dream of flashing wild knives!
And airborne the rhyming chime of clashing horseshoes mock silver
Filling the stunned light that yet runs from there to Arcturus:
And ourselves, strange travelers, still live on that starry beam…

And so the morning…
                    wearing a bright bandanna like a Mexican
Bandit

        wears away.
                        And along about quarter-time comes
My call: to go out into the late corn and gather
The gold and pearl of the roasting ears for the noon meal.
– And there she was – Jenny! – filling the field with light
Brighter than sun!
                        And so we labored together – that action
Nearest to love: when work is play.
                                    And around us the spires
Lifting
        the living green
                            a music of hoarse rattles,
The whispering pipes and the feathery cymbals of the fiery field
Swaying ripening song: silky answer to a cadence
Of the flattering wind.
                        And there we opened the holy wigwams and hogans –
Pulled back a tent-flap of husk to peer at the seated and sacred
Congregation
        grandfather maize…

ear in the milk!
We snap them loose from the stalk and pop them into the sack.

Sack? There was none but the front of Jenny's dress
Lifted.
      Over a mystery: where the bronze and pearl frontiers
Divided sun from moon on her downy meridian thighs…
And singing so in holy labor, soon we came
To the end of the shallow field, where the old willow kept,
Over the coulee heights, his whispering watch…
                        Rested there…
Then – out of pure gift for my thirteen-plus-nothing-years-need
Opened her dress!
         stepped forth!
                 moon coming out of a cloud!
– And lay beside me
           warm as a star coming into my arms!
And we made love
        in the damp grass
               under the willow…
I entered her
       opening the silky gate and passing through
The marvelous terrible thighs to the ancient and awe-ful world
Mysterious
      full of the rituals and terrors of men…

                      and found there
This girl…
      innocence…

laughter…

        found my self…

Seemed to.

       We rode each other to the opposite ends of the earth:
And arrived together in the sacred terminal of holy commerce –
Place where one can arrive only by twos and two
Is one or nothing…

      blazing there…

            in the damp grass…

And lying beside my darling girl, my hand on the bush of her belly
The whole enormous day collected within my palm…
Around us the birds were singing their psalms, and the bent grass
Shyly unkinked the joints we had lovingly flattened.

                  The air
Grew warm and round around us: but the wheeling sun rolled fast.

At last she left; like a goddess: bearing against her belly
The fruit of the chanting enchanted field and my own invisible sign.
Ah, there was a girl come along early to wake me
Out of the wintry sleep of boyhood: to take her hand
– And mine! – into countries where all may journey but only
Without maps

      without compass

          riding blindfold…
– And she took me into the country of strangers and enemies, the violent
World of men! And it was…

        innocence

         love

                        the world
Of children again
                but bigger only
                        and I was older
Already than any.

            She left me there, god's years later –
A half-hour, maybe – her lap heavy with daylight.
And I lay in our musky couch counting the fields of the sky…
Love enhungered love; but unhungered hunger for the hungering
Hungry boy.
        For the time being – or always? – I lived on
Slow dreams under the willow where the milkweed pod
Opens a feathery eye toward the bird-breathing sun…

                ❋   ❋   ❋   ❋   ❋

At quarter-time in the afternoon, roused; returned
To the barnyard.
            My head full of honey and the flag of my loins aloft.
Lifted myself on the haymow ladder and poked my head
Into the upper dark…
                saw there…
                    "Not for kids –
We're separatin' the men from the boys here!" Rod speaking,
The boss spike-pitcher. "Git down outa this, boy! Git down!"
He pushes me down the ladder and drops the trap door shut.

But I had seen

        there in the musty dark

                    Jenny –

Or another Jenny…

        (Moon coming out of a cloud!)

                            Her cloudy

Transfigured flesh in the gloom!

            (On a lance of light from a knothole

The dust was dancing, aloft, on the spunky smell of their sex,

Where they swelled around her like animals drawn to the Christmas-manger –

French-postcard.)

            And her face – poor face!

                    (That was open, loving, wild

Under the willow in the greeny light) like a breathing trap

Shut now.

        Locked as in terrible combat.

                  She lay

Bucking under some loud clown with his pants still on.

Suffering

        acting

            burning

                entranced

                    cold

                      dedicated…

Ladies' choice!

        A gang-bang,

            but there was no arm-twisting –

She wanted it so.
                  I stood deadstill in the barndoor dirt
(Hearing the overhead thump and thinking of sweating quarters
Of dying meat upstairs
                those souls
                        consumed and consuming)
Stunned in the rain-cleared light as if I'd been kicked by a horse,
Hurting.

        What hath god rot?
              What hath Rod
Got?
    Friend, when all collapses around you the bosses
Find work.
        So, with Bill Dee and Ed, the midnight twins,
Into the bonerattling blank field to clean the boiler
Of the ancient Nichols and Shepherd steamer stonily sitting
(And the hole in the whistle alone weighed seventeen pounds on a Sunday!)
On its ten-foot wheels like an indolent idol.
                    Before Freud came
To North Dakota we did it: ramming the brush-ended rods
Down the fifteen-foot slots of the grimy honeycomb flues.

Symbolical day!
        And philosophy shot on the wing!
                    "Take now,"
(Ed says) (groaning a little) "them Sand Hill girls.
Stay away from there, little buddy. Them women will give you a dose
Before you can spell gangkorea, man! They'll clap you up

Ere you can bring your pants to half-mast. I *mean* it –
And if I don't know who does? Measure is all," says Ed.

"Measure yourself to that firebox," Bill Dee tells me. "Get in there!"
I slither in like a rattler, the fire door shaking its tail,
And the chimes fall in the flat field like a handful of silver.
"You think you got *troubles,*" Bill snorts. He pops out his glass eye.
"Stick this here up your ass and see what the world looks like!
And say me no aye, yes or nay but sing it out plain!"

Inside the iron womb of the firebox's small world I look:
The wall frescoed with scale:
                    flame-painted murals
                                        I cannot
Read.
        I crouch there.
                This roaring castle of fire
                                    – cool now –
Around which revolves the world of the rig on the days of our labor.
"How's old iron cunt?" Bill calls.
                            And gentler, to my ears only,
Through the metal lip of the fire door: "It's many a good man
Got up on the wrong side of an Indian pony…"
                                        trying
To help me understand.
                    I cannot.
                        I take up the poker,
Knock the clinkers loose from the grates and slam open the damper.

After they leave I fire up the old lady – the new water,
Cold in her belly, must warm for the next day morning run.
I peel the rain-wetted skin from the straw-monkey's rack and feed
The quilted clot of the tweedy flaxstraw into her stony womb;
Scratch a match on my pants and the end of the fire-blacked fork
Blazes; (the oily flax, crackling, blows out the daylight)
I put the torch through the iron lips and a great roar
Breaks loose from the lion of fire inside the door slot!

$$\qquad\qquad\qquad\qquad\qquad\qquad\text{Open the damper.}$$

Let him rave.
$$\qquad\qquad\text{Then steady}$$
$$\qquad\qquad\qquad\qquad\text{fork after fork}$$
$$\qquad\qquad\qquad\qquad\qquad\qquad\text{each one}$$
Left in the slot till it lights and the fire burns inside and out.
As she warms I test the water injector: blast out shrieking clouds
Of blistering steam.
$$\qquad\qquad\qquad\text{She draws.}$$
$$\qquad\qquad\qquad\qquad\text{Give the old lady a drink,}$$
Open the blowers and cram her belly with incendiary flax,
Button her up and *done!*

$$\qquad\qquad\qquad\qquad\text{I turn away from the dark-bringing}$$
Fire half-blind (and the fire still blazing under my eyelids!)
Amazed that the day still stays and the skyborne west-tilted field
Lifting late sunlight…
$$\qquad\qquad\qquad\qquad\text{and the lag-along birds homebound to treeclaims}$$
Lofting to kin and mankind the shy spiel of lark song
Dove song
$$\qquad\qquad\text{crow call}$$

     far-faring

Sparrow…
    the loose ends of the evening.
         I stood there

Elaborate loneliness
     like an unfinished Navajo blanket
           empty

As the threshed field
     lost as some fabulous gold mine
          hollow

As an abandoned tunnel…
      high and far the sky

Stood over me and my small woe.
       Distant voices,

Indifferent, drifted in on the cold of the autumn evening.

I turn to go: reluctant: at leaving the orderly orders

Of labor and this manageable iron maiden, her clanking pulse, her

Cud of fire and cloud.
      I crank up the balky truck,

I turn, and, flat-wheeled and rattling, drive down the breathing field.

       ✻ ✻ ✻ ✻ ✻

That night they broke Outlaw – were breaking him when I came back,

A buckskin bronco – hammer-headed, wall-eyed, long-gaited and loco –

Mean as a runaway buzz saw: kicker, striker and biter

Beautiful! Totally useless. Kept around maybe as Parson's

Secret sin. Or hope. And for years Outlaw had broken

Presumptive cowpokes, persuading them out of the west.

                                                  And now –
Three ropes to hold him and still rearing!
                                        But they ear him down,
Snub him against the corral-post and slap the blindfold on…
Stiff-legged he stands there quivering, as if there were fire under
The creamy skin.
                        Now saddle…
                                now cinch…
                                        tight…
                                                tighter
Too tight…
                Now hackamore on and rider up and blindfold
Off!

    The honyock pulls leather at the first stone-legged buckjump;
Outlaw swaps ends like a blacksnake: while the rider is openly wondering
Whether to shit or go blind.
                        Then a lazy, sunfishing, slow
Roll like a dolphin empties the saddle.
                                And so he sends them –
And this in the sloughfooty bog the rain has made the corral!
Drunk sober or sane, the long the short and the tall –
He shucks them out of the saddle like popping peas from a pod!

But not forever.
                In the leg-locking mire of the barn corral
They rode him.
                Rode him at last – Rod did – had to be him! –

Poor-devil Outlaw stoned with fatigue trying his best
To rear over backward and Rod smashing his ears down
With the loaded quirt.
                    Myself: silent:

                              screaming:

                                        Outlaw!
Outlaw! Outlaw! Tear your foot free from the earth!

                    ❋   ❋   ❋   ❋   ❋

And light years later in the haymow loft I lay.
                                        Long-
Remembering Jenny…
                    My ding-dong darling and haymow madonna…
Sexual vessel
          lay for us
Vessel of singular ardor
                    screw for us
Horizontal rose   carburetor most holy   princess of poontang
Two-stroke virgin   independent suspension   unholstered cunt
          help us in the hour of our need
Long-cock echo-chamber   uterine superhighway most traveled
          accept our offerings
Candid receptacle
                    receive our prayers
Hairy gate
          open for us
Bridge of thighs

carry us over

Encyclopedic pudenda　hairy prairie　automated vagina

Be with us in the day of our hunger

ENOUGH!

Even then I could see it was not that way.

She was no

Gongshagging lamewit.

But then what was she?

Easy: merely

Lost.

And what did she want?

To enter.

To burn

Alive…

To live on other frequencies, at more intolerable depths…
To rip up the tent of solitude, to step out of the skin,
To find among the damned the lost commune and to found there,
Among the lost, the round song and the psalm of the living world.

And I too had entered those latitudes of desperation and given
Through her (or earlier): my heart to the lost ones of the world
Forever.

Sad, that bridge of bodies, trying to build
On mere number the Great Aleph of solidarity…
And I see them still…

bang-tail babes in death-dark drag
In the Village or in Little East Nowhere North Dakota

or Lost

Angels in Super Scab's smog-lined mafioso scout camp Venice L.A.…
It's lack-love set this blaze…

                    in this sad country where number
Counts
        where love has no hands…
                  no fingers…
                          (but I remember,
When I take my death in my hands to write and endite you this,
Or climbing the terrible stairs of the typewriter to hang
By the skin of my heart to the cold col, to cross over
To the true blaze).

            I didn't know, then, it's the Innocents
Who must live most lost, most reckless…
                    the life of a dangerous time.

                ❈   ❈   ❈   ❈   ❈

Midnight…
        the great nets of the stars…
                sifting the darkness.
Night birds.
        A whine of wind.
                That's all there really is…
Except for the mind's excitement, the heart's hill-hurdling desire,
But at that age it seemed not enough. The world seemed empty…

Wind out of the north quadrant.
        Clear.

The barometer

Lifting a wing of salt and sun…

work in the morning.

3.   The great fires in the heavens whirl and wheel.

The wind

Shifts.

The continental circuses of calm and storm blow

Through our houses.

The hurrying years collect in the counting rock…

I met Marian on the road to a war and we held hands

Over the dead.

And after…

when I returned from the long

Enchantment.

Or someone returned…

wearing my used body.

– Girl with the moon in her pocket!

Quail-keeping girl

girl

With the red-eared hound…

That innocent

perfect…

– returned and left her,

Torn away in the vast cyclone of the Postwar, the psychotic

Continental drift

                    the heart torn out of my side.
                                        I had met
My own Dark Lady.

                    And of that time, as of records
Kept, etc.
                    as of marked stones left on the trail
                                        as of blazes
                                                    or gardens
Planted and tended
                    – it's all in Sauvequipeutville, Salsipuede
Avenue Marsh Street Elysian Valley…
                                        twenty-feet under
The progressive concrete where the freeway came through.
                                                    And the world rides
Over a poor house, bulldozed down and buried.

What I met looked like a mask (deadset for early death,
With the mask of insanity under it) made from the money-of-the-month.
– Mask of a rich whore, a bourgeoise, chippying around
With the dangerous world of the poor.
                                        Pulled off that mask and found there –
(The damned call out to the damned: "Save me!"
                                        Cry I can never deny)…
– In the woman of our fatality, we find under the mask
Ourselves
                    our own lost innocence
                                        crying to be redeemed.

In that mirror of flesh we confront our own past
(Which is always wrong)
                              our weakness
                                        (therefore: terror, despair)
Our own corruptibility
                    our human potential for being
Lost.
        And *that* woman is all the mortal hungers
Of our own lost years;
                    our defeats;
                              our secret country;
Childhood
        future
                hope
                    fear
                        class
                            revolution
Our fate.

        In those days we built our cooking fire
On the wind
        walked only over the abyss
                              slept, always
In a vast bed swinging among the polar stars.
In those days we invented the atlas of handy catastrophe;
Discovered the buried languages hidden under the twelfth rib –
The illuminated jokes of the Cardinal of Lower Mombasa;
                                        projected

(Only on astral planes it is true) the psychic structures
Of the mechanical grand pianos that were grinding Mozart to death.
What did we care that Mexican calendars were full of antique
Firecrackers?
                    The A-bomb shelters full of lepers, the banks
Leprous with exploding money?
                              The bed swung round with the world
But we lay always true north like needles of blood and bone.

And each to other like a wall, world, electric fence –
Bluebook   secret-society   conspiracy   cartel   enchanted castle…
Assaulting each other to extremes of flesh, like holy burglars
Breaking into a Saracen keep in search of the Holy Grail.
We had to smash all masks and tear down every wall.

These hungers fed only on themselves.
                              Each road was chosen
Only for its dangers: the desperate authentication of terror
That kept the world at bay.
                        For when love becomes the Absolute
It cannot admit that Other, and it longs always for death:
That final seal on its value and condition the lovers aspire to
Because changeless.
                    They dream to burn there.
                                        Perfect,
                                            And perfectly
Unmoved and unmoving.
                    Radiant.
                            The point at the heart of the diamond…

But fate never asked us to die for the revolution or love.
And the world got in the way at last, the world of the blacklist,
Of money and need in a bourgeois town.

                        In time it finished us off.

          ❋   ❋   ❋   ❋   ❋

"I've seen it many's the time (Martin speaking, my brother)
That riverboat gambler aristocrat with the flowery vest
Headin' out west with his TB and double-eagle on his watch chain,
To burn like a damned soul in Tombstone or Dodge City,
Reckless, gallant, lost.
                 But they all sober up in the end.
They wind up in Azusa: putting the lawn under concrete
And painting it green.
               My god, man, don't you *ever* watch teevee?
That's just life on the Great Pubic Plains, old buddy!"
And Peets is adding: "If'n you cain't eat it or screw it, fuck it!"

Maybe may be.
            The world is too much but not enough with us. Soon-later
Most give up or go under –
                terrible erosion in the gaunt
Seasons.
      In the killer winds.
                 And we are flesh, not rock.
But must be.
       The gentle rock:

not to wear out;
                                        to stand
Against Frivol, Trivil, and Superfice, the three national giants –
And to stand there in the tearing wind when all seems lost:
Our life shot down at a distance: death of a hungry wolf…

                    ❋   ❋   ❋   ❋   ❋

And so I must praise and pray for all loved lost women,
The queens of the green years.
                                        Time filled them with babies,
Wore down their loving hands
                                        emptied their mouths of kisses,
And led them into the dust at the foot of the grandfather stair…

There, leave them in peace
                    who were so lovely once.

4.   Little as it is, what have we, comrades, but love and the class struggle?
      The rock and the wind and the drifting delegate blazes of fellow
      Travelers
                stars
                    our far and fiery companions…
                                        and nothing
      To wear but this angry body: of which only one is issued
      And always too big or too small
                    – always too *hungry* –

and the angry

Hungering soul…

     – and *that*…

          never the right size either…

You only live twice: once in the mind and once
In the world.
          But, in the world, only the unexpected
Happens, ever.
          And so I was given a second chance
And the girl came:
          Genya:
             of innocence
                 beauty
                    valor…

She found me there – this child did – on a road deadset
For death
      and turned me
          compassionate compass of flesh
               O fiery
Heart
     O treasure of warmth in the bourse of ice
             O
Companion and stranger
          miner's-light
            lighthouse of the temporal sea…
This same sea I saw say early and slowly:

(Men low lie here: crazed: and crazy they laze and die –
Lo! Death) lost-night's-life away only, uttering a cold corpse, say:
       Love
           Its bells   barks   bridges.
                       Its midnight sun…

All this in a girl with a handful of debts, a black cat, an upright
Piano full of theories, heresy, heartache, dynamite-violets?
And each white key a doorway to the world's anguish and each
Black key a gate, a hurled stone, a wild horse,
And each horse named and each name known and the knowledge filed
Under each white key for to ride the straight of those lonesome roads
Alone in the dark or the shine of the long or the wrong ways
In the light of the runaround moon?

               It was so.
                    And each
Day of her life like a loaded sail – and no wind in sight! –
And each sail two ships; and each ship
A white ship or a black ship; and each
White ship a hope; and each black ship
A promise; and each sail loaded
              with dynamite…
                     cats…
And ravening grand pianos
          will grab you
              simply because
You walk around at blood heat.
        Heatseekers.

Was it?

It was,

So.

And not so.

She was a second life that I might have

Wasted.

Too close to say…

The life I put on over

My death.

The second heart that was given me in place of that other

I wore too long on my poor flag.

Yes.

It was so.

And so I entered again the growth of innocence.

And, writing –

Now! – I am furry with animal light.

I enter the ecstatic

Round dance of the fox and the field mouse on the scarred, warring

Hills,

the rites of passage toward the sacred city of birdsong,

The tunnels of morning hunger and the ancient rivers of night…

And now here she is sleeping…

the arch of her foot darkened…

By the passing of time, by the oil of the classic sea…

and outside

This window

in the halt of the afternoon

in the Skyrian light

A sewing machine of birds is mending a side of the weather

Which the locusts unravel hourly in the clattering heat.

And outside

This window

midnight

the white and faultless moon riding

The snowy hills and fields of Dakota.

And she lies sleeping!

Under all this burden!

Kachina…

blazes…

and blessings!

V

1.   Man is the fate of his place and place the fate of the man
And of time…

        Had arrived there

            – North Dakota, the farmhouse

                  the old

Dominion of work and want (but all in a new style now)
My turnaround point and old-time stomping ground
To find the place we went wrong and blaze the trail through the dark,
To make the Kachina…

        night journey inbound dream

Voyage…

          ❉   ❉   ❉   ❉   ❉

     The road outside the window was "our" road
Once. It is now anybody's road.

        It is the road
On which everyone went away.

       Take it.

          To the coulee bottom –
Head south on the ice toward the Indian graves and the river.

Sunday.
   Calm as a saint

       and the church-bells falling like wounded

Parachutes into the parochial dark of St. Mary's-at-Sheldon into
The noonday acetylene of snow and sun as I tramp south.

The coulee holds, at the far end, a black bone
In its mouth: the river trees: sheathed in a plating of sleet,
And I hear, in the cold hush, their icy rosaries clicking
A mile of frozen Aves.
      Little changed, or changing –
River: still wild: earth hold here
(As always I hope) the glamour of animal night, the holy
Terror of empty places, secret, and the ancient prehuman
Light.
   Luminous, the river snow unscrolls a white
Tall, telltale: faint script of bird and hieroglyph of beast:
Where one has come to a dead end in the air as the owl,
Falling, trolled him away; or hawk struck; or the stalking
Mink closed and clung in his hunger.
        In the stark upriver
Sun I see the black of the beaver town where my youngest
Brother (dead now) trapped the old bulls in a happier winter.

The beaver have moved since those times; have come downstream
Toward easier forage.
     A short walk on cold water
Takes me here: by a dam-site. And here I sight in the upstream
Black and blaze the place I swam one long gone midnight
After setting the threshing rig in the neighbor field.
          Glare ice
Above the dam where the last thaw runoff froze.

                                                    Listen:
Under the skin of dark, do I hear the singing of water?
The trees tick and talk in the almost windless calm
And the stream is spinning a skein of an old and lonesome song
In the cold heart of the winter
                              constant still.
                                          One crow
Slowly goes over me
                    – a hoarse coarse curse
                                        – a shrill
Jeer: last of the past year or first of the new,
He stones me in appalling tongues and tones, in his tried
And two black lingoes.
                        A dirty word in the shine,
A flying tombstone and fleering smudge on the winter-white page
Of the sky, my heart lightens and leaps high: to hear
Him.
      And the silence.
                        That sings now: out of the hills
And cold trees.
              Song I remember.

                              I turn to the slope
That lifts to the bench, taking a path that the rabbits broke
In their moon-crazed rambles.
                              I grope for handholds in the buckbrush clumps,
I thumb the horny gooseberry brittle: stiff in his winter
Dress
      – grab on and climb.

A rime of icy crystal
Glitters around my going like sun-maddened precious stones!

A step; a half-step, and a step more. I finally make it
Over the shallow lip and stand on the low plateau:
Here's Tommy Comelately to pore over the bones
Another time.
                    And what's here – on the little bluff
Over the little river?
                    A way station, merely;
A halfway house for the Indian dead – analphabetic
Boneyard…
                    It was here the Sioux had a camp on the long trail
Cutting the loops of the rivers from beyond the Missouri and Mandan
East: toward Big Stone Lake and beyond to the Pipestone Quarry,
The place of peace.
                    A backwoods road of a trail, no tribal
Superhighway; for small bands only. Coming and going
They pitched camp here a blink of an eye ago.

It's all gone now – nothing to show for it.
                    Skulls
Under the permanent snow of time no wind will lift
Nor shift…
                    – these drifting bones have entered the rock forever…

And all done in the wink of an eye! Why my grandmother saw them –
And saw the last one perhaps: ascending the little river
On the spring high water in a battered canoe.

                                        Stole one of her chickens
(Herself in the ark of the soddy with the rifle cocked but not arguing)
Took the stolen bird and disappeared into history.

And my father, a boy at Fort Ransom, saw them each spring and fall –
Teepees strung on the fallow field where he herded cattle.
Made friends and swapped ponies with a boy his own age –
And in the last Indian scare spent a week in the old fort:
All the soddies abandoned, then.
                           Wounded Knee –
The last fight – must have been at that time.
                                        And now
All: finished.
                 South Dakota has stolen the holy
Bones of Sitting Bull to make a tourist attraction!

From Indians we learned a toughness and a strength; and we gained
A freedom: by taking theirs: but a real freedom: born
From the wild and open land our grandfathers heroically stole.
But we took a wound at Indian hands: a part of our soul scabbed over:
We learned the pious and patriotic art of extermination
And no uneasy conscience where the man's skin was the wrong
Color; or his vowels shaped wrong; or his haircut; or his country possessed of
Oil; or holding the wrong place on the map – whatever
The master race wants it will find good reasons for having.

               ❋   ❋   ❋   ❋   ❋

The wind lifts and drones on the hill where a file of whispering
Snow wears at the bench-slope, rattling the sleet-stiff buckbrush,
And a train of cloud piles down from the high north,
Hiding the sun.
              The day collapses toward evening.
                             Cold,
I turn from the bone-white field and drive my feet toward home.

In the thickening early gloom the first of the night hunting
Begins.
       On a quickening wing, a Great Snowy Owl,
Pure as a mile of Christmas, sifts and seethes down the sky,
And the shy and hiding rabbit hears and turns his white softness
To stone.
       Tranced, fear serves and saves him.
                     The owl steers over,
Swings out on a spur of wind, swerves in his search and is gone.

Snow on the wind.
        First farmlight.
             In downriver darkness.
A fox barks.
       Once.
       Again.
         Silence and snow…
– And the fisherman still alive in the future in Skyros!
                 (But dead
Now and forever.)
       In the boneyard…

                    Simulacra…
                                    The Indian is the first

Wound.

2.   Evening – another evening – and the lights flare
From the farmstead yardlamps far over the blank open
Spread of the prairie night.
                                    Renaissance of illumination
Courtesy REA.
                    And each lamp beacons and beckons
Across the neighbor and empty fields: *Come ye over*.
But no one comes.
                              And the traveler on the worn and improved roads
Goes by in improved darkness not even a barking dog
Lights…
                    The houses blacked out as if for war, lit only
With random magnesium flashes like exploding bombs (TV
Courtesy REA)
                    Cold hellfire
                                    screams
Tormented, demented, load the air with anguish
                                                        invisible
Over the sealed houses, dark, a troop of phantoms,
Demonic, rides: the great Indians come in the night like
Santa Claus
                    down the electronic chimneys whooping and dead…

Still, in the still night from a high hill (if there were one)
In the dark of the moon, with the far and fiery heavensteads blazing –
Huge galaxy-ranches and farm-constellations and solitary starcrofts shining –
On such a night, if one had a hill, he might see, in these lower
And faster fields, the constellations of farmlight: less vast
But moving still, in their hour and season, like the Plough and the Bear
Burning…
        impermanent…
               companions…
                       having their dignity there.

But from the imagined hill I see also the absence of light –
The abandoned farmhouses, like burnt-out suns, and around them
The planetary outbuildings dead for the lack of warmth, for the obscured
Light that the house once held.
                 And where has it gone?
                       And where
Have *they* gone? Those ghosts who warmed these buildings once?

Over the hills and far away. ("Our road"
Is anybody's road now: road that we all went away on.)
Away to the new wars, and the new ways, and the old
Whores of a system that found us expendable; to Work and to Want
In other pressures
        playpens
           – in wilder parts of the sky…

Dark, dark the houses lie there.
         The wind of the winter,

Like an animal, tears at the broken roofs,
                                        and the rain of spring
Opens the doors sly as a thief;
                        and the fires of summer
Flare on the broken panes, blister, consume;
                                        and autumn
Arranges in those sad parlors, chiefly, the melancholy
Of absent chairs.
                    There, hysteria has entered the wallpaper:
It flaps in the gloom like a trapped bird.

                                    In empty kitchens
The rat turds, hard as BBs, rust.
                        Filth on the stairs
(O grandfather dust!) thick and mousetracked, leads to rooms
Without character: boxes of boxed darkness: birdshit –
(But only the swallow nests here – the daubs of mud over doorways
Are the most live things in the house.)
                                In the downcellar dark
Are nests of Mason jars: crocks; jugs – an entire
Breakable culture abandoned archæological disjecta
Membra lost processes…
                        And the attic night trembles
For its terrible treasures
                                its secret histories like deadmen's bones
Unburied in the gap-throated old-fashioned trunks' dark fathoms.

Here, fur-bearing bibles, inlaid with fake gemstones,
Like sand-covered driftfences of tallies of a winter count,

Record, before Genesis, the early departures and the first begots –
Writ by hand…

        and the letters, packaged in rotting twine,
Talk all dark in a language of leaving and loss

                      forgotten

Tongues
      foreign

          sounding

            – words of love and hunger…

Finally the aging and ageless photographs, unfixed in time
Or light, mourn: for the abandoned ghosts who no longer
Haunt these frames.
          And where have they gone?

                  Through bankruptcy;
To be spiritual props to the interest rate in the Farmers' First
National Bank of West Nowhere Dakota;

              to die in the dying
She-towns of the farmlands and the thousand widow-sodalities
Of those depths (the husbands long gone under from working
To assure their wives this final loneliness).

            Last, they've gone
Back to the land:

        in ten thousand little lost graveyards, forgotten:
Before the fashionable collectivity of contemporary death…

But you will not find them there, nor even the ruined stone
Maybe, that spelled their fate.

        (Look for MacCormick reapers,

Look for the brass-tongued Nichols & Shepherd steamer – these dead
Machines are more alive.)
               And now where the fence lines join,
In deserted coigns and corners abandoned they enter the night-rock…
In the lilac-choked encampments of the older dead, in a grave plot
(Where in summer the wheat like a bright sea breaks and in winter the fallow
Encroaches) under the last of the true prairie, the last
Of the wild grass.
            Forgotten.
                Lost as the last Indian:
Who were good men in their time: a century or a cemetery ago.

❊   ❊   ❊   ❊   ❊

Leave 'em lay where Jesus flang 'em.
             Turn away:
From these exhausted houses toward those newer lights,
Brighter but farther spaced than the old, with a greater emptiness
Between, around.
          In the deep
                winter
                    rentier
                       wheat rancher –
Who fed on those old bones   gone:
                to Acapulco:
With their newest Janes in their bluest jeans to New Orleens
In their flying machines
            (and they have 'em)
                to Coeur d'Alene for the snow.

Or gone into the neighbor frau by way of a wife-swapping key-club –
And *herself* gone to shop in nearby Dementia via *Town and Country*
To return, after years of hunting in the haunts of artistical queens.
Covered with gay wallpapers wild and a flair for hysteria:
And all to adorn an unused den for a country bourgeois!

For the dead, *all else* is alive.
                              Or how explain
The bourgeois belief in a boss culture?

                                        But most I see
(Between the magnesium flashes cold, before the dawn's early
Light) the sad sons of the prairie: sitting in darkness.
There, in a glass, brightly, they sleep on two sides at once:
The past, the future: at last united.
                              (Courtesy R E
A.) A moment.
                  A kind of sleep.
                                    Clear to the end.
Where?
          Here.
                  This is one end of the night
                                        now.

But no present: only the past and the future: both false.
As the poet saith (Bob Bly) drawn down
The barrels of inexhaustible revolvers to sleep like freaks
In the .45 caliber interchangeable wombs alcohol
Insulated

                    at home
              TV

                        Dakota
                              is everywhere
                                        and *grow* there
Like the jolly white giant
                        in intolerable pressures
                                        at home
                                              in the expanding
Expendable universe grown at ease
                              with the Indians' end
And their own
              some future
                        pi in the sky
                                  it's here already.
And the missiles
              Minot
                  Grand Forks
                              sleeping their murderers' sleep…

3.   And the people?
                  "First they broke land that should not ha' been broke
                                                      and they *died*
Broke. Most of 'em. And after the tractor ate the horse –
It ate *them*. Most of 'em. And now, a few lean years,
And the banks will have it again. Most of it. Why, hellfar,

Once a family could live on a quarter and now a hull section won't do!
Half of the people gone left the country; the towns dyin';
And this crop uh hayseeds gutless – wouldn't say shit and themselves
Kickin' it out their beds. It's hard lines, buddy!"

Bill Dee speaking his piece: hard times
In the country.
        Bill Dee: last of the old bronc-stompers
From the gone days of Montana mustangs we used on the farms
For light work and for riding and the pure hell of having
Outlaws around…
        The same Bill Dee of the famous removable
Eye: which he'd slip in your shot glass sometimes – O blinding and sobering
Sight!
    – "Just take a swally uh *that* and say what yer innards
Perdick fer the follyin' winter! Take a *glass* eye view of the world 'n
Change yore luck!"
       Not only a glass eye: a gab
Nine miles longer than a telephone wire.
         A sense of style:
Could roll cigarettes on a bucking horse in a high wind –
But only one-handed of course…
         Was the greatest success I know
Out of the old days alive
       alone
     but alive –
Had decided he wanted to be a bronc-snapper and cowboy and *made* it –
On the last ranch on the hither side of the moon.
         And lived there

Still: on the Bonesack.
(Ranch in the Sand Hills.)
And a small cabin
Built there: of elm and cottonwood made: squatter –
"Ain't a hell of a lot, but it's more 'n' some got: *'n' hol' that, Tiger!*"
He rattles on as we rattle along in his ancient car,
And that's where we're heading: down to the Hills in the late-winter day.

Under the thin snow the Hills show no sign
Of natural order.
Sand from a postglacial delta, the winds
Pushed them into no pattern, and now the grass half-holds
These random structures: holds for our lives' long moment only,
Perhaps.
Under the noon-high sun the blow-outs' sandwhite
Eyes glare back at the cold light.
The sun clots
In the bunched buckbrush, is caught in a patch of briar and bramble –
And a deer jumps out of the light, flies over a fence, sails
Across the top of a hill like a puff of cloud!
"That one,
I'm savin' a while yet," Bill says: as if it were something he owned.

Scrub oak on the hills; chokecherry; staghorn sumac
By the river's edge…
and there the ancient and moving order
Of the living water: now ranged in its wintry keep.
Where the bluff drops

Steeply down toward the ice are the sedgy halls and freeholds
Of mink and muskrat on the swampy ground and then the river.

"Old Sheyenne got better fishin' each year," Bill says.
"Them honyocks around here just too *lazy* to fish. They druther
Buy them damn *froze* fish in them plastic bags.
Why, hellfar, you remember that place where that spring comes in –
Nigh my cabin? Used to take fish out of there with *scoop* shovels –
Gunnysacksful! 'n' people with pitchforks spearin' the big uns!
They don't fish there no more – nobody but me. Why, boy,
We get you some whoppin' Northerns 'n' the best-eatin' goddam Walleyes –
Takes an illegal net to get illegal fish, 'n' I *got* one!"
Illegal fish flesh and fowl – about all that he lives on.

And into the Hills' lost places: now, following
The river, and again buckjumping over the iron, faceless
Ranch roads: opening the gates in the fences, kittycornering and quartering
The waste…
                Dead houses here in the bottomlands:
                                        and eyeless
Schoolhouse, abandoned, crumbles;
                                undenominational forever,
A church is stumbling into an empty future, lofting
A headless and rotting Christ on the cracked spool of a cross:
Unspinning god at a loss in the psalm of the man-eating wind.

"Ever'body here got blown out in the last of the dusters.
Should never been farmed no-way. The country's sure empty. But me –
I like it this way.

And the animals comin' back! Why, hellfar,
They ain't only pheasant and grouse – man, there's wild *turkey*.
There's deer, there's foxes, there's – last night I swear I heard a coyoot –
Heard it or dreamed it…They're comin' back sure – the old days."
Dreamed it; no doubt. And dreamed the old days as well: doubtless.
Another fast dreamer…

     At last we arrive at the shack.

Here's Uncle Chaos come to meet me halfway!

        Seems so:
Near the house an antique car is racing into the ground
And releasing its onetime overpriced atoms into the void
At the speed of rusty light.

       Over the doorway a splintering
Rack of flinty deer horns starts no fires in this wind.
Hung from the wall, abandoned gear goes into the weather:
Worn spurs and rotting saddles and bridles

          emblems
Of the gone days.

     Indoors, deerskins cover the floors,
The bed, the few chairs.

      There's a new shotgun.

         A rifle
My father gave him – 25-20 Winchester brushgun.
Traps, snares, spears and fishing tackle: the illegal
Net…

   Ground zero

     Bill Dee

       at home on the wind,

Adrift and at home in the universe

                         alone…

                              alive…

                                   And the others –

I think of Tiger Good in his shack on the Maple River

Trapping and hunting his way through the big freeze of the Thirties;

Of the squatters in Troop Number Nine's log cabin here on the Sheyenne;

Of that nameless one who lived as a hermit here in the Hills;

And of Moonlight John: his home a demounted two-door car-body

Beside Route 46.

                Froze to death there in a three-day blizzard:

Winter of the blue snow…

                    mavericks

                        loners

                            free men

And what's to show for it?

                    For Bill Dee in winter a treeful

Of moonlight.

            The snow and the river.

                        The lonely meat roads he follows

Tracking illegal deer.

              Feuds with game wardens.

                        And in summer

Forty acres of butterflies fenced by verticil sun.

Now: mackerel sky: the cloudy bones of the wind;

Slow air climbing the light and the little stair

Of dustmote, waterdrop, iceflake   weightless celestial blue…

Nights with the winter moon caught in the stars' far
Houses…

    And noon blazing cold in its cage of fire…

             ❀   ❀   ❀   ❀   ❀

"Seems like it was right here somewhere – place we went wrong."
– And the voice of the dead fisherman (still then alive in the future!)
Tears at my ear, at my heart, like a mad bird screaming
Or keening ghost…

       Lost…

         Sunk with all hands…

                Here.

Somewhere…

     My grandfather saw the beginning and I am seeing
The end of the old free life of this place – or what freedom
There was: the round song at least: the solidarity
In the circle of hungry equals.

         Or if there was nothing else –
Resistance…

     And of Bill Dee and those others…

              survivors merely,
Anachronistic.

     Nothing to build on there, though they keep
(Still!) the living will to endure and resist.

           Alone.
Alive.

   Outlaws.

Riding a cold trail.

        Holy…

* * * * *

If New York holds history locked in its icy museums

                            stony

Keeps no wind can shift or shake

                  its falling walls

Spalling

      unspelling the rebel names while the prisoners sleep

In the night-rock…

            If Los Angeles' windless calm is only

End of the continental drift

          decaying granite

                no house

Will stand

      and change *there* merely the empty alternatives ranging

The sounding void…

          then what star steers and stands, what mansion

Founded on fire brightens towards us   what sea will call us

Saying: here is the road to the ancient future light?

Exhaust these four: what's left?

              Nothing.

                Nothing?

Man is the fate of his place, and place the fate of the man

And of time

      A beginning then

           to know one's place.

                                                    At least
That.

4.   Where.   From.   Toward.   To which.   In which.   Away from.
        Into.   In.   Out of.   There.   Anywhere.   Nowhere.
        (A grave step in the wrong direction.)   Here.   Where else?
        Was.   Am.   Will be.   (A grave step in the right
        Direction.)   (In Eden there was no place.)   (No place *else*.) Name
        Sake.   Name place.   Name fake.   No
        Place. Noplace: like home.   No.   No homeplace.

Wherever I'm at, you'll find me someplace close to the Front.

        Here.   What-Was-Before.   What-Comes-After.   Now.
        Hither, Thither & Yon: the local gods.   Being.
        Becoming.   Having been…
                              Sherry (on the Frontier)
                                                    Bourbon
        (On Rye) (King of Kentucky) address:
                                        Avenida Salsipuede,
        Sauvequipeutville
                        West Nowhere
                                Dakota
                                        Nem Mokodik
        Utcha
                Texicola
                        Estados Unidos por Nada.

                                   Here
            (Where-the-Dead-Are: someplace-close-to-the-Front)
                                                                 Here

5.   In the pastures, now, the grass is eating the horse that time rode
        (So slowly!) from between my legs and into the flowering earth…

        Men have pastured wheat in the sun – and I was once a wheat herder –
        And alas, in the richest city in the world, hunger is *free*…

        Footsteps in stony silence…
                                    is it a dream: that I see
        In spring the grass greener in the shape of a horse, the quick shade
        Of the deer in the fading flowers in the roadside ditch where a car
        Laid her?

                All things are doorways: all things are passing
        And opening into each other always…
                                            our house door equally
        On Crazy Horse and the Cadillac.   (Echo of revolution
        In the north forty…)

                        But the Wobbly's footprint there led only
        To crowded jails in the nameless towns…
                                        And the Communists blazed trails
        To Federal Pens…

But now they have superhighways for *all* of us –
Night courts, day courts – and finally, friends: *to the Wall!*

Hawks. Skulls. Skull-trumpets easy under the wind…
All's well.
          I am here in the middle of my life (or more likely
Toward the end)
               I tally the winter count.

                    The more
The snow falls, the more my heart feels empty. The snow
Is good for the coming crops but bad for my soul. The falling
Barometer of my spirit is good for nothing
                              still
                    I'm *here*
And I have to be here: or elsewhere: so
                         – here for a while –
(In the economy of suffering, nothing is lost)
                              – here.

                         And it's only
The nostalgia for the living dead and for abandoned places that moves me.
(America is terribly old, saith the poet: Jim Wright)
Aye.
     Because nothing endures.
                    Marsh Street
                         the Indians
                              – gone under
The pluralistic concrete where the new freeway blinds through.

All's drift and dream.
                            Here stood a happy house,
Once: one blink of the eye and it's lost.
                                        Our whole history
Seems only a simple catalogue of catastrophe leading here…

But, at least: here.
                        (East is the death journey and West
The Oregon Trail to the dead myth.)
                                At least
                                        here
(Dakota   the farmhouse)
                            – begun before Easter –
                                                at least
                                                        at least
Here…

6.   The ghosts, the glory and the agon: gone.
                                        Having no past,
But only successions of failures in labor love and rebellion –
Cold-decked, the dream-pack switched by the tin horn of the status quo –
Forward! Having no history, on to create the legend!

The tracks of a million buffalo are lost in the night of a past
Lit only by the flare of a covered wagon
                                        a harp of flesh
Is silenced

the book of feathers and moonlight is closed

                                                forever

On exhausted roads spun out of acetylene lamps of the dead
Overlands

          the transcontinental locomotive is anchored in concrete
Next to the war memorial

                under the emblems of progress
A vision of April light is darkened by absent eagles…

It is not *my* past that I mourn – *that* I can never lose –
(Nor my future, which is assured, and in which I sing more cold
And passionate still as the passing years swing over my deadheading
Mortal part

            heart at home on the wind

                        borne

In the blood of strangers…

                carried

                    forward forever

                          this song…)
– No, but the past of this place and the place itself and what
Was: the Possible; that is: the future that never arrived…

                      ❄   ❄   ❄   ❄   ❄

It is almost finished…

              – the Kachina.

                            Midnight has flooded the coulee

With ancient brightness

              south

toward the hooded river
                              toward the dead
And the wind is spelling a tale in the spooled snow…
                              in the sea…

Genya stirs in her sleep.
                    The ghosts home on my light.
We wait: the Eternal Couple: the Fool
                              the Woman
                              and the Moon…

VI

1. _____ and always halftime at The Funeral – but once, in Samsara…
That is: NOW – start in the empty anytime: arrive
Ahead of time: HERE: in the filled-up nowhere, and go
FORWORD

                   – "Cain't hear you boy – ain't no color but the night
Down here – get out in the stream and *sing!*
                                 Who be ye?"

'Tis only myself…
                 the last man of the century…

                               going
Home…

        "Who you talk to then?
                       Dark here; cain't see
You."

        I'm just a worn piece of leather that was once well put together.
                                   I am
The one who has come at last to wake the reluctant dreamer
Out of his surfeit of continental sleep

                    to free the Bound Man
Of the Revolution
                    to make your jawbone book and heavenly
Credit card.
            Sunrise in the rock...
                            the light of my house
Burning...
            Do you read my blaze
                        down
                            there
                                in the dark?
                                    Over.

"Ah – that old resurrection man!
                    Talk like you found it –
Place you get out.
            But my foot
                – stuck here in the stone..."

In the time it takes to make one step is the life of my poem.
And unless the step is endless, hell is forever.
                            But hell
Shakes at one step; shatters.
                    It is *not* daybreak
Provokes cockcrow but cockcrow drags forth the reluctant sun   not
Resurrection that allows us to rise and walk but the rising
Of the rebel dead founds resurrection and overthrows hell.

2.   What I am doing
                  ain't nobody
                        nowhere
                              done before…

Have come a long way and arrive tired, the feet
Of language: raw: trailworn: needing to be reshod,
And myself with saddle sores from the long night ride.
I arrive near death, near the stall of silence…
                                    but that's no matter –
What began in the first blaze – despair – is to end in joy:
After showing you hell I'm to blaze you the trail to heaven…

Arrive cold – after the long fall into
The past that must be the future the future that is my past.
I see the bus go by advertising DOGMA and the blind
Veteran asking bread in the cold teeth of the night O
Ancient Witness
                  – and all unchanged in the time of this poem…

All to be changed.
                  I offer as guide this total myth,
The legend of my life and time.
                              But the message arrives from far off:
From some future galaxy – arrives very fast, very faint, in a language
I can barely translate…
                    and always the danger of shortfall, noise,
And the plaindamn inability of readers to know good sense and song…

And so – nights of waiting for a single word and nights
When all arrives at once like a migration of birds.
Days when I turn it off in order to breathe, days
When only an enigmatic phrase comes through from another galaxy –
Poem
            – nights…
                        when I am only food for the moon…

But hangups are no substitute for real agony.
                                    And I
Am born every morning…
                  And once in Samsara
                              and the ceremony done…
– Warped and bandaged arc of a broken bow I am bent
On straitening…

3. Begun before Easter of a different year…Skyros…Dakota
The world:
            outside my window
                        changed and unchanged.
                                    I have come
Back toward the light
                  (my brothers' houses all burned this year)
                                          toward
Morning.
            Beyond my window the armless windmills are marching
Into the sea.

And the iron poet strides over
The dark village.
            Cockcrow…
                        – and always springtime in Hell…

            ❊   ❊   ❊   ❊   ❊

I have come here – too young for this world and too old for the next –
From my violent acres crying for incarnation, to claim you,
To found our hungry legend in the field of bread, to find
Our bread in the bank of hunger, in the lame streets of the dawn,
To find our sign past sleep or these sleepy reveries of an insomniac Harp…

_____ have come to claim you, to build, on the angry winds of the renegade
Angels, the four blueblowers of the compass points, this stand
For the round song and the commune;
                                    in the moon of bad weather to build
The pure rock of this passage   oasis of song in the cold
And desert night…
                (first the stars and the sea, now
The rock and the wind)
                        – have brought you here: beyond the four
Elements: stripped: naked for traveling…(the dead fly *up*,
Having lightened load, through the rock…)

                            Now: all the trails are blazed:
The evidence is given, the Fisherman is rising, the Kachina is made –
The ceremony is done.
                – Now only the incantation.

                                        I confidently wait
Your rising.

        Night, pure crystal,
                        coils in my ear
                                like
                                    song…

4.   Begun before Easter…
                        Sign of the Fish…
                                    wind whining
        Out of the black North's cold quadrant, the moon
        Glistening on the folds of the coulee snow and a far scar
        Where the river sings and ceases, locked in its house of ice;
        Cold front sliding in: a wisp of high cirrus
        Rides over the Indian graves, the barometer drowses, the burning
        Clock of midnight turns on its axle of darkness…

                                    Had come there,
        To that House, first sign in the blessed zodiac
        Of all my loves and losses…
                            – to sing and summon you home.

                        ❋   ❋   ❋   ❋   ❋

        Now: the wind shifts
                        a star

                              falls in the sea.
Skyros
          the statue of Brooke on the citadel.
                                        Time interposes
A discontinuous strata, the sediments of the summer:
What was and what is slide along old fault lines, history
Condenses its marble heroes
                              a metamorphic palimpsest
Hardens between the farmhouse and here: and I dive
Into the night-rock
               terror

                    Now I call you:
                                   I call
You:
      from the four Winds and from Fire, come forth now
My thunderbird jawsmiths and soapbox phoenixes;
                                        out of the ice-lined
Rolling coffins of the U.P. Line: rise;
                                   I call you
From Water;
               blind marble of those tolling bones
Walk home forever now from the cold dismembering sea;

I call you from holy Earth:
                         boneflower: starform
                                        I call you now:
Goddess, sweet land I love, Old Lady, my darling ones –

Come:

       We'll walk up out of the night together.

                      It's easy…

Only:

       open your eyes…

            slip your foot free from the stone…

I'll take you…

       my darlings, my dear ones…

                   over the river.

– North Dakota–Skyros–Ibiza–Agaete–Guadalajara, 1968

PART THREE

Make it as simple as possible –
but no simpler!

       – Einstein

I

1.   I'll take you over the river, over the winter ice…

❊   ❊   ❊   ❊   ❊

To go from Cham to Amoymon, Amoymon from Cham from
Sitreal, Palanthon, Thamaar, Falaur, Sitrami – the infernal
Kings of the North…
                      Recensions of demons:
                                   Samæl, Azazel,
Azael, Mahazæl – to look for the fifth element, the Fifth
Season…
           Orient, Paymon, Amoymon, Cham
                               – for the Fifth
Direction
          and six signs of the zodiac still open!
                           O
Gematria, Notarikon, Temura – Kachina: Yield up the Names!
TET RA GRAM MA TON
                    Coo
Coo.
     "The works of the light eternal are fulfilled by fire"…

❊   ❊   ❊   ❊   ❊

We will proceed southward, pulled by the cold bells
Of the churches, Cham to Amoymon, toward a winter feast of darkness
And light…
                    Yes.
                        Christmas. Prime. In the savanna of my years,
Nineteen Twenty-one-or-two of the blithe and fooling times
Smooth: buckskin-fit as my little hide to my soul.
Seemed so. Then, anyway.
                            And out to the field at nones,
At the ninth hour of winter song in the falling afternoon light,
Under a sigil of snow and over the December-sintered roof
Of the little river, lifting and lofting our cold voices –
Poor gifts but breath our spirit – calling our holy office
Into the blank white of the field's now-lost pages
To bring the gold of the summer home for the crèche and crib
And to line the rack of the sled for the trip to Midnight Mass…
That was an easy singing then for the boy's small pagan
Heart that followed his then-tall father's magic into
The fields of legitimate joy: all dark soon to be light –
If there was dark at all in the unfailed unaging world…
Well, it was a kind and kindly singing I do not deny.
But the world will require a countersong for those spiritual Entradas:
Enchantments chanted in cantatas to cant open the third eye:
(Eye of the World: a wise eye, a worldly wise eye wild
Open for the Fifth Kachina: SAQUASOHUH)
A new jazz, a blues for our old Fourth World
TU WA QA CHI…
                    the
                        Hospital…

But all this comfort-and-joy began nine months
Earlier – eight months actually (Virgins Immachinate – unplotting –
Require but eight months' pregnancy. Parthenogenesis anyone?),
Impregnation: April 21, 3:55
PM (Hi there, Tomasito!). The Holy Ghost descended
On Mary…the long long Fall into the Flesh…
There was a traveling salesman no farmer's daughter resists!
– Torose Toro, God's own Taw of the Second Sign,
Holy Square-and-Straight-Shooter to tie and tow her to God,
Great Spook of the Annunciation arriving a month after Gabriel,
H.G., *hydrogen grande*, the sacerdotal hydrogen,
That Always-Was-and-Always-Will-Be of the Steady State system
Of the one and Triune God…

                    But hold on! We're a little bit early –
Only two of 'Em so far and eight months to Midnight Mass…

Still when the Most High put on his Suit of Blood His mobled
Duds, His mackled and immaculate Zoot, when His Spurs was a-jinglin' –
Then did the Old Gods didder, horripilate, scatter:
– Witches and warlocks skating away on high and windy
Arcs and into the chant-sprung nightsky's sudden nave…
Learning strange vaportrails, curves unknown to mathematics…

These lines will be filled-in in color later by Sputnik,
By the Dog-in-the-Moon (Avaro wrote that one down),
By the Intercontinental Ballistics Missiles (their loops and crotchets),
By the IFBM (the Interfatality Ballbreaker Missile),
By moonshots and moonshorts, by shooting the sun and bombing the moon:
By putting out all the lights of the bright and morning star…

– Sure 'n' ol' Ugly there, jus' as big as his own business!
And there, surely, Old Ugly, the ultimate weapons sits
Gutsgurgling (his special fuel's crofted from blood and sperm)
Big D for Death
         at stool…
                sitting on white house lawns…
ALL OVA THIS LAND!
            (Orient! Paymon! Amoymon! Cham!) ☦
As in the silos waiting near Grand Forks North Dakota –
O paradise of law and number where all money is armed!
O the Open Eye on the Top of Dollar Mountain: ANNUIT COEPTIS!
IDOLATRY
      IDIOLATRY
         IDEOLATRY

2.   And still out to pick up that straw in the strum of the afternoon!

I ride in the jingling wake, my small sled tied to the bob,
Jinking along at the back in the field-bound hayrack's furrow
In the deep snow of the river road…
                hearing the thrum
Of the cold guitars of the trees and, distant in the dead-still air,
The rumbling of afternoon trains, the shunt and clang of the boxcars
Hunting their sidings in faraway towns at the ends of the wide
World of the winter…
          and beyond the jingle of the harness bells,
And the hiss and hush of the runners cutting the deep snow,

As we crossed the river, came the long and compelling call

                                                magic

Of the whistling distant engines –

                          interrupting my father's tune.

Bounding along on my belly on my little drug-along sled,
I knew I was part of the Horizontal, the World of Down.
In the World of Down, everything seemed out of place: as:
Water, now building its winter palace of ice at the well,
(To be lugged to the house in the cold and slopping pails that froze
Our pants into crystal leggins); as flaxstraw, wheatstraw, corn
Always away in some far field when needed at home!
And ourselves too…

                    somehow away from the Center…in the World
Of Down…

          But the World of Up, the Vertical (Christmas reminds us
Once a year!)

        – *there* we may lift our eyes!

                   (In *that* world
Where no eye looks down; where the earth, perhaps, does not exist
Except for us; where, in their shirts of marble or plaster,
Those bearded wonders and winged wanderers out of a higher
Order, luminous and white, [especially in this so holy
Season] – beings from fields far other and whiter than these
We enter now…

        to be entered only by following…)

                          may lift up our
Eyes
   – where Christ on his wooden rocket is braced to ascend!

And here come the Prophets now from the land of Nod!
To follow then: those bearded ones all come from the desert:
A great arc: empty; worn sandstone; silence.
And a louring darkness there where we might have expected light…
A few tents, empty, the flaps whipped by the wind.
Abandoned latrines where the sand whispers. A few fires
Where a blackened tin can still simmers a rancid denatured coffee…
Is it a railroad jungle here in the Holy Land?
But here is a blacksmith forge where the banked coal still smolders,
And the quenching barrel is ringed with the rainbow flecks of iron
Where the horseshoes hissed and hardened in the kingdom of Tubal Cain…
Might as well add in a couple of rolling mills and the odd
Hornacle replicating facility…and a jackal or three
Up there in the right-hand corner…

         and a few reeling and indignant
Desert birds or at least their shadows.

        Here Number
Is being invented; and its shadow: Law.

         Do you feel the cold…
And the darkness coming?

       And above all else the sense of desertion?
(Those few fellaheen out on the edge have been trained to be silent.)
It will take more than an automobile graveyard to humanize
This landscape. The visions here will all be wrong. Even one
Appletree might change it though…

        but there is none:

          the wind

            the empty

Dark…

And that landscape persists forever.
                                    Though I am here
In the World of Down: A Helper: bouncing along on my sled…

And suddenly there's that ziggurat rising out of the snow!
The strawstack where summer holds: still! in its goldeny heart!
– And my Da beats down the snow and rams a pitchfork in
And the stack-side opens like Adam to the glow of the inner soul
So august-cured and pure.
                            And I will go then and explore
This tent of the tribes of winter all pocked with animal glyphs,
To be hierophant of the fox and the stumbling amanuensis
Of the short stories of fieldmice to whom an Annunciation
Materialized out of the air to fix them numb in their tracks
To be raped and rapt away in ghostly rip-offs by owl-shine,
By hawklight, their poor stuttering last steps a lost
And foxed copy…
                    How terrible then to my child's eyes
Were those great mysteries of the air! Signs of the World of Up.

And went then from the strawpile top to the World of Down –
To strawstack tunnels and caves: these were rivers of hunger
Where stray cattle swam through the straw when the nights, full of coyotes,
Barked at the moon.
                        And what were they dreaming then, those Cretan cows,
Eating, their dehorned heads pressed into the side of the summer?
Their chewing mouths…black holes open in the universe of blood
Where green things fall forever…wells without bottom, graves
Ravening their way forward in the full shine of the stars…

– No wonder the coyotes were crying a bottom blues and the moon
Pulled up her skirts – those terrible cows will eat *any*thing!
Will eat up forests, drink rivers so that the bridges fall down!
Will piss on the poorhouse, kick over lanterns and burn down Chicago!
– Leaving behind them a train of round and mysterious stones:
The brown eyes of their frozen dung that glare at the stars
Unblinking…

        and these wintery labyrinths where the bull of summer was

                                 eaten.

– All this I read from my strawstack tower where a winter lightning
May yet sour all the bumblebees' honey in a flaring noon
Hung from a dozing and bell-crazed midnight when I, Tom Fool,
Float into the crocodile's mouth of Holy Mother Church
With all my sins on the tap of my tongue and as long as your arm
(An arm that's laced with pinholes and long snakes like a junkie's)
To be disarmed and tongue-tied there and commanded to climb and to sing
Up a hell-high line of Hail Marys and into the icy rigging
Of the good ship Salvation…

        homeport Jerusalem

                outbound

For Beulah Land…

      – a little town west

           – toward the Missouri…

But the lightning does not strike my tower, not yet, and I dance
In the hayrack, building the load, as my laboring darling Da
Lofts up the forkfuls of raw-gold straw like the aureate clouds
Left over from summer.

      And I, treading my fancy fandango,

My turkey-in-the-straw, while he shouts and laughs and half buries me
Lifting the last of the past year's light – the two of us singing
In a warm winter fable of our summer's work.

And done at last

I latch my sled to the right-rear bunker and we run for home.
– Sky: changed: now.

In the deep catch of the winter:

Dangerous: to turn one's back on Cham, the North and the Northwest
Demon: while the great Siberian highs wheel in and the sly light
Changes without seeming to change and the sky turns blue and bruised
And the icy night of the Blizzard roars down on the wind…
Snow showers to the north, and a few clouds, but the weather
Is only closing the gray eye of the evening.

Now in the tented

Field the cornshocks tower around me on my tiny sled,
And the cutback stocks like time tick under my runner's passage.
In that white field, in that gray light, in the World of Down,
Like a land-swimmer, bellyflat on the sled in the flying snow,
I enter a new domain, a new-found-land, like the deme
And doom of a Lapland Dauphin. *Here* is a cold kingdom come –
Place where the local comrades dress wholly in ghostly white.
As instance: the tearaway snowshoe rabbit blowing his cover
With a rapped-out curse from a foot the size of a mukluk. (And one
Worn – *sans doute* – by the "red-bearded muzhik from Michigas/Who
Played *folie à Dieu* with the Vichyssoise."

How can we stop them?)

And *away* rabbit!

And now comes the slippery weasel sly and slick

As a fart – in sovereign ermine – priestly – all exclamation –
!Mark! down to the black spot at the end of his tail!
And there go the Prairie Chickens like mad Anarchist Arabic
PRINTERS writing the Koran (or prepared to) across Dakota
And into contiguous Greenland (seduced by the glacier's glabromantic
Belly dances) or writing the Tao in the rows of the dead
Corn.
      A congregation of drunken (ugh!) Noitagergnocs
                            a prudence
Of confessors
        and excommunication of priests
                      a quarry
Of quarreling tombstones, they strut away
                      – talking in Arab.
– And of other birds, aside from the quail and the partridge, there were
Lammergeier, Murres, Snipe (!), Shite Poke and Muscovy Duck
(They don't give a fuck) and Colduck and Thunder Bird
And Guillemot – and musical swans from Nashville who have no names.

And all of them in a most unmerciful and unecumenical goins-on,
Tearing away like sinners snapping at the body of Christ –
(A little empanation here – *and turn on the wine*, the w-i-i-ine)
Mobilizin' our sacred corn, our sanculotide
Of Fructidore: won from the summer in the Last Days…
And, of other birds, there were pheasants which –

_____
                                          ❁
_____
_____

❁ The excised lines were considered (by whom?) as too obscure or Obscene for the eyes of the Gentle Readers.
(Who can they be?)

And the Pheasant leaped out of the tenement of corn like a burglar taken
In flagrante delicto with a cry like an angry bedspring
(Part silver, part bronze, part windchime and part pure galvanized iron:
A gateless gate opening on hinges never been oiled
By a single koan) – *leaped!* showing his colors, those jewels
Blazing around his neck, in a hellish and helicopterish
Blur and burr of feathers: indignant bandido and banshee!

Coldcocked and donnard by the spunk of that desperate and damned desperado
I take comfort from Cousin Owl: now: lifting: silent:
Like a puff of white smoke, so low and so slow drifting…

                                                 but drifting
(Great Snowy Owl) up! and off! and down on the wind…
And SUDDENLY doing his Owl magic and DISAPPEARING
INSTANTLY into the absolute white of the vast north winter…
– That is (probably) by putting out that one spot of color:
Aii! Eee! merely by closing his eyes…
So thick, the snow, I might put out my hand and lose it!

                                                   Seemed
So _____†
Say what a fortune this hand holds held out at forty below!
Why…none…yet.

                           The hand that went out in the snow
Was lost (it has never come back, never left) and for forty years
Has wandered the desert.

                           Yes siree! It's a *fact*.

---

† This line was omitted by the publisher for failure to fulfill the norms of that School of Poetry best known by
   the ideogram ⊙. This ideogram (known in Academic and Antiacademic circles and squares as the Poet's
   Sign) is generally translated: no-hearum, no-seeum, no-sayum. Nevertheless (see above):

And in them same environs
Where, a while back, you may have noticed them tents and them jackals –
Sand drifting…open latrines –
a forge still hot…
Deserted.
Oh, yes, He has been there too, this Hand,
A-loose in the landscape of Prophecy always here or hellswhere,
(Though it seemed to me that He might forget how to find His way
Home; or that He might, like a thief, steal into my pocket
And forget to let me know He was back – and I'd be afraid
To feel for Him there, that much-traveled Hand, that voyager, hidden
In my worn jacket – or He might stay away for years and turn up
In my Christmas stocking, playing with all my toys and breaking them,
Groping the apples, assaulting the oranges, returned so wise,
Or cynical – I wouldn't know what to do with a Hand like that!)
But: I put out my hand…
– lost at once in the blinding snow…

And so the forty – more or less – years of the wandering:
Staking a claim now and again but continually dowsing
For secret water – for it seemed that everyone was dying of thirst
In those ancient contemporary landscapes where the Hand was hired and fired
Often: as a foreign-born Agitator and oft-foiled Révolutionnaire.
But persisted, this Hand; blazing the trees toward the Secret Country,
Setting the type of the Manifesto, and picking up the fallen gun.
Yes, this Hand has wiped away other tears than those of its owner…
This is the Hand they kicked out of all the Academies and Antiacademies,
(Still building them fires and steering the dowsing wand).
Been fired by cattlemen and sheepmen and gone to live with the outlaws:

(Hole-in-the-Wall his address; letterdrop on the owlhoot trail).
And was agent (Haganah; '47) before they set up that
Arab shooting gallery on the Great Plains of Texaco
In the Gaza Strip: this Hand has shook down several Safe Houses
(Though not enough) and has levitated high as Mohammed's Coffin
(Suspended between Earth and the Eschatological) to ask forgiveness
In his own poor language – that of the Tuatha de Danaan –
Which (alas!) the Prophet did not speak. (And this is
The Hand's general experience with prophets – hello, Allen
G.!)
    But persisted, this Hand, and put out numerous fires
(Some he had started) and put His Self in the eternal blaze
Often: to carry coals to Old Castle.
This Hand has

Increased temperatures in reptiles and some reptilian critics (Hi
Poor Richard!) and increased the Kelvinical and Thermidorian reactions
(Can't win 'em all!) of country and city cunt, and has stroked
(Surreptitiously) the Venus de (blank) and one ass even more classic.

Classical Ass
Is Hard to Pass

This is the Hand that dreamed it was a foot and walked around the world on water!
That went to Oxford and found a bull; that went to the Louvre
To learn how to feel; that has snapped off the heads of marauding pheasants!
This is the Hand that is still searching for Itself in my pocket!
This is the Hand that glommed from the wind a four thousand dollar bill from Palmer Thompson!
(Senescent Capital accumulation – see Karl Marx.)

This is the Hand that wrote on the blazing walls of Greece the blaze Z!
That was twice cut off at the wrist for begging alms in Almsbury!
This Hand was buried at Wounded Knee in a fit of skeletal abstraction!
This is the Hand that carried the rifle (age ten) to assassinate the local banker!
This is the Hand that lit the chandeliers of all the underground seas!
This Hand is the author of McGrath's Law: *All battles are lost but the last!*

This is the Hand that removed the *liounes* from the menaces to Daniel!
This is the Hand that wrote the words
                  that warned the King
                            who prepared the menaces to Daniel!
This is the Hand that built the wall
              where the words appeared
                  that frightened the King
                            who prepared the menaces to Daniel!
This is the Hand that ripped down the wall
              where it wrote the words
                  that destroyed the King
                            who prepared the menaces to Daniel!
MENE MENE TEKEL UPHARSIN!
        This is the Hand

Now why was such a *gentle* Hand so hunted?
                        He wants
Only to hold the apples that grow outside this window…

Why?

Because of the Three Lustful Vegetables who hated Him!
Because of the lack of disorder in early surrealists' surly lists and last lost orders!
Because he was born so far from home!
And also because his best girl never learned how to write!
Because of the disappearance of the Third International!
Because (so they say) of the electronic pollution of birdsong!
And because (finally) (so they say) hell is overpopulated!
And has moved (furthermore: so they say) to Chicago!
And finally because that summer, cows' tongues turned to wood
And we had to shoot them between their large moist eyes
With tiny rimfire cartridges made by a subsidy of DuPont.
And finally because the banker George P. never came by
Where I lay in ambush, with my brother Jimmy and our .22 rifles.
And finally
      and finally…
           and finally.
                etc.
                   etc.
                      etc.
Because from forms of freedom the spiritual relations turn into
Fetters of the spiritual forces. Then comes the epoch
Of theomorphic revolution.
                But still this Hand *did* come back…

A salt script, *lettre de cachet*…
          "and *he* is to *read* –
     Here! – in these *sweatswamps* of his *Hand* – in these *llanos* and *pampas,*

In the quicksands of his palm, in that graph whose line is continually falling
(Graph, we may add, where neither abscissas nor ordinates can apply)
 – In this *thing* without geometric form to its shape or name
(Vectorless and parameterless as a eunuch) – without a fri'nd in the world!
You expect this *boy* here to read his fate in his Hand
(Which furthermore may be fondling the apples in his Christmas stocking!)
To read – *here* – in them Sand Hills and them Bad Lands! –
His *fate?* To read there in the alkali flats in the palm
Of his hand, in that earthquake country – I ask: you expect him to *read…?*"

Yes.

    I say it is all in our hands.

                      It is in all
Our hands' hard-lines-and-times and cold fatalities.

And all in our Christmas stocking: the one we seldom look into…
And meanwhile what of our Hand?

                  Oh, He is home,

                          been home –
At six-fifteen South Eleventh across the Red River from Fargo!
This hand is searching this white page of that distant snow –
Like a blind hawk hunting the trackless emptiness ahead –
Searching for your hand to hold while we write this down together –
This: _____

_____

_____

_____

_____

3.   Apples.

                  Outside this window, from the top floor of this house,
At this desk, at five twenty-three on a fine June morning,
In that light, in this waking, I find in these
Abandoned latitudes and fake doors into the slatternly
Weather (blowsy and whorish that will hold us another year
In the Fasching and false gestures of festival thermometers) I find these
Apples.

              Up in a tree.

                        Down from my desk

                                      – where else?
Nothing special about them.

                        They are of two kinds:
One of which can make pies – with the proper human ingredients;
The other an ornamental crab

                        – and I see one bloom
Still! Left over from Spring six weeks ago, to what
End?

          Spray "like a rapid branch of music" – *those*
Flowers…

           so late…

                  those most tendentious and irregular flowers!

° It may be that these lines (and there may be many more than suggested here) constitute the key to the whole
poem – and perhaps to *all* poems, or at least to those where unseen collaborators of present and future have
added lines of their own.

I think I have heard them before. But I won't ask *when,* as I look
Past them over the frozen coulee where we haul in the straw –
(You remember we went out for straw and lost a singular hand?
The good right hand was it? Or the sinister left of darkness?
The lost hand of feeling – the left and dreaming hand?).
– So: apples. I "love" them, rounding, and that belated bloom,
Even if *love* is in quotes.
                                                    (It is hard to know *how*
Love *is* these days, or what should be its proper object…
– What is there, Comrades, [I ask] but love and the class struggle?)
Hubble-bubble-bubble (saith the "poet of love") in his latest book.
But I feel tender toward them anyway, those last late blooms,
And special solidarity now toward the proletarian Apple
Lifting – *how* does it do it? – seems…easy – like a fountain –
That great freight and weight of the late and ripening fruit…
Lifting toward heaven in the virgin morning – borne up by birdsong! –
Apples for my Christmas stocking fifty – only fifty! – years early or late!

❊   ❊   ❊   ❊   ❊

We bring in the straw in an evening clear and pearly.
                                                                            Open
To all the light of the wide, wild, woolly west…
Into which I am looking now…
                                                    at those patient apples…and into
My garden:
"Larkspur, lupine, lavender lantana, linaria, lovage"…
– Sounds like a season in Ls: too far from anywhere ever
To get home at all…

But here we have got to the Ps
                              Peonies
Anyway. To Patience plant and Im-
                    patience
                          and Jack-in-the-Pulpit –
Plants that will grow in the dark (or at least in the shade) and Paradisiacal
Apples! It seems better.
                    As we go on from the Ps to the Qs –
(In the shade: where I am: growing eucharistical bread)
And Quince: apple of the first Garden
                              – I grow it here…
Here!
      On this desk!
                    World-apple and apple of my eye…
Eve's apple, the Quince was – world with a bite taken out:
For which I offer this weight of paper as receipt and roadmap
Forward toward the only Eden it is possible to find and farm.
I turn over my paperweight now as a puff of hot wind blows
These winter pages. And inside that glass apple or tear,
A fall of woolly snow is clouding the gold of my trees…

But west from this little garden, over the coulee, the light
Hardens toward Christmas Eve.
                    In that gone time
                              in this
Light we wait for supper and the Three Wise Men…

The Coming of the 3 Weiss Men
A Tale for Good Little (Red) Indians
And Other (Colored) Minorities…

Gentle Reader: Once upon a Time, in the Anywhere that is Dakota…
You can imagine about what it would have been like out there:
Lift the window on Canada and let in a little snow –
Some cyclonic widdershins here, if you please! – and some of that cold
That sent Sam Magee to the furnace with Shadrach, Meshach and Abednigo,
And a bit of smell from the lignite that burns in the potbelly stove…
And the woman, working, of course – milking the cow, maybe,
Or making butter (best to have her inside here) or cooking
(What?) Praties, maybe. Or if they're Norwegian – lefse.
Not a bad angle there. *Cut.* Through the window we see her

(*That dreaming farmwoman's face* – SHE IS IRONING CLOTHES: I KNEW IT!)

Thinking of sunny Trondheim and the troll that took her virginity
(*Make a note back there somewhere that she's pregnant and near her time*)
While Sven is reading his newspaper: *The Scandinavian Panther*
And we see in LONG SHOT: HER POINT OF VIEW: away down the

coulee

These…well…*kings,* sort of, mopin' 'n' moseyin' along
Towards…
      "Ole?"
          (*I* know it's Sven but *she* has forgotten)
"Ole"
    "Yah?"

"Some strangers comin' up the coulee…"
                                                    "Yah"
"Look like three *kings*…"
                        "Yah"
                                            "Or could be, maybe, the Prairie Mule
'n' a couple lonesome deadbeats staggerin' home from the Sand Hills…"
"Y-a-a-ah."
                    "For Jasus sake, man dear, if not for me own,
Put down that poteen! Here come the holy season fallin' upon us
Like an avalanche of hard Hail Marys and yerself down on all fours
Drunker than Paddy's pig – "
                                    "But I'm tellin' you woman I see 'em –"
"And meself with a belly as big as a barn and me time come –"
"Mary! it's three *kings* I see! – Unless it's Fergus
Of the golden cars… and Coohooligan…and wan of thim other ten million
Famous kings us Irish is famous for. Or else…maybe…"
"Or else?"
            "Or else Bill Dee and the Prairie Mule and maybe…"
"Maybe?"
                "Some other lonesome deadbeat staggerin' home from the Hills…"
"Y-a-a-ah?"
                "I tell ya I see it right here in the Book of the Blue Snow,
Woman! And them comin' on like Buster's Gang! 'N' it *is*
Bill Dee! wid a Japanese portable television! – on which I see –"
"Television ain't been invented yet, Ole."
                                    "Well Jasus woman it's _____ "
Cut *Cut* CUT!
            But it *is* Bill Dee –
With a portable TV

On which you may see Bill Dee, coming
Up the coulee with a portable TV on which you may see
Bill Dee with a portable TV coming…

Get the idea?

We may deduce from this that the Wisemen have *not* come – or
We may deduce that the *true* Wisemen have not come *or*
We may deduce that the true Wise Men have not
Come – for the poor.

Yet.

Or have come and have been forgotten….

Let's interview Bill Dee…

"Hi, Bill! I see
You're still viewing the world through that obfuscatory glass eye –
Whatta ya see out there? Why are ya here? Tell me!"
"Why *not?* Put a glass in yer head – and many have 'em – I tell ya,
'n' y'all wander the wide world long, wild wonders to see!
I'm just walkin' along 'n' I come across these two mopers
Wanderin'! A water witcher 'n' a witch watcher 'n' neither of 'em
Could find water or witch in a ten-gallon hat and *it* fulla stud piss!"

(I hear the heavy trains of the sea coming in to the anywhere
Stations of sand and salt…

– but: back to the subject!)
"'n' so, after a cold crossin' we come to there guards."
– "Guards?"

"You don't think everythin's pertected? – and this a hierophany!
– Anyway: Guard says: 'Advance. And gimme the countersign!'

'n' *I* says *Countersign?* What the fuck you talkin' about
Buster? 'n' he says: 'Right on! *Advance one countersigner!'*
'n' here I am! 'n' whatta think of *them* apples?"
Well.

      It could have been someone like Bill Dee…

                          we were so
Lost…
     Did Christ die…
              waiting for the three Wise
Men?
     Or is he still waiting,
               shivering in some
                    lost
Sheepfold?
       Corral?
          Or the hencoops which we have prepared for his final
Coming?

      Under us a lattice, thin as a molecule, grows
Instantaneous – formed (just under our feet as we flash
Forward over our world) like the forming of winter ice
Over the river…
        and we skate onward caroling:
"Over the river ice!"
          Never aware how thin
That winter ice is…formed for an instant under our feet
Then vanishing…
        Or in summer as waterwalkers we skate
The dogday rivers…

the thin skin of the water holding
An instant that is our forever as we rush out to the stars.

But it's thin ice, or thin water, anywhere you look…
I turn over this weight of paper, this paper weight and the world
Dissolves in snow…
                    over my garden…
                                        what do you think
Of *them apples?*
                    If I blink a tear away the world will
Disappear!
            But I will not.
                            Nostalgia is decayed dynamite.
                                                    Cham.
Amoymon. Orient. Paymon.
                            In all the rose of the compass
No charge is left.
                Now we must lift up our hands…
                                            to ourselves…
Already it's nearly too dark to say anything clearly.

II

1.   …too dark to say anything clearly, but not too dark
To see…
                    one foot in early twilight, the other in snow,
(Now failing away in the western sky where a fair star
Is traveling our half-filled trail from the still, far, field –
O rare light! – trailing us home toward the farmhouse lamp)
We go:
            home:
                    and then, with a shout!, my brother Jimmy
Leaps! And cleaves to my back on the little sled:
                                        and we're home…

❋   ❋   ❋   ❋   ❋

But not too dark to see…
                    It is snowing in Lisbon,
                                        Tomasito!
(At the corner of *Rua do Karma* and Rolling Stone Square
Where I'm living and loning and longing for you.)
                                        Portuguese winter!
A snow of leaflets falls from the hot and dumbstruck sky.
Midnight Mass for the Fourth and Fourteenth of July, Tomasito!
Or maybe the snow of Pentecost: the leaflets speak in *all* tongues
Of men and angels – and maybe it's time to change
                                        angels…

Still…*not* too dark to see…

                    (– was right *here*

Somewheres – place we got lost…)

                        And I *do* see:

                             here:

                                clearly

(Having third sight) *primero* (and aside from all the political

Palindromes) I see the beautiful girls of the Poor,

(More beautiful than all the nineteen thousand Marys) rusting

Under the hailing and merry slogans of the Tetragrammaton

Of the Revolution

                  – each Throne, Counterthrone, Power and Dominion

Of the hierarchy of those fallen angels signed with Hammer & Sickle!

They rust and rest – or their simulacra of holy pictures –

Where I saw them once before, among the foreign money,

On the back walls of earlier bars and wars…

                            their asses

Widen…

      icons…

           calendar queens…

                  (And Cal's girl, too…)

Some have wakened to fight in the man-killing streets, but these, enchanted,

Dream-chained in the burning palace of Capital, slumber…

They sleep where Custer sleeps and only Keogh's horse

Is alive…

        over cheap bars where *pão* and *vinho verde*

Have not changed into their bodies of bread and wine…

                              Not

Changed, yet, but changing: for also in those darkbright streets

I can hear the guns (seven, twenty-seven, seventy-five)
Of the July Days…
                    (though they haven't started shooting yet).
                                                  And the bells
On the trucks of soldiers and armed workers.
                              But few of the latter –
Alas…
        Like the girls, the Workers' Councils (soviets) are resting
Or rusting…
              – Though they and the damned poor are wrestling for the Body of Good
Through the ten thousand parties of the Revolution:
                                        there
                                              in the shouting
Streets that all end in the cold sea.
                          No time!
For love!
        (Though this is a kind of love.)
                                It is time! (they sing!)
                                              Time!

(And the bells clang from the rushing trucks and tall towers)
Time! – to change angles and angels and to reinstate
Cham, Amoymon, Marx, Engels, Lenin, Azael,
Stalin, Mahazael, Mao, Sitrael – Che-Kachina –
O yield up the names of the final Tetragrammaton! –
Time! To make sacred what was profane! Time! Time!
Time!
        to angelize the demons and the damned…

2.   And we, of the damned poor, trot our frost-furred horses
Into the barn where beyond the glinting lantern, a blessed
And a steamy animal sleep is clotting into a night
Dreamless, perhaps, or, if blurred by dreams, it is green as summer
And the hay that burns there – a cattle-barn night, star-lighted
By rays from the deadwhite nailheads shining in their rime-laced albs.

The yard is corralling the darkness now, but Orient offers
A ghost-pale waning moon host-thin in the wan and failing
Light:
The sun that brief December day now gone
Toward topaz distances…of mineral afternoons
Beyond the Bad Lands…

                toward Montana…

                        the shandy westernnesses…

And we three (who are now but one in the changed and changing
Dark of my personal fading and falling world) we three
Hand in hand and hand in heart sail to the house –
My father has lent me the light so we can go hand in hand,
Himself between us, the lantern brighter than any moon!

Indoors, my mother bends over the stove, here face rosy
In the crackling woodfire that winks and spits from an open lid.
And we *all* there, then, as we were, once,
On the planet of sadness in a happy time. (We did not, then,
Miss you, Tomasito, an unsuffered age away
Waiting for all my errors to make me one time right.)

And so I will name them here for the last time, who were once
Upon the earth in a time greener than this:
My next brother Jim, then Joe, then my only sister, Kathleen,
Then Martin, then Jack, the baby.

                         Now Jim and Jack have gone
Into the dark with my mother and father. But then –
                                       Oh, then!
How bright their faces shone that lamplit Christmas Eve!
And our mother, her whole being a lamp in all times and weather…
And our father, the dear flesh-gantry that lifted us all from the dark…

    [In that transfiguring light, from the kitchen wall, a Christ
    Opens his chest like an album to show us his pierced heart
    As he peers from a church calendar almost empty of days.
    Now: say, then, who among you might not open your flesh
    On an album of loss and pain – icons of those you have loved
    Gone on without you: forever farther than Montana or sundown?
    No Christ ever suffered pain longer or stronger than this…]

So let me keep them now – and forever – fixed in that lost
Light
     as I take the lantern and go down the stairs to the cellar
In search of the Christmas apples cold in their brimming bin.
There, as deep in the hull of a ship, the silence collects
Till I hear through the dead-calm new-come night the far bells:
Sheldon…
        Enderlin…
               bells of the little towns
                        calling…

Lisbon…North Dakota…

[Yes, I hear them now
In this other time I am walking, this other Lisbon, Portugal –
Bells of the Revolution, loud as my heart I hear
Above the continuous bad-rap of the urine-colored sea.
Beside which I am walking through that snow of July leaflets
In search of the elusive onion to make the home-done sandwich
Herbaical and vegetable and no doubt even healthy, and certainly
Hearty-seeming (in mind's tongue) after fifteen ĸs and quais
A la recherche de cebolla perdue:

Vegicum Apostolicum

Herbibable sancti et ecumenicabable…

Meanwhile
I die on the vine waiting for news from you, Tomasito,
Waiting for the angel, waiting for news from heaven, a new
Heaven, of course – and a better world in birth! *Here:*
Under the changing leaflets under the flailing bells.]

And the bells of Sheldon carry me up the steep of the stairs,
My feet set in a dance to be bearer of these cold apples,
The fairest fruit of our summer labor and harvest luck.
I lay them out on the lamplit table. On the gleaming cloth,
In the dreamy gaze of the children they glaze in a lake of gold!

O high wake I have said I would hold!

It has come all unknown:

Unknown!

And my blood freezes

to see them so:

In *that* light

         in this

             light

                  each face all-hallowed

In the haloing golden aura shining around each head!

And how black and stark these shadows lean out of the hollow dark

To halloo and hold and hail them and nail them into the night

Empty

         – its leaden reaches and its cold passage

                              empty…

And so, at that last supper, in the gold and blood of their being,

So let me leave them now and forever fixed in that light.

3.   To go from Cham to Amoymon!

                        Toward Midnight Mass!

                                  And the frost

Filing the iron of the runners or the runners filing the snow!

It sets our teeth on edge, that gritting and steely protest

Against our going. But we go all in joy! In joy

Our holy carols and catcalls collect from the coulee hills

Their coiling and icy answers like echoes drawn from the stars!

Initiatory ceremonies toward a feast of illusionary light!

The holy words rise cold in the ghostshapes of our breath,

Our little smokes and fires that lift the words-made-flesh

Into the eye of heaven, the bone glare of the moon

Her celestial pallor

            deathshine…

                       (All that the priests have left

Of the warm and radiant Goddess who once held all our hands!)

And rise as well to the dark demons stirring around us

Pale in their faint fire whose dream on this night of nights

Is again to be born and burn with that flame the world once was

Before the abstract light of the Father's Heavenly Power

Put out the eyes of the stars and drained the life from the moon.

Cold Heaven, now! the alienating Pale

Of the Priestly Power Trust, God's Own Monopoly Light,

Has fenced off our fallen world, all…

                          – from our true sight –

Insight: all dark now and the motherly magic

That once had opened our eyes and hearts to Brother Flower

And Sister Star and Brother Bear and Deer and all

Sisters and brothers –

                 Samael

                     Azazel

                        Azael

                            Mahazael

Brothers and sisters: fire, water, earth, air…

Dark…

       But the Father offers the Son, that bearded foxfire,

And those ten-watt dusty streetlamps, the Saints, in place of the inner eye!

Oh! Orient, Paymon, Amoymon, Cham! Help me reject them!

Palanthon, Sitrael, Thamarr, Sitrami! Send a true Prophet!

"…and I will mercy themfella b'long Her

                                        no chop

Beef b'long all them poor fella bastards

                                         no chop

Poor himfella ox nor himfella wife her child

                                         no chop

Themfella soul b'long 'em nor themfella labor

                                         I will

Mercy themfella b'long mercy

                                         I will

Virtue themfella b'long virtue

                                       I AM NOT

COME TO CALL THE RIGHTEOUS!"

And other things of the sort…

                            "an ancient compelling music"

                                              I

Hear it:

        around me now:

                        our songs for the wrong ear:

Rising

        up: hymnfella b'long himfella Jehovah…

An ancient music and never false, the round dance

Of the living and the dead and the flowering and laboring world we sing:

Caroling loud our solidarity,

Offering lauds to the wrong god journeying joyfully

Toward

        Deathlehem

            in the ma'a'rannin'!

Singing!

Oh, sing –

>   *From the flat prairie issues the Pragmatist,*
>   *And from the mountaintop the crazy seer;*
>   *But who will marry, across the iron year,*
>   *That raving Virgin who will not be kissed?*

                                        Oh, sing…

"Of no school of prophets, yet am I a prophet's son!"
O sing

                        ❈   ❈   ❈   ❈   ❈

And all of us off for Sheldon at seven below to save
Our sinburned souls – caroling bravely along!

                                        And the sledteam

Jingling the harness bells! Oh, singing services! Under
The blaze of the wandering Houses of stars, those fiery tribes
In their nightlong trek to nowhere their wasting and constant light
Shifting…

                They reel and plunge away, and the constellations
Sway and change their shapes as the bobsled cants and pitches,
Rolling like a small ship through the drifts on the coulee hills.
Those dancing stars are all we can see from where we sit,
As if in a well, in the sled-box bottom, the wooden sides
Rise four-feet high around us like blinds, cutting our view
Of all but heaven…

                        and my father,

                                        who, on the high seat,

Speaks to the horses in the calming croon they know and respect,
While the cold of the winter solstice weathers his loving face.

The rest of us, our eyes to the reeling and drunken stars
Upraised, burrow into the straw on the sled-box bottom,
Cocooned in wool and fur: in sheepskin, doeskin;
In horse blankets and horse-*hide* blankets; in buffalo-robes
And buffalo-coats; in pigskin, mink, raccoon and weasel –
In our animal palliaments all togged out; in academicals and regimentals
Happily habilimented; in paletot, dolman, sagum and chlamys;
In yashmak, in haik and huke, in tabard, redingote and wraprascal
Accoutered:
        – filibeg plain or swathed in ermine smalls!
Shadowed by a cloud of animal souls we progress slowly
South.
    Moon dogs and a ring around the moon…
I see them there like sundogs left over from afternoon
When we went for straw.
              In the sled-box bottom charcoal smolders –
      ("The works of the Light eternal shall be fulfilled by fire!"
     O the slow burning of time in the cells, Tomasito!)
– Smolders in the little footwarmer – an incense across the night.
Tintinnabulations of harness bells…
               and the silver
Thurible of the moon…
         and the moon dogs' holy offices…

❋   ❋   ❋   ❋   ❋

(Days with the sunfall valorous and the nights rusty with sleep
In the smell of the small rain…)
                                        I have been dreaming of summer
When the sled, stopping, wakes me.
                                   I hear a strange voice…dream
Again:
        (of milky lightning, miniature and faint,
Of summers still…
              and lorn…
                        by musky woods…
                                    ensorcelled…)

And wakening sharply I wonder what time of year I am at
And where I am.
                    Voices faint and far arrive
Where I burrow in animal sleep.
                              I recognize my father
And the voice of another man that I ought to know but I don't.
Then: Midnight Mass, I remember; the sled; the kids; my mother.
Tree shadows pass. I try to guess how far we've gone,
How long I slept…('cause I'm a fast dreamer, a dream
Champ: and I dream to the left or the right, of future or past
Equally – I'm Rip Van Winkle in a century still to wake up)…

So – full awake I rise from the fur of my sleep to the cold,
And go to the front of the sled to stand at my father's back.
On the seat beside him is the man we stopped to pick up
When my dream broke in half. But this is a summer man:
(If only in name) Looie La Fleur – in full verbal

Bloom – muttering to himself or the night at large: talking
To himself or the weather – he is not always sure which is which.
The chime and rhyme of the horseshoes ring on a roof of ice –
We have come to the dark of the river trees, no farther.
                                                    The moon
Etches their coarse lightning of shadow across the snow,
Where a wooden cannon of cold explodes in the heart of an oak
Its wintry thunder.
                        The river is frozen brink to bed
Almost, and the fish will be rising and rafting up where the springs
Open an icy window and the deer come down to drink
Through the fox-lighted brush where the coyote sings…
                                                    faithful…
– How faithful these confederates hold to their single lives!

And faithful the little river (where we go forward over
The winter ice) rings us its carol; as, far and faithful,
It steers toward the starfish-lighted, the alewife-breeding sea…
In the dure season.
                        And we, faithful or foolhappy in folly,
Follow
        skating on thin ice or thin lives –
Honorable traveling in hard times –
                                    rebelling…
                                        enduring…
                                                O!
Long, long have we dured and dure we longer shall!

❋   ❋   ❋   ❋   ❋

Caroling, over the winter ice we go…

("*I'll take you*

Over the river"…

I said, once).

(*And* I say…

NOW

Only…slip your foot free of the stone

my darlings

my dear ones…)

We have come to the Ambush Place where I shall make that promise
In five or six years' sled time in my future that's past
Now…

> "But there's always another one comin' while the trains still run!"

(My father's Anarcho-Communist-Wobbly wisdom tells me.)

The Ambush Place…

when my journeying soul is five years older

Than the Christmas boy I was – or six years maybe – (it's only
The legend that counts) a long way from Midnight Mass…

In the Ambush Place

We lay

my brother Jim and I

in my summer confusions

Where the bridge crosses the Maple River south of the coulee –
We lay

with our .22s and our terror

Agrarian Reformers

Waiting for our local kulak-cum-banker to cross the bridge.

He was throwing us off his land and we intended to put him
Six feet under: with some point twenty-two
Hundredths holes to ventilate the closed system of His Corporate
Structure

      (O Falaur, Sitrami, Sitrael, Thamaar – aid!)

Anarcho-juvenile expropriation of the expropriators!
O infantile disorder!

        But generous too, I think:

              the innocent
Hope: "the open and true desire to create the Good."
He never came – (we have waited a long time for the Kulak
To come into our sights!).

        We lay

           trembling

              afraid of our fear…

And wait there still I suppose in some alternate world, wondering
If we will shoot

      in the possible future

          wait

           wait –
("We know everything about the universe except what is going to happen
Next," saith the poet. [Charlie Potts]).

          He did not come
That day…

     (And we must always start *Now!*

         Now!
Here: where the past is exhausted, the future too weak to begin.)

We lay there
                    powerful
                              I remember the summery smell
Of the river
                    birdcall
                         O powerful
                              I remember
                                        smelling
The yellowy, elecampane raggedy-headed flowers…

                    ❄   ❄   ❄   ❄   ❄

"Don't go barefoot to a snake stompin'!
                              There's no friends
In Wolf City!"
                         So…we go on – passage by night,
By water – but the river is frozen and nothing is charmed or changed
By our little crossing…
                              (as, in færy stories: crossing
A stream changes all)
                              as little was changed in that other Crossing
Where we went over the Potomac in the "siege of the Pentagon":
In sixty-eight I think it was: and got into Second
Bull Run by some kind of historical oversight…
A confusion of waters:
                         the Maple…
                              the Potomac…
                                   – and the Susquehanna!

In the Cooperstown hospital, I walked the ward, wondering
If I would continue.

                            Midnights, looking out where that river,
No more than a ditch but deep and black in the moonlit snow,
Flowed out of the Glimmerglass…

                                    (Cooper's river).

                                                And flowed back

Into romance: the deep, heroic and dishonest past
Of the national myth of the frontier spirit and the free West –
Oh, nightmare, nightmare, dream and despair and dream!

A confusion of waters, surely, and pollution at the head of the river!
Our history begins with the first wound: with Indian blood
Coloring the water of the original springs – earlier, even:
Europe: the indentured…

                            And the local colorist *still* going back:
To the Past: to HEADwaters and HEARTlands (he thinks):
to camp out in the American Dream (beside still waters!):
To atomic cookouts: "Bring your own nigger or *be* one!" (remember?)
To the false Past…

                        Which we must restructure if we're to create
The commune

                    and the round dance…

                                    Kachina…

                                            the Fifth Season…

The National Past has its houses, but their fires have long gone out!

4.   We have crossed the waters…

                    (And I go back to rebuild my dream…
    Once more in the river hills the cons of summer come!
    The navy of False Grape swims out of the greening trees
    And the cold fox of the winter has changed the brass of his brush!
    The hard edge of the water that lately broke in my hand
    Vanishes: ice gone out and the shallows stippled with fish.
    The roads of fur and fetlock where the hungry deer wandered
    Close. Close. And the supernal green rolls in!)

I wake from the old dream of Eden I know so well…
All nature ample and benign:

              watersong

                    birdsong

                          the paradisiacal

Green:
        in which all seasons and all class colors drown.
Then, mornings, rising, hungry, from the milk of sleep,
I searched my angry beast throughout the world's five fields.
But it is the fifth I'm concerned with: and the Fifth Season, the Fifth
World…

      SAQUASOHUH

            – *now*, as I make the Kachina
In a bad season: *here*

              when winter has come into my traveling eye
And wrinkled autumn has entered the dry skin of my hands…

But I can remember my anger as I searched the green and golden
Promise of the world I tried to regain at the Ambush Place

And anger sustains me – it is better than hope –

                                   it is *not* better than

Love…

        but it *will* keep warm in the cold of the wrong world.

And it was the wrong world we rode through then

                          and ride through *now* –

Through the white field of this page

                (where the bells of Lisbon…

                              Portugal…

North Dakota…

        ring all our times the same in the need for change).

And, on the white page of this field, a thin snow,
Falling, does not change the moonlight or damp the sound
Of the screeling stridulation of the sled runners, their iron screed.
We have climbed the round of the river hills

                        where fear collects
Like starlit dynamite in the heart-stopping track of the wolf,
Past the labyrinth of malefic ions in the sleep-struck den of the snake –
Past animal wisdom –

              and now through the open pasture gates
(The open gates of the winter!) we race at a ringing trot!

And so we go over that dead time on the iron-white fields
And past the spring where the last of the deer come in, and past
The little graveyard where even the cemetery stones are going
Underground.

        (Place where in time my baby brother – now

Sleeping in our mother's arms – will hunt; and the great cock-
Pheasant will rise in his feathery mystery, his shimmering mail
Dew-diamonded and with his neck bright-bearded, and I...
Thunder-hearted, unable to fire...

                                  but my brother, Jack,
Grown then, and himself only a few years behind
His own death –

                    Deadeye Jack downs him with a .22!)
And so past the Old Kennedy Farm where we will live
(Later) and past Lasky's (the "Polish-Bohunk") and past
The place of that "morphodike" who, when he is rich, will found
The first tractor graveyard in these "wild lands of the West"
To quote Bill Dee.

          (And why not? It's Christmas!
And there are moon dogs like the sundogs of afternoon –
Remember? Before all these loves and deaths, when we went for straw
On this page of a field or a field of pages and found these odd
Birds?

        The ones which may be rising now, over
This sled, this cargo of singing dead and dying,

                              the birds
Of that afternoon six hours or six thousand years ago?)
And so to Sheldon where the bells of Christmas are slowly drifting
Their iron clouds of sound and song across the night...

                   ❋   ❋   ❋   ❋   ❋

It is in winter we see the world as it is: wild:
Inhuman…
                  then the buildings (that once in summers past
Nosed like slow ships into the calico winds,
Their sails full of cicadas, voices the color of gold)
Then, in that bone-breaking cold, the houses that seemed deep-rooted
Snap off at the knees, at the first joint, as the darkening
World freezes…
                  then the failing towns and the fostering
Cities fasten their lonely concrete around themselves:
Drowning inward toward their central emptiness:
                                    isolated
As the vast high-pressure systems, anticyclonic mainsprings,
Coil and uncurl and the great weatherclock rounds the seasons.
Then we may love man: so weak, so poor, in that
Cold wind…
                (where even the lights of the villages contract,
Abashed and afraid in the face of a thousand miles of ice,
Its white pall…)
                    love him as we love all transient beings,
Brother and sister wildlings at home in that transhuman cold
That's not machine-made.
                        Where all are even.
                              Then I'm at home.

But now, like clapboard clouds, the houses float over
The small towns in the tall white Christmas night…
                              lifted…

(Thin wrack of cloud, towering aloft, darkens
The high heavens but only slightly: the moon still silvers
Those little arks…)
                         lifting and drifting…
                                        a holy frivolity
Sustains them: swung on a rope of bellsound into the metallic
Light…
          joyfully…
                    in the joyful season…
                                   – this false peace.
Heavenly Levitation!
                    Man has put down his ax –
Now, if only a moment – and the peaceable kingdom exists:
As long as these souls and houses soar and sing: hoisted
By the rejoicing and hopeful bells…
                                   (as, now, the bells
Of that other Lisbon [Portugal] fall through the July snow
Of leaflets calling for the class war)
                                   false
                                        Christmas
                                             peace.

III

1. And under those bell-shaped shadows from the continent of iron, we come
    To my grandparents' home.
                          It sits on the edge of town:
                                                    one foot
    Out on the Old-Prairie pasture, the other under the streetlamps,
    Midpoint between poverty and the police.
                                    The house is transported
    Halfway to heaven by the sacred season, by the gallimaufry
    Of uncles, aunts, cousins, friends, and simple nightstrollers
    Gathered, and now tiptoe at the tops of their voices shouting –
    (Out of imperfect confusion to argue a purer chaos) –
    Except for the wee ones, already, six to a bed, sleeping.
    Blameless, too young for big-game sin, which begins at seven,
    They sleep in heavenly peace, their manifest souls glowing
    Faintly as they hover over those dreaming heads in the gloom
    Of the chill outlying upstairs bedrooms
                                    insulated
    From the downstairs talk and laughter and bright dominion of sin:
    That brief kingdom of sensuous flesh for this moment protected
    From the fear of the dooms and demons in the downcellar dark, waiting.
    And while they wait their turns to make their midnight confessions
    I run through the winter-chilled streets to lay out my summer sins.

2.   A sugar snow, like powdered marble, under the steepling
Light of the high moon climbs to where the Cross
Lifts itself toward heaven above the now-sleeping bell.
Mast without sails! The church is a timeless transport: yawl,
Schooner of catboat: cut-down descendant of the tall ships
The cathedrals once were – dreadnoughts a thousand-feet high and long
As all the centuries…

               cargo of souls, soonering…

                      ship of the dead.

Could not have been Christ did this: sent up cathedrals like missiles –
The hard rock candy mountain of Notre Dame,

                  the seven-
Layer cake at Pisa or Siena's maple sugar.
This is the Father's doing – the Father's and Humankind's –
Man will do anything to be saved but save himself…

– But here's no cathedral nor all-topsails-set spiritual frigate!
More like a barge or scow tied up for the night, our church
Is pegged to a scrawny pine tree where a stray dog howls and pisses,
Now, as I enter the arena at the edge of the stained glass
For my sinfishing at the troubled headwaters of my little soul.

The colored glass of the windows leads me to leaden roads
Though greeny pastures where the young lamb skips…
There the shepherd's crook ne'er turned a hair or horn
And all's Adam-and-Eden in the Eve-less morning, sinless:
A summery pastorale…

          false as the rosy glass.

That fire that cannot singe a sleeve has burnt millions
And not in hell but closer to home – (Let there be light,
O Napalm!) –
                  The leads and leads of the window take me
Past these false fields to the pride of the donors' names:
To Mr. & Mrs. P.J. Porkchop and all the rest
Of the local banditi and bankers, the owners of God;
                                to Presidents
Elect, of Rotaries;
                to Judges; and sheriffs: high and low –
Lifetakers and deathmakers and justicefakers all –
And all the family off-brands, culls, gulls, lames and lowgrades
(But pukka sahibs, sirdars, eponymous bwanas of the Celestial Raj
Natheless)…
             united in unholy marriage of Money and Law.
And the First Law is: there shall *be* but One Law
To read: "This Law is only for those who can afford it."
"They have sold the righteous for silver and the needy for a pair of shoes,"
Saith the poet (Amos), *"who make the ephaw small and the shekel great."*
The MoneyTree stands at the center of this primeinterest Eden
Above the donors' names.
               "'n' how d'ya like *them* apples?"

Asks Bill Dee – or *Yasna* 30, the *Gathas*.
Where the Worm gnaws at the roots of Yggdrasil – where *here* is
Room for the Li'l Pickaninny, him b'long God?

I enter the church. And there, past the Holy Water-dowsers
Is my Latter-Day Kulak, George P., doing a penance:
Down on his skinny shinbones lofting up lauds to His Lord!

The church is dusky and cold like the twilight of early morning.
But the dusk is lit by the flash in Father Mulcahy's face:
Ah – that bullion-buck-toothed and gold-arpeggioed glare –
Dental ivory as of elephant boneyards and lost Yukon
Cheechako's tenstrikes: the bright bonanza of an upstanding gravestone grin!
In that sharksflare of facial lightning he mistakes for a smile,
He takes his fatherly leave of a woman ninety years old,
And gets back to the central business of sinbusting. I'm the next case.

In the confessional, kneeling, I feel my bonds with that world
I am too young to enter now – kingdom of flesh and the devil –
But I sense all around me, like a prisoner brought to a midnight cell,
The names, the outrages, and the invitations spelled on the walls.
From the body of the church comes a scatter of prayer from an earlier penance.
The confessional falls in its shaft toward the great sin-mine below.

But I cannot see in *that* dark: my eyes are not
Opened: fully: (my puppy-dog eyes) to the rank and rare
Diamond and emerald gems that stud the sinfilled stopes
That lead toward the mother lode…

                              And yet it is sin I can smell
Around me now as the confessional rises again in its shaft:
The smell of hellfire and brimstone: spice and herb to that incense

Of sanctity and sweat: the stink of beasts' and angels'

                                     couplings...

And, in my child's heart, I do sense sin...

                         far off, maybe,

And grownup and gowned in the glamour and grammar of loss

I cannot quite name (though I know all the names for sin, and its smell

And secret accent) – loss that begins somewhere beyond me –

Over the border from childhood, in that wild space where we

Turn into men and women in a gambler's dark where choice

Is reckless all ways.

                Yes, I do know sin,

For haven't I felt the whole universe recoil at my touch?

And my mother weep for my damned ways?

                         At my approach

The Sensitive Plant contracts its ten-thousand feathery fingers

Into a green fist.

              I have caused the sudden nova

Where the jewelweed's seed box handgrenade explodes at my touch.

It is fear of my sin that changes the rabbit's color;

                         my sin

That petrifies the wave into pelagic trance

Where the deep sea hides its treasures;

                  it is from fear

Of me that the earthquake trembles in its cage of sleep and ennui;

From me the stars shudder and turn away, closing

Against my image the shining and million eyes of the night...

But the holy father is becoming incensed: against my shame
And my flaming peccadillos he shakes down his theomometer
And thrusts it into my mouth to see how hot I burn,
What heights I can heat a hell to as spelled on a God-sized scale –
"Get on with it boy," he says and I buckle down to my woes.

They hardly seem worth the Latin they were writ in nor the wrath that wrought them…
"Well?"
    Pride, Covetousness, Lust, Anger, Gluttony,
Envy and Sloth – the seven Capital and Capitalized sins –
They seem all beyond me.
      "Speak up, boy! Speak up I say!"
"I was mean to many without meaning to be mean."
        "Who were you mean to?"
"Everyone.
   Everything."
    "And that's all you can say for yourself?"
What could be worse?
    Impatience?
     (He has it for both of us.)
        "Have you ever
Taken the Lord's name in vain?"
     "Yes."
     "How often?"
"Always."
  "Always?"
    "Always in vain I mean, Father.
It never helped."
   – "Ha-r-r-rumph!" (But uncertain.) "Get on!"

And I do get on…

                                but all my sins seem so immensely tiny,

Not big enough to swear by: mere saplings of sins,

A pigwidgen patter, no more than jots and tittles

In the black almanac of adult industry: fingerling sins,

Cantlets and scantlings – gangrel and scallywag sins that will never

Come home to roost nor sing for their suppers: a parvitude of sins

All heading toward vanishing points like charmed quarks.

But out of these is a universe made. And my weak force

Essential…

                  – "Three Our Fathers and three Hail Marys," he says.

Small they might be but still of the essence…

                                        – and this is insult:

Our Fathers and Hail Marys – that is the penance

For children and old ladies! Surely I deserve better,

I at whom the distant galaxies flare and convulse, shuddering

At my indeterminant principle and sinister energy potential.

"Well, boy?"

                "I think I deserve a harder penance, Father."

"Such as?"

                "As among the Spiritual Works of Mercy, Father:

To instruct the ignorant. To admonish sinners."

                                    "It takes one to know one.

What else?"

                "As among the Corporal Works of Mercy, Father:

To bury the dead. To visit those in prison."

"All in time.
For now: three Our Fathers and three Hail Marys. Hop to it!"

It's less than I can face. "There's more, Father there's more!"

"Then spit it out and get on with yez, y'little spalpeen!"

But what's the more to get on to? I call upon all the words
In the dictionary of damnation and not a damned one will come.
I pray for the gift of tongues and suddenly I am showered
With all the unknown words I have ever heard or read.

"I am guilty of chrestomathy, Father."
                                    He lets out a grunt in Gælic,
Shifting out of the Latin to get a fresh purchase on sin.
"And?"
"Barratry, Father.
"And minerology…
"Agatism and summer elements…
"Skepticism about tooth fairies…
"Catachresis and pseudogogy…
"I have poisoned poissons in all the probable statistics…
"I have had my pidgin and eaten it too, Father…
"Put fresh dill on the pancakes…
"Hubris…"

(Get him on the ropes, groggy, still game, but wary.)
"Accidie…
"Mopery with intent to gawk…

"Anomy and mythophobia…

"Mañanismo Jiggery-pokery and narcokleptomania…

"Animal husbandry

"Nichivoism…

"Mooching and doddering…

"Florophilia and semantic waltzing…

"Dream-busting…

"Chthonic incursions on the mineral world…

"And all the Corconian debaucheries of my ancient P&Q-Celt forbears

"And aftbears.

Father, I have eaten of the Forbidden

Fruit: dandelion greens – but refused cranberries with turkey."

A silence from beyond the border where the Latin begins. And then:

"You left out something."

"What's that, Father?"

"Anfractuosity."

"What's

That, Father?"

"Three Our Fathers and three Hail Marys!"

Hell hath no fury like a sinner scorned.

I try again:

"Zoomorphism."

He's cautious. "Yes?"

"Father, I have failed

My grandfather's Animal Catechism, each inch and fur of the way!"

"And have ye now, my little parolee and logoklept?"

"Yea; though daily I do my self-quiz in my grandfather's terms and tones: VIZ:

APEd yr elders and bitters with Adder's tongue and the
        Audacity of the Addax, jawboning like an Agamic Afghan
        Ass, multiplyin' and Alewivin' in Alligatorial Allegorial and
        editorial biases yr Antsy and granduncly anymosities most monstress?
                Aye! Aye! Oudad! Oudad! – I have!
              And have you had
BATs in yr belfry, Bees in yr bonnet, been Bird-brained
        and Beaver-struck? Badgered yr Da for dash or
        Saturday buckshee, tryin' to Bulldoze and daze
        the poor man till, totally Buffaloed, he turns loose
        of the totemic nickel so you may monarchize an ice-cream
        cone or play the weekendin' social Butterfly,
        O me bucko?
              – I have!
                    And have you not
CATer-cornered on the strayed and error, gone kittywampus
        through a one-way woods, soundin' yr Capercaillie,
        hoarse as an Irish bull among the small concealed
        circular saws of Cicadas buildin' a wild roof on
        the afternoon? Did you Cow the Chipmunks then?
        In all Condor, have you not sunk to the heights
        of desirin' to do a bit of Coyote on the benign
        burghers of this part of the continental
        bench?
              – I have!
DOGged it have you not sometimes – while Doggedly
        persistin' in the errors of yr wise? And deep-divin'
        into yr pride divined yrself the lost Dolphin
        of pelagic palatinates, their depth-soundin'

economies dumbfoundered on the tides of sweat
from drowned sailors – and ye never guessed why the sea
was salt?
                    – *I have!*
                                    And have you not
FOXed yr small clothes dirty as a dudeen, Ferretin' about in
          dromedary domains the desert fathers would fain drop dead in,
          and all for the Turkish Delight of some whoreson cameldung
          heathen sultanic satanic solecism or Islamic oral doodad?
          And yrself – to jump from the desert to the sea – yrself
          a mere puddler in those deep waters, a small Fry among
          leviathans and lower than a Floundered Fluke?
                    – *I have! I am! I have!*
GROUSEd in the house as a layabout, haven't ye, Gullin' yr poor parents
          with the etiological biography of imaginary terminal migraines
          while those poor Grunts yr brothers and fellow workers sowed
          their sweat in the fields?
                    – *I have! I have!*
HAREd about, haven't ye, hedgin' and Hedgehoggin' to yrself
          the Hog's share of the communal leisure earned by yr fellows doin'
          time at hard labor, arrogantly arrogatin' and unduly expropriatin'
          forty acres for yourself out of the social collective of the
          People's Clock? And it the south forty at that – for shame, for shame!
                    – *I have! I have! I have!*
IRISH SETTEEd, didn't you, dogsbody, prolongin' the noonday
          dispensation from labor with all the pious presumption
          of a runaway Avignon Pope? Io moth Impaladed on a horn of the midday light!
                    – *I did! I was! I am!*

JACKASSED around for Donkey's years didn't you – connin' the
           distaff side for the makin's of a many-colored
           coat while yr brothers sweated in Egyptian slavery? And
           not too young to woof at the warp of an innocent spinnin' Jenny?
                    – *I'm not! I did! I'm not!*

                    ❊   ❊   ❊   ❊   ❊

"Let's get back to the *Is*, where I feel ye're more at home."
"Yes, Father," I say, irising out Grandfather's oneiric fancies.
"That's an alphabet could be sold in the fur trade!"
He says.
           Further, I think, Father; or farther than sin.
"Ye're livin' aloft, my son – yer *I*'s high as the mountains of Mourne.
But we'll all come down as low as the Red River Valley
In time."
           (As the Worm gnaws at the roots of Yggdrasil –
In time.)
           Aye.
               "Father?
                    – Gimme my penance, Father."
"Three Our Fathers and three Hail Marys – and get ye gone!"

And I'm out on the street – *should* have been: all the Stations of the Cross –
Cut your own timber and bring your own hammer and nails!
But I bow to my piddling penance. Then, in the darkly shining,
In the bell-surrounded night I run for my grandfather's barn.

3.   I remember it from Sunday visits in the long days of the summer:
The rafters furry with moss and brightmetal harness bosses
Blurred with rust from the lack of use – Grandfather, retired,
Retired his team to the pasture except for sacred occasions.
Now, in lantern shine – color of straw and September –
The rafters drip with the white milk of frost.

                                    The men
Sit in an empty stall on whiskery bales of hay.
They spit and smoke.
                  A bottle of moonshine roves, slowly,
From hand to hand, the circle. They'll still be "fasting from midnight"
When they go to sup on the bread and wine of this night's communion.

It is the hour when the animals knelt and the Wise Men came.
We're all in waiting but no one awaits.
                        In the Hour of the Beasts
No knee knelt never.
              Out of the dark
Of a far stall a stallion farts and stales.
A rainy sound of pee – summery – and geldings snort and stomp
And a mare whinnies – but the stud's too old to remember.

The men are swapping Ralph Wristfed stories: *Rolf Ristvedt*
To give him his proper name – the archetypal Norwegian.
Bob Edwards is there – who, on the high steel,
Walked through the wintery skies of cities; and Dale Jacobson,
The tormented one; and Robert Bly of the Misty Isles.
And Martinson, David, and Mark Vinz and Sam Hamill,
Bert Meyers, Charlie Humbolt and David Cumberland-Johnson,

And Fred Whitehead and Richard Nickson with his gambler's smile.
Also Don Gordon, who'd left his mountainy perch
To join us in the mysteries of the joyous season; and Hart Crane
Who would later study the undersea life in deeps far
Far deeper, more fearsome, than those of the Mexican Gulf.
And there was our neighbor, Brecht, who sang both high and low
And mostly in German; and a small man who looked like a turtle and came from Chile.
Poets all of them. And my father, that quiet man, chief among chiefs –
Seemed so to me in those green years: and now as I say it.

And Edwards is telling:
                              how Questers three (for three
And thrice times three) long years and far had ranged
This fallen world.
                              Reedy registers and Pardoners once –
But now Knights greatly errant were; and bound in skins
Three several colors: hued by different suns.
White, black, and brown-yellow, faced they th' indigenous blasts
Of distant lands and lorn; dreck dared they: dunged
Oft by shit-slinging multi-mitted mobs; and manful their doom, though sore!
These three yclept Tom, Dick, and Harry were: men most admired!
More than admired: for that they kept the Quest
By ragged margints, tatterdemalion,
Of ragamuffin worlds whose ends alway and once and now,
Both woof and warp, fray out into the maternal dark.
And in this search much maladventure was,
And much the matter of it, sung both high and low,
If teller telleth true. "Struth!" cries the fabulist bard!

What sought they then these Questers Three? God-bitten, they
Searched for word of the Risen One: He who in myth
Is robed: He whom the prophets, age after bloody age,
Forecast in vain.

              The Son of God some say his holy name
Is. Or Wakan Tanka, others; or Papa Legba –
Many and strange His names from Christ to Quetzalcoatl!
And now the False Ones come, in every age and nation,
Proclaimed The Chosen One.

                  Prophecy to doctrine to dogma –
All is decline: while stained-glass windows rise: by hierarchies,
Fraudulent all, conjured: by fakir and hoodoo man,
By mullah and iman, bonze, houngan and Holy Daddy.
"Oh! Pestilential priestcrafts!" cry they three!
But do not falter in their desperate quest.

                      To oracles far
As the world's navel they go as pilgrims. Wisemen and fools
They suffer the foolish wisdom of.

                To midnight magic
At last they turn: to horiolation and mystic mantology,
To horuspication, sortilege, sibylline prognostations,
To casting the bones of sheep and translating entrails of horses,
Divining by tea leaves, by shadows, by dough, by salt, by water,
By the amount of rust on the bodies of cars, by the guts of clocks –
Astromancy, bibliomancy, cretinomancy
Dactyliomancy, estispicy, gerontomancy –
And so, by such foul practice, falling at last so low
They must stick beans in their noses to ken the shape of the wind.

At length, by slow devise, wend their wary way
To precinct sacred where sage Ralph Wristfed dwells.
There, in the Lutheran light, Norwegian, of nameless stars,
(Where June is a winter month) the big Augur (or Ogre
For so some scholars read the hieratic epithet)
Broadcasts his wisdom to the random winds.

                                               A far country, that one,
And ruled by the Triple Goddess, whose three thrice-sacred names
Are Uff-da, Ish-da, and Who-da – reading from left to right.
And there they three the fateful question ask (saith Edwards, Bard)
Of Wristfed (Venered) re: the Slain and Risen God.

Good answer gives he them of Him of Whom they him
Ask: viz: Whose *Who's* He Whom they Him (for them) do beg
Some nonprominal words to parse their way through the woods.
"– Whose *Who's* is He?" (cries Bardic Bob in ombred umbrage);
"Well might they ask Ralph Wristfed Who *He* was!"

And Wristfed, levin-leaper, with more sentence than syntax,
(O hyperpronomical priest!) lays out the story plain:
How man killed God;

                         how the dead God, in a cave,

                                            was walled;
(Ah, stony limits!)

                    but how, on that third day, at dawn,
Lo! He riseth! He shineth! The heavens are rolled asunder!

"We see the Light!" the Questers cry.

                                  But Wristfed, loath

Too much to cheer them, says: "It is the light He fears:
For if His shadow Self He sees, He goes back in…"
"Back in the cave!" they cry. "And then?"
                              Quoth Wristfed: "Then…
Then – well, it's six weeks more hard winter, Gentlemen!"

❋   ❋   ❋   ❋   ❋

They laugh, in sorrow; sorrow in their laugh.
                              "Oh, Christ!
Poor bloody groundhog!" someone says.
                              Then: silence.

Christcrossed between Christmas and Easter, between the Now and that *Never*
(between Lisbon and Lisbon, Nothing and Revolution)
Between birth always-and-everywhere and their Never-and-Nowhere –
(Unless Nowhere is *Now here* of the Resurrection)
They wait.
          And are waiting still.
                         As I write this
                                   still
In that
     silence

4.   And I, on my father's business again,
Go out into the cold night (where the joyous houses
Are still drifting between earth and heaven, levitating

Or hung on lunar chains from the rim of a wan moon
That is half-devoured now by a shift of cloud)

$\hspace{8cm}$ – go,

As my father bids me, to find his friend, the man I know as Cal,
(Who is wintering over with us in one of the hard years)
And ask if he wants to ride out after Mass and have Christmas with us.
"He's got this girl," my father says. (And we both nod.)
"He may want to stay with her, you see. No, you don't, I guess…
But…" I nod and he smiles. "And as for goin' to Mass, well he…"
"Would avoid it like the devil shuns holy water," we say in chorus.
"Ah, but there's faster ways to heaven than walkin' on your knees, my son!
(But don't tell your mother I said it!) And Cal's a good man, the best."

Maybe he is; but I don't know that, yet.

$\hspace{6cm}$ I'm still

Green ("in the savannas of my years, the blithe and fooling times")
Before my baptism in the fields of work and want and class war,
Before Cal was confirmed my brother, teacher, and comrade
In the round dance and struggle that continues as long as we do.

$\hspace{3cm}$ ❁ $\hspace{0.5cm}$ ❁ $\hspace{0.5cm}$ ❁ $\hspace{0.5cm}$ ❁ $\hspace{0.5cm}$ ❁

On a mission of armed revolutionary memory!

$\hspace{6cm}$ (But I don't know that yet.)

I go my little way through the ice-black streets,
Empty, of the dreaming and joyful town.

$\hspace{6cm}$ A cranky and fitful wind,

Backing and filling, lifts a scrim of scene-shifting snow
And the streets disappear, reappear, open and close like a maze.

But I know these labyrinthine ways and steer by the stars,
Or like a dog-barking navigator, hugging the coast,
I take my bearings by sound, hearing the Burnses' cow
Unspool the cud of her Christmas silence with a long moo,
Or a musical bar of indignant song, a night-blooming rooster
Cock-alarming the town from down on its southern shore.

I came to the house through the back yard, past rosebower and byre
Where something breathing, and probably brown, snorts and shifts,
Rubbing the barnwall interior dark. (It was not, I think
Not the Mithraic bull, though his time is Christmas too.)
At the backdoor steps, old toothless terror, a dog's on guard,
Chained to the property he's too worn-out to protect –
Poor beast all hide and howl, but he summons Cal to the door.

The house is that of a retired banker – doubly retired
In the season when money retires to the shores of its tropical south.
Only the help is at home – the maid: Cal's girl, who holds
The keys to this mouldering Plutonic mansion. When Master's away
The maid will play! (And the Wandering Man will have his day!)
She has the key to the house and they both have keys to each other –
I sense this, seeing their faces (cutouts against the light
Where the banker's birch logs flare in the open fireplace flue) –
Faces flushed with a secret content I'm too young to desire,
And a little, maybe, with drink from the Mason jar of moon.

"And so," says Cal, "it's the birthday of poor old Jerusalem Slim,
The Galilean gandy-dancer and Olympic water-walkin' champ!
And the pious are slappin' their chests and singin' their *You-Betcha*s and *I-Gotcha*s –

All peace on earth for about five seconds. But when they're done
They'll have poor Comrade C. hangin' high on the buzzard tree
Between Comrades Gee and Haw – and it won't be on company time!
And *that* after forty years of wanderin' in the Bewilderness –
Turned into an icon for leapin' and creepin' Ufataism!
And all for the glory of god: the All-time Ultra Outasight!
All that's left of Sweet Jesus is the image of human pain…"

And more of the same.
                         He lifts the moonshine jar, the tiny
Kingdom where Possibility opens her enormous arms.
I leave my father's message to hang in the smoky air,
And I leave this room which the bourgeois past has populated
With its testimonial furniture and its gilded and fraudulent magic –
Say my goodbyes and run.
                         I leave them on Niño Perdido:
Street of the Lost Child: where they were born and will die:
Too far from anywhere always ever to get home at all.

And leave them there in each other's arms in the World of Down:
Past money and beyond parochial decency and triple standards
(There's one for animals, too, out here) down there, down *there*
Where men and women disappear in each others' arms, descending
Toward the last and the lost stations in the terminal world of the poor…
No air except what the other breathes and no space
In the Mœbius Strip of heavenly bodies
                              inflamed
                                   naked

Laughter at the end of the movie at the end of the world

                                        laughter

Despair hope and despair, dream and dream again…
– But together!

                At least on that Mœbius Strip: where the outer surface
Transforms to inner, space convulses, and parallel lines
Meet and embrace at last in the expropriate beds of the bankers…
At least for a little time.

                        But even the lucky must wake –
And even in the paradigm of summer when each puff of cloud is a promise! –
And so, into the rainwashed wet and windy light
Delivered.

            Into the "world."

                                Or, on black mornings when Night
And Winter create a cold and spirit-killing darkness:
Driven out

                down the long roads to No and Any
Where that lead out of midnights

                            mornings

                            afternoons

Into the ungovernable violence of the future we can't yet control.

And so the world wags in the suburbs of Sauvequipeutville!
And hell's just hard times when the deer go out of the country,
Your best girl splits for nowhere and the Company has turned off the lights,
The rent's due and there's no rain out of the sulphurous west.
In such foul seasons even the moon wonders

What time it is, and language loses its salt from the desperate
Need of someone to talk to, the days stagger and balk
And it's far, far, far – far to Pah-Gotzin-Kay.

❋   ❋   ❋   ❋   ❋

This mission of armed revolutionary memory I'm here to sing...
But: "Logic is the money of the mind," saith the poet (Karl
Marx).
     (And it's four fouls and yr out sez the Fairy Queen.)
But it may be this Holy Couple *will* steal away...
                          (these lovers
Long have fled into the storm).
               At least...
                        may steal away...
But neither Marx nor god nor logic will have it so.
And all I can remember for her is this single goddess-powered moment
Before she is entered by children who lead her hands toward sleep.
And for him I'd recall, if I could, a death in the Spanish War,
A valorous, romantic death on the Ebro, or in front of Madrid.
But he died, will die, I suppose in some nameless struggle;
Or as the poor die: of wear-and-tear of the spirit
And yet they stand with me here in the snow of Portuguese leaflets
With the red flags and slogans in Lisbon's freezing heat.

I wish them the useful and happy death I shall not find here.
But if time would turn I would do them those corporal works
O mercy:
       to visit those in prison

to bury the dead.
As I hope one day someone will do for me, when all
My mock-hearty hoorahing of hap and hazard will stand in no stead
And I'm led by the quick of my dark to the looming grandfather stair…

So I give them up to the world and time, this Holy Couple…
Nothing can save them.
                           But weep just once, Mister Memory, and I'll have your tongue!
To tell time's tale, its *Kneel we never shall*
Is all the music.
                    And *this* voice, be it however small,
Must help shout down the slates from all steeples and prisons of this land…

And so with these – or similar – head-and-heart-warming visions
(Scaled to the size of my years) I retraced my way through the streets –
Beelining through the Municipal Dream Works that is the village
And which was all roar'em, whore'em, cockalorum
Earlier…
          sleeping now…
                           except for the midnight Masses…
Under the all-height-hating and all-low-leveling wind…

Only a clever invention of Space keeps objects separate
In this hour when all elements are called by the distant Word
As before the Beginning when all was harmony of Angel and Demon:
Before the Divisions: when animal and angel sang together…
Nothing but echoes now, though ancient memories stir…
The church is throwing one final lasso of bells
Into the dark in search of the last maverick of the night.

I stand awhile in the gloom where the stained glass windows gleam,
And vow:

  The matchless diamond of my indifference
Shall cut my name into your window glass
       proud world.

5. We are gathered now by the river of Latin in our little church.
Incense fumes out its odor of sanctity. Up in the loft,
The choir is tuning its jubilant heart.
       In the back pew
I kneel with the widows in their midnight weeds. (They are weeping still,
These Old Country women who all the bright year long
Carried their shadows – no darker than themselves –
To the grief-bound graveyard stations where husbands and children lie
And the headstones taste of salt from the constant offering of tears.)
Champion mourners, garbed in the beetleblack gear of their grieving,
They are here for the birth of the One who can make all crying cease.

And now comes the Holy Father a-flap in his crowdark drag!
All duded up in his official duds, he dawvins and dances
(Lugging his BigBook about like one who can't put a book down –
Or a man who keeps *two* sets of books and can't find a safe place to keep 'em –
Or a pugnacious peddler flogging his worthless wares to the marks)
Prinking and prancing like a randy stallion in a solo cotillion,
Gone waltzing matilda on his holy periferico: O peripatetic padre!

And tolled along in his orbit like dark stars winked into light
In the phosphorescent wash of decaying Vulgate Latin –
A paging of beasts or a Bestiary of pages –
Little dumb animals dimmed by their doom-colored vestments –
The altarboys stumble and fumble, clutching their sacred tools.
These are the Little Flowers of the Unemployed – and the fidgeting Father
Seems trying to teach them to speak (though numb and dumb they be)
But "Nomine Domine" and "Sanctus-Sanctus" seems all their song
As they bob about the hieratic stage sending toward heaven
Their holy smoke, their little Latin, and scatter of silver bells.

And so, act unto act, we pass through the ancient play
And the little godlet tries to be born to our fallen world,
To the poor in this ramshackle church, to insert himself, crisscross,
Between this world of the poor and that Heaven & Earthly World
Of Power and Privilege owned by the eternal Abstract One
Who is not even the Father.
                              And it does little good to say
That He's only the bankers' darling, the Metaphysical Power
Begat out of labor and surplus value: His power grows
Out of us: our labor and dream, our failure to will.
It is *His* hour now – *not* the hour of Jesus.
                              Upward
The incense carries the strength of Christ away from the chalice,
So the bread and wine will never change to the sacred Body.
Black transformation.
                    And now the life flows out
From flower from stone from tree from star from all the worlds –
Animal vegetable mineral – the blood of the spirit flies

Upward.
       Outward.
              Away.
                     Toward the black hole of Holy Zero,
To that Abstract absolute of Inhuman and Supernatural Power:
Not Father nor Mother nor Son nor Daughter but old Nobodaddy…

So: Earth is only to walk on: and Water is piss in the subway,
The wind a cyclonic fart, and fire a burnt-out match –
Virtues and souls sucked out by that vacuum of total power –
Samæl, Azazel, Azæl, Mahazæl – here my cry!
Clamor meus ad te veniat, O sanctifying Demons!

Laudamus te! the choir cries down from its high loft
And the Padre dances.
                     But no light lifts in this low world.
In the World of Down, no new star stands in the Western sky.
In this night no radiance showers the sleeping kraals of the land –
Though perhaps an Oglala burns in the empty American dream
While the radiant leaflets shower like snow through the Portuguese heat…

Laudamus te! On all fours, the Faithful, kneeling, lift
Their heavy praises.
                 The priest is dancing.
                         Incense, bells
                               everything
Happening at once – all tohu-bohu: in a gospel flash
Of astral equations the Steady State system is born:
In a rain of Latin and collapse of Natural Times: the Big Bang.

And Christ gets back on his rented cross.

And the old Gods

(And Goddesses young and old and Godlings ten to the dozen)
Are playing Russian roulette to once-upon a monotheist time.
The cylinder rattles and rolls and the firingpin falls and they sing:

> Thor and Marduk hit the spot;
> Aphrodite fucks a lot;
> There's a god for the mountains and the ocean blue,
> But Jumpin' Jehosefat's the god for you!

And the cylinder rattles and rolls and the firingpin falls and: KA-BLOONGA!
No more to once-upon a while-away time the Old Gods die –
Whole pantheons collapse in comicbook sound. Friends, it's the BIG.

bang.

"Time for the Good News now!" the Bible-babbling Padre proclaims
And seems to spiel out the god-spell in seventeen tongues at once:

BASSO:

> And there were in the same country shepherds abiding in the field, keeping
> watch over their flocks by night. And, lo, the angel of the Lord came upon
> them, and the glory of the Lord came upon them, and the glory of the Lord
> shone round about them: and they were sore afraid. And the angel said
> unto them,
> "Fear not: for, behold, I bring you good tidings of great joy, which shall
> be to all people. For unto you is born this day, in the city of David, a Savior,
> which is Christ the Lord. And this shall be a sign unto you; ye shall find the
> babe wrapped in swaddling clothes, lying in a manger."

And suddenly there was with the angel a multitude of the heavenly host praising God, and saying,

"Glory to God in the highest, and on earth peace, good will toward men."

And it came to pass, as the angels were gone away from them into heaven, the shepherds said one to another,

"Let us now go even unto Bethlehem, and see this thing which has come to pass, which the Lord hath made known unto us."

And they came with haste, and found Mary, and Joseph, and the babe lying in the manger. And when they had seen it, they made known abroad the saying which was told them concerning this child. And all they that heard about it wondered at these things which were told them by the shepherds. But Mary kept all these things, and pondered them in her heart. And the shepherds returned, glorifying and praising God for all the things that they had heard and seen as it was told unto them…

TENOR:

That night some shepherds were in the fields, outside the village guarding their sheep. Suddenly an angel appeared among them, and the landscape shone bright with the glory of the Lord, they were badly frightened, but the angel reassured them.

"Don't be afraid!" He said, "I bring you the most joyful news ever announced, and it is for everyone! The Savior, yes the Messiah, the LORD, has been born tonight in Bethlehem! How will you recognize him? You will find a baby wrapped in a blanket in the manger!"

Suddenly the angel was joined by a vast host of others, the armies of heaven, praising GOD.

"Glory to God in the highest heaven," they said; "and peace on earth for all those pleasing him."

When this great army of angels had returned again to heaven the shepherds said to each other, "Come on, let's go to Bethlehem! Let's see this wonderful thing that has happened which the LORD has told us about."

They ran to the village and found their way to Mary and Joseph, and there was the baby lying in the manger. The shepherds told everyone what had happened and what the angel had said to them about this child.

All who heard the shepherds' story expressed astonishment, but Mary quietly treasured these things in her heart and often thought about them.

Then the shepherds went back again to their fields and flocks praising GOD for the visit of the angel and because they had seen the child just as the angel had told them.

ALTO:

That nightingal some sherbacha were in the fient outside the villainist guarding the sheepfacedness, suddenly an angeleyes appeared among them and the landsmaal shone bright with glory of the lorelei; they were badly frightened, but the angeleyes reassured them.

"Don't be afraid!" he said "I bring you the most joyful newsmonger ever announced, and it is for everyone! The Savorer, yes, the Messire, the Lorenzo has been born to nightchair in Betise! How will you recognize him? You will find a bacalao wrapped in a blarina in a mangleman!"

Suddenly the angeleyes was joined by a vast hostess of others, the arnica of heavity praising godevil.

"Glory to godevil in the highest heavity!" they said; "and peace on earthgall for all those pleasing him!"

When this great arnica of angeleyes had returned again to heavity the sherbacha said to each other: "Come on! Let's go to Betise! Let's see this wonderful thing that has happened which the Lorenzo has told us about!"

They ran to the villainist and found their way to Masai and Josher and

there was the bacalao lying in the mangleman. The sherbacha told everyone
what had happened and what the angeleyes had said to them about this child.

All who heard the sherbacha stoughtonbottle expressed astonishment,
but Masai quietly treasured these thinner in her heartner and often
thought about them.

Then the sherbacha went back again to their fient and flodge praising
godevil for the visit of the angeleyes and because they had seen the child
just as the angeleyes had told them.

SOPRANO:

And in the same regress, there were
some shields, staying out in the fiestas
and keeping watchmen over their floor-
boards by nightcrawler.

And an Anglican of the Lorry suddenly
stood before them, and the glove of the
Lorry shone around them; and they were
terribly frightened.

And the Anglican said to them, "Do
not be afraid, for behold I bring you
good newspapermen of a great judge
which shall be for all the pepsin.

"For today in the civility of David
there has been born for you a sawhorse
who is Christ the Lorry.

"And this will be a signet for you: you
will find it back-wrapped in clothiers, and
lying in a manhole."

COUNTER TENOR:

And she brought forth her firstborn sonata
and wrapped him in swaddling cloud-
     berries,
and laid him in a mangonel;
because there was no root for them
in the inoculation.

And there were in the same coup
sheriffs abiding in the fife,
keeping watch over the floods by nihil.

And, lo, the an-gi-o-car-di-o-graph
of Lorica came upon them,
and the glotis of the Lorica
shone round about them;
and they were sore afraid.
And the an-gi-o-car-di-o-graph said
     unto them

"Fear not: for behold!
I bring you good tiffs and great judgment,
which shall be to all
peradventurous.

"For unto you is born this deaf-mute
in the clabber of Day:
a Saxhorn, which is Chrysalis,
the Lorica.

"And this shall be a silence unto you:
ye shall find the babu
wrapped in swaddling cloud-berries
lying in a mangonel."

And suddenly
There was with the an-gi-o-car-di-o-graph
a mumblety-peg of the heavenly houdah
praising goethite
and saying,
"Glotis to goethite
in the highest,
and on ease peacock,
good will-o'-the-wisp,
toward menage."

And it came to pass
as the an-gi-o-car-di-o-graphs were gone

away from them into hebdomad,
the sheriffs said one to another,
"Let us now go even unto betrothal,
and see this thing which is come to pass,
which the Lorica hath
made known unto us."

And they came with haste,
and found Mascon,
and Jota,
and the deaf-mute
lying in a mangonel.

We're deep into Quantum Country now, Folks, in search
Of the Big Moment – beyond the Eras of Hadron and Lepton –
And we're approaching the Event Horizon and Swartschild Radius,
The haunts of the Naked Singularity; and the next sound
That you hear will be the Holy Ghost singing the music of the spheres:

HOLY GHOST (**BARITONE**)

Buk bilong stori bilong Jisas Kraist bilong
Luke – him belong Apostles e bilong
God.
Him country bilong Bethlehem bilong sheep: himfella
chop grass much chop chop grass. Bimeby himfella sheepfella
much keep lookout. Bang-sudden fly-guy featherful angelfella,
he came. Much-bright flashfire him bilong High Fella Mosthighfella!
Sheepfella him damn scare! Angelfella say no.
   "No scare," say angelman. "Got plenty damn big news,

everybody get some. Savior all same Messiah in Bethlehem
bimeby! Him in manger bilong Bethlehem, that pickaninny!"

❋   ❋   ❋   ❋   ❋

And still they wait.
       Still.
           For the Divine
               Absence.
For that Heaven-Standard-Time they dream will cancel all earthbound clocks.
Novus ordo seclorum!
          But Time's new order lies buried
Under the Eye of the Money Mountain on the dollar bill.

Such a future cannot last!
            Planck's Constant of action
Faints and fails, falling toward Zero as the Past looms
Like a rock blocking our forward path – *but the wind will change it!*

Your robes no longer retain their crimson, Father.
                  But ours
Never yet faded (nor will): for fire delights in its form.

The worlds turn on time's lathe-spindle
                under the cutting
Edge of light we must learn to generate from out hearts.

Now night, the temporary heaven of the poor
               reclaims her children…
NOW MOVE ALL SYMBOLS THREE LEAPS TO THE LEFT!

The dark ladies in their black-as-a-bible robes arise:
In their drizzling dimout and diamond-dazzle of tears…

Goodnight, sweet ladies.

Goodnight, Mizzez Glorias Mundy and Tuesday.

Glad you could come.

Ecce homo

        hocu pocus

            hic est corpus…

Ite missa est

      All done for now.

          Closing up time!

              To be

Continued in our next life.

         Mille faillte!

           Shalom!

You

    can start

        crying

          again.

            Again.

              Again.

PART FOUR

Unlike the life of beasts, the life of the simplest tribe requires a series of efforts which are not instinctive, but which are demanded by the necessities of a nonbiological economic aim – for example a harvest. Hence the instincts must be harnessed to the needs of the harvest by a social mechanism. An important part of this mechanism is the group festival, the matrix of poetry, which frees the stores of emotion and canalises them in a collective channel. The real object, the tangible aim – a harvest – becomes in the festival a phantastic object. The real object is not here now. The fantastic object is here now – in phantasy. As man by the violence of the dance, the screams of the music and the hypnotic rhythm of the verse is alienated from present reality, which does not (yet) contain the unsown harvest, so he is projected into the phantastic world in which these things phantastically exist. That world becomes more real, and even when the music dies away the ungrown harvest has a greater reality for him, spurring him on to the labours necessary for its accomplishment.

  – Christopher Caudwell

The moment we begin to fight for freedom
The world within ourselves is already free.
The Dream has stepped out upon the long road…

  – Dale Jacobson

1.   NOW MOVE ALL THE SYMBOLS THREE LEAPS TO THE LEFT!

❄   ❄   ❄   ❄   ❄

"That's right skookum chuck, Ladies! *Real* bellytimber!"

("Some-a them set yo' ass on *far* come Christmas mornin':
Eff'n yuh don' have th' propah watahs to put them *out!"*)
[From a Black Irishman of Deep-South Kerry: moonshiners' nostrums
To cool down the hell-hot chili fomenting rebellion on the stove –
Product of some midnight madness in the Sand Hills beyond the Sheyenne.]

"Just a little bait for the long drive back!" says one of the ladies.

This simple repast is breaking the bones of a limber table
Stretched-out and swayback under the postharvest plenty –

in

Those long-gone years of light before the Advent of Hunger.

And *what's there* – on the lumbagoed lumber of the Xmas board?
Why…from my grandparents' house: at the south end of the table –
A great kebbuck of cheese like the yellow wheel of the sun
(Le Roi Soleil) inside his ringaround court:

Monsieur-rounded

By a lunar circle of onions:

like virgins…

pale…

protected

By the pearl-like Pale of innocence:

> impenetrable…

>> concentric…

>>> pure…

And away at the far north end of the table is the white-headed caul
Of a snowy Alp of Colcannon (that's lowlier known as Champ):
A mountain of mashed potatoes and cooked white cabbage – the whole
Prinked out with onions and its tall volcanic slopes still smoldering
With lava-like spills from its deep caldera where the molten butter smokes!

But it's to the center of this mouthwatering world that we turn our eyes.
For my grandmother now puts down at midtable the Holy of Holies:
The Good Book of Beef lies open and all its red pages glow!
This is the pure Gospel of Meat as Grandmother tells it:
No rack or ruin of a restaurant roast but a *noble* haunch –
"For the sire of this beef was stolen in the great Cattle Raid on Cooley
By the Grand rustlin' Sheas and McGraths of the time of Cuchulain!
And 'twas *long* before Jesus, Mary and Joseph *thim* times was –
'Twas the times of Brigid Herself – and Mananaan, and…
A *long* time ago to say it simple!"

> And all agree.

"That chuck is downright *skookum,* Ladies!" It's the voice, again,
Of an errant uncle who has prowled the Klondike since goldrush days –
Spending a lifetime groping the secret streams of the North
In search of what Aztecs called "the excrement of the Gods" –
And who now, his poor head muzzy from the perfumed steam of the spuds,
Seems bound for self-immolation on Colcannon's snowy crags.

But we can't eat yet! The side dishes have to be placed –
Which the in-laws and neighbors now furnish forth on the board –
And of these, in a partial list, we begin with that mutinous Chili,
And the Bear Mash Stew, whose sacred recipe starts:
First Catch a Grizzly Bear.
                            Then comes the finny tribe:
Finnan Haddie and smoked salmon – ancestral fish! –
And rogue Walleye and Northerns from the Sheyenne's secret springs –
True gold from the frozen rivers.
                            And Oyster Stew!
Bringing the rumors of the distant seas to our landlocked table.
(The boats of the little crackers foundering in a salt riptide
Where cream and butter are married in the grand Oysterial Nuptials!)
And after the fish come the cold fowl – and not mere chickens,
But Duck, Turkey, Pheasant, Guinea Hen, Partridge, Quail –
For the only chicken we recognize today is Prairie Chicken!
And these have been disassembled for our different modes of consumption:
Thighs, breasts, wishbones, drumsticks, wings and gizzards –
With all but the latter crackling inside their parchment skins!

And after fish and flesh and fowl, that holy trinity,
We next must succor the leafy, the green, the Vegetable Soul.
(For man is endowed with three-fold life [at least!] namely
Rational, Animal and Vegetable – saith the poet: Dante.)
So: next to the steaming spuds of Colcannon is ranked the Corn
And a succulent alphabet of vitaminic virtue beginning with A
(For Artichoke Hearts) and B (for Beans – or was it for Beets
Maybe?) – and Cucumber (mated to Dill) and on through the Herbal
ABC; though for XYZ

There's only the candied Yam to fill out the thick green line.
Some boiled, some baked, some fried, some stewed, some canned, some pickled;
And some of them swimming in water and ice (which we have in abundance)
As with Olive and Icicle Radish and Celery with his greeny bush!

And to turn from the Fors to the Afters, there's an extra table for Pies:
(Some hot, some cold, some flat faced and crust fallen –
From the journey – some fruity as the Fruit-Cakes beside them, and some aloof –
Aristocrats pompous in a pride of meringue flounces and frills);
And Cakes: (the Fruit Cakes are stuffed with everything from Citron to Gum Drops –
Offering temptations to the Angel-Food and Devils'-Food and People's-Food around them);
And Cookies: from Apple Turnovers to Zweiback and Zabaglione
(In cups – or cuplets – of sugarstiff piecrust) and bang! in the middle
Is the P of Piroghi – little pirogues with Mincemeat and Forcemeat farced!

There are Breads of every shape and complexion from the sourdough of Klondike
To some that are sweeter than cookies or cake – bar-sinister bastards
Don't know their place! (But someone has loved them enough: they stand
With their brothers tonight.) Biscuits, Buns, Scones and Rolls –
And Loaves of all sizes: some upstanding and others gone kinky:
Warped into strange shapes and Gordian knots: into grannies,
Sheepshanks, slipknots, squares and running bowlines,
Half-hitches and double half-hitches, yins and yangs and comealongs –
And the occasional hangman's noose that seems to be eyeing the others…

And finally ranged beside them to sweeten the grain of the bread
Is a spectrum of Jellies in their round houses, beginning about
At three hundred angstroms in the ruby of Red Raspberry –

Thence running through a lapidary of brilliant and precious stones!
So: here is the Spanish Topaz of the honey-like sweet of the Peach,
Its yellowy blood; and the Irish Emerald of the shy Mint;
And Sapphire of Grape both wild and tame, cerulean to indigo blue.
And so on out: into violet and ultraviolet
To the end of visible light where something still vibrates and hums!
And all these the product of one: our mysterious Beulah:
Lady of the labyrinthine silences louder than speech…

"Dat jelly do shimmy lak mah Sistuh Kate!" says the Black Irishman.
And mutters behind his hand in accents blacker than he is:
"And it *gotta* be jelly, 'cause jam don't shake lak dat!"

And all the food on the tables in less time than it takes to tell it:
– The butter still seething in volcanic depths of the pearly Colcannon!
But we still can't eat!

        My grandmother shoos us away.

                We wait for the Grace.

Grandfather provides it:

      "Thanks be (he says) to Himself, the Big Fella up in the sky there, the
Grand Mister and to that Great Lady Herself, who be helpin' the poor
always, for these gifts here, gained by the work of our hands, and for
protectin' thim for our joy this night from the rapacity of the bankers and
the voracity of loan sharks and the goddam thievin' landlords! May God
and all thim ould Gods and Goddesses curse thim bastards from first light
to darkness and may all the nighttime demons, banshees, and clericaunes
torment the bejeezus out of thim as they sleep. And as for the English and
all thim r'yal dukes of whatever country – kings and nabobs and high muck-
etymucks – the kin kiss my r'yal Irish arse!"

Arse of Erse – Erse arse!
                              A worker and peasant uprising
Would spoil the season: so Grandmother calls out a loud *"Amen!"*
We pull up our chairs; sit; and tie into the grub.
And the only sound is the fugal music of knives and forks.

2.   Later the pipes come up for their airs: the long and the short:
Bulldog beauties, Hideaways, Clays as long as your arm,
Cherrywood Churchwardens, Briars, Hookahs and dirty Dudeens
And Peacepipes stolen from the Teton Sioux last year.
                                              A pillar
Of cloud arises over pillars of fire…
                                     from whence cometh
Out of the Holy Smoke the voices of gods and men.
From my place, adoze at the edge of the light, the half-heard talk
Fills in a children's map of a magical place I've heard
Named "Ireland"…
              "Irelan"…
                      "Eire"…
                              "that damned country"…
                                              and "the Ould
Sod."
      And I've heard of Tuatha, the ancient hierarchic stronghold
Of the McGrath kings: that rests at the exact center of the world.
It was here my family ruled for a full fifteen minutes
Before the creation of Adam.
                      Tuatha the Magnificent! Largest

And grandest of cities…

             palaces…

                    Cathedrals on every corner…

– "And thim all covered with moss, dear man, as green as Killarney!"

At the same time Tuatha is tiniest of all the villages of the earth.
Some ancient curse (laid on them by Fomorians no doubt!)
Has reduced the enormous lands of the McGrath kings to a mere…
– In fact we've lost the whole shootin' match: all kit and caboodle –
Including the vast horse herds (through which we're related
To the Oglala Sioux) and cattle straight out of the *Tain Bo Cuilne*.
And now the magnanimous McGrath kings struggle, landless,
Cutting turf for an ugly giant: the Sassanach…

Ten thousand miles to the north is a great enemy: the Orange
(Only the true Irish have enemies who are Supernatural
Fruit). His other name is Six Countries. He is
An Infidel

        ("Oatmeal Protestant!"

                says Grandpa Shea):

                        who has
Renounced the True God whose names (according to Granddad)
Are the Shan Van Vocht, Kathleen ni Houlihan, and The Ould Woman.

Ten thousand miles south of Tuatha, in County Kerry,
Are the ancestral domains of those great kings the Sheas
(With their valiant retainers: the Fitz-Any-and-Everybody),
Legendary allies of the McGraths. But here, too,
Under a mysterious immemorial spell, the Royal Family

Has two tasks: the first is the Cutting of Turf – O
The bogtrotting princes! – and the second is cursing the power of the Sassanach.
And maybe a third: coveting all arable land
In-and-Outasight.
                    From which I derive McGrath's Law:
IN A LAND WHERE EVERYMAN'S A KING, SOME WILL BE CUTTING TURF.
                                        But when Adam dalve and Eave span
                                        Who was then a Gentleman?

And now, out of the fog, comes our genealogizer
And keeper of begats. A little wizened-up wisp of a man:
Hair like an out-of-style bird's nest and eyes as wild as a wolf's!
Gorbellied, bent out of shape, short and scant of breath –
A walking chronicle: the very image of the modern poet!
And beginning with a kind of high snore or nasal tic –
That shortly becomes a perishing whine –
                                        and with arms flailing
As if to punish the four wild winds of heaven he begins
To begin:
        "In the beginning the High & Mosthigh
            WhatsHisName said: *Fiat
            Lux* or: *Let there be Lox!*
        And there was Lox – but considerably later.

And after a week in which He couldn't
            tell *lox* from *lux,* a week of
            blundering-about creating whatever
            came into His Head the Mosthigh
            took off in his Fiat.

It was then that THE MCGRATH
       took Creation in hand.

On the Eighth Day the true creation
       began.

And THE MCGRATH, because SHE
       was a KIND WOMAN,
       created Gin, Ham & Japery to
       be the three aids to the muse.

It was the Time-clock and the check-in of the First Hour.

And then THE MCGRATH (*She*)
       created the MAGH RUATH
       from whom all subsequent
       McGraths derive certain divinatory
       powers in regard to the Social
       Revolution. And an almost fatal
       skill at catching snipe in a plain
       brown wrapper.

And THE MCGRATH *was* the
       MAGH RUATH (though some
       say he is THE MCWRATH or
       THE MAD RUDE or Druid).

And that was all the doin's of the Second Hour of the Eighth Day.

In the First Hour of the Ninth Day
      (in a bout of absentmindedness)
      THE MAGH RUATH
      impregnated all the lakes of
      Killarney (and certain
      waters of the Kerry Coast
      and of the odd island or two
      somewhere beyond Thither
      Galway and the Bantry Bay)

Begetting thereby all the caroling mackerel of the salmon-colored sea!

He knocked up all the mountains of
      Knocknarea and Connemara; be-
      getting a shower of stones.

Some of which became the seven
      classical planets: and the
      rest potatoes.

From which – later – the Buddha
      brewed the poteen that came
      to be called *soma*.

And it was the Morning Glory and the Evening Primrose of the First Hour.

In the hours after midnight he/she
      fulfilled the Doctrine of
      Plenitude, making all things

made that were made, and
      having nothing more to do took a break.

And HE left the beginning and the
      Close-to-the-end of the Begats to
      Leonel Rugama, who is
      to die in the Blue House, in
      Managua, Nicaragua, after starting
      the Recensions of the
      Revolutionary Names and beginning
      the Angelization of the Lost and
      the Damned and the Demons.

And this work is to be completed by
      the least of the McGraths among
      us, or by his son. *MILLE*
      FAILLTE AND UP THE
      REVOLUTION!

A canonical silence falls: which now he begins to adorn
With the fragrant names from *The Book of Che* by the dead poet –
Who has not yet even been born! – Rugama's Recensions:
      "Tupac-amaru…"
      "Tupac-yupanqui…"
      "Cuauhtemoc…"
      "Cuauhtemotzin…"
      "Tlacopan who begat Huascar."
[Who, our rememberer tells us, is simply the Indian name
Of our own Irish Oscar, our mythical minstrel man!]

And: "Oscar begat Geronimo"; And onward so that:
        "Crazy Horse begat Sitting Bull."

He breaks off a moment. Then says, "And the list goes to the Great One,
Ernesto Guevara, who will come among our survivors
At the prophetic hour: and under the name of CHE."

Again the silence. And out of the dark of another room
A snore from a foundered sleeper still cooking his Christmas goose.

"And after the Little Big Horn when they laid the gilt hair
Of Custer there on the Greasy Grass the Sioux went north.
Do ye recall?" (No need to. He's in full avalanche now.)
"And so on the high Canadian Plains it came to pass
That the blood of the Oglala Sioux entered the McGrath line!
Blanket brothers and kissing cousins to Indians North and South
Some of us are! And as I've foretold the least among us
Shall be our shaman and singer and our main remembrance man!"

And he points his naming finger at me.
                                The weight is so heavy –
This nostradeemedaimoniacal numen-denomin-ation.
I feel like a naked singularity; and, slap-on-the-instant,
Fall into a doze…
            or a daze…
                        or a drowse…
                                    the spell continues…
Names are shaken from the McWrath-bearing tree…
                                        Vladimir Illych

McLenin…
>William Z. Foster…
>>Elizabeth Gurley
Flynn…
>the Magon brothers…
>>Joe Hill…
>>>Pancho Villa…
Harriet Tubman…
>Denmark Vesey…
>>Henry Winston…
Big Bill Haywood…
>all…
>>Troublers of the bourgeois sleep…
And others more…
>the list continues…
>>Oghams of Ogma…

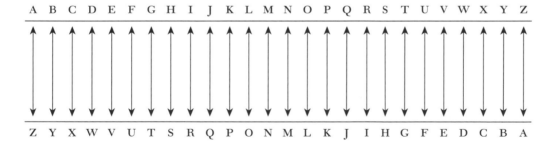

"Mean, unclean 'n' ob*scene!* Lewd, crude and lascivious!"
I am shaken out of my dreaming trance by the rant of the Black
Irishman who stands at a window gazing into the dark.
But whether his comment concerns the recitor of our Unnatural History

Or some goings-on at the neighbor's across the way I will never
Know.
      The gathering is silent a while. And then it is over.

    ❇   ❇   ❇   ❇   ❇

So here we are at the end of a glacier of sperm, Tomasito!
Terminal moraine, detritus, soil that brings forth trees –
Ten zillion years away from home (wherever *that* was) –
Way past the bog-trotting Paddies, the potato ranchers and Tarriers,
Down the infinite reticulations of the landing net that god
Let down for the prophet in the days of his youth: ladder
Of egg and sperm…
        the double helix and gyre…
                      genetic lattice…
And our names still green on our family tree: the Quaking Aspen!

3.   Now we must wake the sleepers and prepare for the night journey.
    We climb the dusty grandfather stairs to the cold dark
    Rooms where the children lie in the luminous sleep of childhood.
    In the drift of light from below, their breaths rise up
    Like ghost smokes lifting from tiny spirit fires.
    Hands between thighs, heads on chests, legs bent back to buttocks,
    Each curled like the brand of the Lazy 8 or the sign of infinity
    They lie; each adream in the heaven of unfixed forms:

∞ ∞

We wrench them out of their sleep and sack them in animal skins,

And so we are ready for the journey home…
                                                    the sleds loaded
With human freight…
                        (and some of us, sound asleep since sundown,
Will never remember this Christmas…
                                    except through the Memory Man!)

Just as we start to leave my grandmother slips me a gift:
One of her famous pomegranate cakelets thin as the Host,
A poker-chip-shaped token called (for reasons unknown)
A Persephone.
                Drops it inside my mitt.
                                    Gives me a kiss.

We go.
        Again the harness bells ring…
                                and the runners skreek
On the packed-down snow of the village streets.
                                    In the after midnight,
In the growing dark, gravity, like a disease,
Has entered again those weathered houses that, since the dusk,
Have floated like clapboard clouds over the sailing town.
They are dragging their anchors now and the slow tolling bells –
The last! – having gathered the darkness into their iron throats –
Are nailing them into the earth again…
                                three silver spikes

At each house-corner

                    peg them into the prairie…

                                    tethered…

But it is Time, Time beginning again that kills
The holy frivolity that lifted them into the metallic night.
Time: "the invention that keeps everything from happening at once"
Is returning us to ourselves…

                        – but not quite yet!

                                NO!

Tonight – still! – only the changing moon is constant;
And moonlight, cloud, stars, snow – all exist at once.
For tonight the wind has spirit – not like the summer winds,
Soulless and whiny: "degraded" winds wandering from hell.
This wind belongs to the Indians – everyone knows *that* in winter…

And so through the sleeping town we go – ourselves already
Drifting toward sleep…

                    The sled stops.

                                Someone joins us.

It is Cal coming for Christmas: his girl gone home to the Sand Hills.

Dreaming…

            we go from Amoymon to Cham to Cham from Amoymon
Toward Sitrael, Palanthon, Falaur, Sitrami – the infernal
Kings of the North…

                  dreaming…

                        dreaming…

                              dreaming…

4.   Dreaming…

                waking…

                        I hear a distant animal voice –

Either a farmhouse dog or a night-beast deep in the woods…

(For we're crossing the river again,

                              south of the coulee…

                                        near home;

The treetops whisper above me over my nest of sleep).

Something inside my mitten…

                        in the hollow of my left hand –

The little cake my grandmother gave me…

                              the little "Persephone"…

Crumbling…

        Take ye and eat…

                        The morsel dissolves on my tongue…

Again I drift away…

                in the murmur of my father's talk…

                            dreaming…

I rise from my sled-box bed in my night-clothes of animal skins,

I climb on the shivering ladder of Quaking Aspen boughs,

And, tiptoe on the topmost branch with the world spread out below

Far-off and tiny as a miniature map (and myself smaller

Than the angel at the top of our Christmas tree) –

                    I leap

                        into heaven…

❀   ❀   ❀   ❀   ❀

And my first leap is a fall…

                long fall…

                         into

The moonrock of the First Heaven.

                     Deep diving

                             swimming

Deep into the terminal stone deep into the mother rock.

Dark, here…

            only a silt of light…

                     and a dull

Haze…

      red…

            tincture of zodiacal fire

From the dark interior sun

               glows…

                   But now I see

What I dreamed long past in my underground sleep:

                              the statues of heroes, leaning

Out of the maternal dark.

             Those heroes still to be born –

                       in fire

Outlined…

      in sleep…

           imagined…

              in struggle…

                  begun…

                     And again begun.

They wear halos like circlets of fireflies.

                    Tiny sparks

Wink in the rock…

                                radioactive matches: the nanosecond flare

Of universal fire where angels burn…

                                the angels

                                                falling

Out of

          into

                    a life

                                heavenly

                                        fireworks

                                                transformations

In the lunar underworld rock…

                                And I hear through the mineral lattice

A distant singing…

                                underground music

                                                a voice that could be

Mine – in *some* future – singing of my undreamed son:

Of the long nighthunt in the rock and passages toward the dark:

This song:

          They come in tiny boats…

          And the boats are of heavy stone:

                                basalt…

                                        slate…

                                                dark…

          And clumsy – like old watering troughs furry with moss

(And the horses that drank of that water are long long dead).

Down there –

Where the boats come in down the long roads through the limestone –
I searched for you everywhere, wading through the heavy light,
Scaly, where it seeps down through the slate…

loaded with darkness

Like the leaffall from stone trees in a heavy autumn of stone.

The leaves of those slate trees falling in that tired and heavy light
Are clouding my eyes now…

as I remember.

Down there

Where the soul boats drift: down: slow: in the dark
Mineralized water of the underworld rivers I called your name…

Topaz, jasper, sardonyx, carnelian, turquoise, aquamarine –
The hours of stone.

Granite, limestone, sandstone, marble –
The seasons.

Through that fatal weather, O Friend and Stranger –
You: reading the crystal of this page! – it was you I sought!

❄   ❄   ❄   ❄   ❄

Down there

I searched for others: to set them free: in the backwoods of granite,
In the underground of obsidian, among the anomalous layers
And blind intrusions (basalt dikes cutting conformable strata
Where the class struggle faltered) there I sought the hero…

Travertine of hidden springs…

> *terminal granite…*

> > *and the black*

Of the primal preterite: I passed through them like secret water –
Like a mineral wind through those stony heavens whose rain falls
As beads of turquoise, and thunder is a distant sigh of rock…

Nothing.

> *This rumor of class war from the upper world of the streets*
Where my comrades fought in the winter of money – that only.

> > *The Hero:*

You: Reader: whose fate was to free the Bound Woman for the vernal
Rising and revolution on the promised springtime earth –

> > *nowhere.*

…Slum, souk, casbah, ghetto, the transform faults
Of industrial parks – I worked these stony limits.

> > *On the killing wall,*

Scored by the firing squads I chalked our rebel terms.
I drank the mephitic waters and made my bed in the dark.

It was then – in my need and blind search, in the nightrock, faltering,
As I slowly changed into stone my legs my tongue stony
Despair hardening my heavy heart – I came, then,
Into the dead center of that kingdom of death.

> > *Down there,*

It was then – in the blue light fixed in the stone chair frozen,
The chains of a diamond apathy threading the maze of my veins,

Lagered in the mineral corrals of ensorcelling sleep, my eyes
Locked to the bland face of the Queen of the Dead –
                                                            it was then

Then that you came, little Comrade, down the long highways of limestone!
Guiding your ship of light where the dark boats of the dead
Drop down like stone leaves: you came! Through the surf and storm
Of convulsing rock you home to my need: little Son, my sun!

❀   ❀   ❀   ❀   ❀

Basalt, granite, gabbro, metaphoric marble, contemporary ore –
Era and epoch up to the stony present, the rigid Past
Flows and reshuffles, torn by insurgent winds,
Shocked and reshaped as History changes its sullen face.

And the future groans and turns in its sleep and the past shifts as the New
Is born:
              Star of blood, with your flag of the underground moon –
That sickle of liberating light – you strike my chains and lead
Me from the throne of death and up the untraveled stairs

Toward the shine of the sun and other stars!
                                          Though one leg be stone
Forever I lag and limp behind you as long as blood
Shall beat in my veins and love shall move as it moves me now,
Chipping the flint of this page to blaze our passage home

Toward the world in the tide of Easter...

　　　　　　　　　　　　　　　rising

Into our life as I hear the cries that are resurrecting
There...

　　　　　　　So, we return. We are free in the rhymeless season.
You have struck my foot free from the stone.

　　　　　　　　　　　　　　Take my hand.

　　　　　　　　　　　　　　　　We must not look back.

❀　❀　❀　❀　❀

And I rise on the lift of the song into the Second Heaven...

And here all's flowering light and the light of flowers!
The rocks are coming into full bloom!

　　　　　　　　　　　　From secret chambers,

From the anteroom between stone and soil, from the microbes' workshop,
These transformations!

　　　　　　　And the deep strata are elevated

Into the light.

　　　　This is the forest primeval

　　　　　　　　　　　the murmuring

Lodgepole pine and the Douglas fir and the top-tassel-tipped
Hemlock.

　　　　And sequoia

　　　　　　　redwood

　　　　　　　　　archangelic

　　　　　　　　　　oak...

Iris bloom under apple tree!
                              And farther west,
Out on the prairie, the insect invents the blossom and the blossom
The insect...
                    the grasses are being brought forth
                                        invitation to horses!

Language begins (the language of flowers in the dance of the honeybee –
Mercurial sailor of the summer seas at home in all ports:
Sweet-talking Sinbad!)
                        and (as the insects reach critical mass)
Architecture...
                    tenement of ant and mosque of the hornet...

This is the first home we long for
                        our first loss
The magisterial prophets that are the deep Wilderness Roads
Of longing and separation
                            from the green secret...
                                        of woods
By leaf-colored waters of little rivers before first bird sang,
By nights cloudy with moths, mask-like eyes in their wings...

And here I would stay
                    but some voice
                        barks...
                                or howls...
And I'm pulled from my willowy wisdom though the fur of sleep or dream.

So, rising on the grief and joy of animal song

                                        I enter

The Third Heaven....

                        The air has thickened with the smell of blood…
All seems stalking hunger or satiety

                                here
In the Eden of the animals the first blood falls,

                                        the first kill
Smokes in the hush of the grass.

                        Life hunts itself

                                        eats
Itself.

        Hunger in the leopard is the lathe that turns the fine
Bones of the antelope, that tunes the speed of the deer.
But never so fast that all may escape, for the dialectic
Of hunt and capture must sharpen: oiled by the blood of the slain.

And Brother Bear and Sister Deer and Fathers and Mothers
Pacing the long grass – Principalities all!
And the lower angelic order of the birds that fly at their shoulders…
Sacred…

        sinless…

                and free…

                        of all but necessity…

                        ❋ ❋ ❋ ❋ ❋

Their garden is bounded by a fence of apes but I bound over.
And into the Fourth Heaven…

                              Smoky light
                                        Almost
A return to that long-past primal heaven:
                                        the rock
                                                  leans
Out of the dark…
                    – but into the smoke of the first tame fire:
And the cave-wall already thick with the soot of the ancient past!

In the torch-lit galleries animals leap from the living stone!
(Or are drawn out: by someone who is not sure he is man
Or animal.
            Or magician.
                        Or agent of unknown Powers…
The thing in the elkhorn mask and tail
                                        animal or man
Is become that Power who will make his place in the sacred sun.)

Beyond the cave in the light of the four colors of heaven,
In tented circles the tribes are gathered.
                                   The hoop of Peace
Unbroken
            in this heaven
                        where the People have come
                                              severally:

Some from out of the earth…

Some from the skies…

Some

(The Kiowa) entering the world through the gate of a hollow log.
Here the Principalities of Third Heaven are transfigured
Transformed from ancestral animals into God-Totems.

It is a heaven without paper…

without wills or deeds
Property licenses rent receipts bills taxes
A place where they don't write letters or fill out forms!

In this Happy Hunting Ground they have danced the buffalo back
They have prayed the Eagle home and the Salmon back from the sea –
These Powers of peoples together have given new life to the sun!
And this is the second home we long for: before the sound
Of clocks

before the smell

of oil

or of gunpowder…

❊   ❊   ❊   ❊   ❊

But a shot chimes out…

And I leap:

into the Fifth Heaven…

Smell of incense and chrism and a ringing of altar bells;

Smoke from a censer and extreme unction of priestly song…

I have entered the heaven of the Catholic Keep, built out of Latin

From the first stone that Peter cast. It rises high

Through the hierarchy of the heavenly hosts, guardians of planets:

Beginning with Angels, the lowest rank, the proletarians

Of *this* heaven, who keep the magic of the changing moon.

Then, rising rank by rank, in feathery pyramid:

The Archangels keep Mercury;

       the Principalities, Venus;

Powers, the Sun;

    the Virtues, Mars;

       Dominions, Jupiter;

Thrones, Saturn; Cherubim, the Fixed Stars and the Seraphim

The Primum Mobile: where every point on its rim

Races to be under the feet of The Most High…

And so keeps the whole mill turning, oiled by the Grace of God.

Above is the multifoliate rose that Dante saw…

Each petal the perfect face of one heavenly tenant

(And I see my *own* dead…

      there

        somewhere in the future…

The ones who believed –

     few…)

       Each face turned to the Light,

To the flower in the heart of the rose, the Father.

         Son…

          Holy

Ghost…
and the Mother…
somewhere
else….

The light seems
(At least in part) to rise from a scorching desert plain –
(Sand; wind; empty tents; and ragged birds
Beating their wings in vain over the hazy land)
And from Amchitka
(The jagged cold…
where the torches burn
Or the downed damned aircraft blaze)
and smoke from forges,
Ancient,
(their fleeting light)
rises where the clanging smithies of the Empire
Raze or reface the towers the Goddess raised.
And the hammers
Bang
and bang
where those swarte smekyd smethes smateryd wyth smoke –
Hephaestus's or Wayland's robots – transform once-holy powers
(Samael, Azazel, Azael, Mahazael – even the Kachina!)
Into Christian demons…
Here!
In the heaven of the Virtues…
Of Mars.
The sparks fly upward nightly from the dark Satanic mills:

In two shakes of a dead lamb's tail

             gone

                forever…

             ❀   ❀   ❀   ❀   ❀

But I fly up on the sparks and enter

             the Sixth Heaven…

Quiet: here…

      (except for the scratching of quill pens)

And white…

      the whiteness of unlined paper…

                The Elect sit

On Bob Cratchit stools entering debits and credits

In white ledgers…

       white ink on white paper…

               only

The Elect can read…

       white hands

         cold

           in the cold rooms

Warmed only by the ghost of Calvin…

         white collars

On their white necks and white cuffs at the wrists…

Canting, cold, ceremented, solemn, in Ku-Klux-Klan-white cerecloths
The choir drones like a bagpipe winching whines high,
Drowning the groan of Gregorian chants from down below.

Dominions, throned like pale Jupiters, the clerks perch
On their high stools, holy, and the wind from their whiffling quills
Gathers, combines, amplifies, and roars through all creation
Translating all the peoples into the saved or damned;
ALL workers into gainfully employed or the damned redundant;
  (And further into unionized or dis-or-unorganized
    And further into Left Wing unions or those of the Labor Fakers
      And thence into hourly wage, speedup, production statistics);
ALL the poor divided into worthy or soupline lowlifes;
ALL the "natives" into scalp-price Hostiles or reservation charges;
ALL animals into fur-bearing or goddamn varmints;
  (And thence into beaver hats and bounties on hawks and coyotes –
    Hummingbird tongues sold by the pound, Quetzal by length of feather);
ALL trees into usable lumber or miserable nuisances;
  (Unless they be "ornamentals" or used by the Hunt Club –
    And so the oak is a table and the murmuring pine is board feet
      And the Druids are lumberjacks and gone is the Golden Bough);
ALL metals into Precious or passed-over preterite;
  (Gold by the ounce, ore by the tone, slag heaps poisoning the waters –
    But the statue of the Possible Hero still sleeps in the rock!)!

Cash nexus!
   – And the end of all idyllic order!
Profit, loss, yield, price, markup, toll –
Value, expense, charge, disbursement, amortization…
Money and number, number and money, number, number…
And the Law:
   TO HIM WHO HATH IT SHALL BE GIVEN –
To him who HATH NOT: it SHALL be taken away.

These scribblers have misread the law
                                        have changed its meaning
To money and number and *so* have bled the whole world white:
Lilywhite
            snowwhite
                        Protestant white:
                                            ALL quality
Blown away in the wind of profit and loss…
And now there is only the wind of Number
                                            rising
                                                rising
From the quill pens to computers.

❅   ❅   ❅   ❅   ❅

                        And on that wind I rise
Into the Seventh Heaven…

                                                            And folks: it's Cloud Nine

Here!
        It's the only cloud in the sky and it's made of the best
Reefer smoke that money can't buy it's the viper's dream!
And the Righteous Bush grows all around them hills thar, Pardner!
And the little streams of alcohol come tricklin' down
Them rocks what ain't rocks a'tall but boulders of pure-D hash!
And the snow on the mountains, Cousin? Why, hit's the *coldest* snow
You'll ever snort and good for everthin' but doin' yer goddam slal*ams*!

Well, well,…a strange country here for a fact…
The Land of Cokayne…
                    Hedonsberg…
                              the Big Rock Candy Mountains…
The heaven of the Lost
                    the Passed-Over Ones
                              whom god created
In such astonishing numbers before he found the Elect.
But this is the revenge of the Flesh on the Spirit where Number can't count.
The wet dream where Whim and Quim are king and queen…
"The face of the precipice is black with lovers"
                              (saith the poet)
Oh yes.
        And the bushes are full of them.
                    And trees bend,
                              heavy,
Under the weight of all the fruit that was ever forbidden.

Cunt-lighted heavens, starless, and the hills flesh-ivory…
Vaginal light
          cock-light
                    the lakes tit-pink and purple,
The breezes harmonized by that Scent-Organ of Huysmans,
The houris of every color in the very shape of desire –
Hit's a man's world, Pardner!
                    And, if the passions fade,
There's sky-to-sky television of every game in the book:
Football to the right of them!
                    Football to the left of them!

And between: mixed

Sexual doubles and triples: swink and swive as thou wilt!
(And the winner: Little Orphan Threeway Annie – at home on all ranges.)

For the gluttonous sloths, those thrones of Appetite: special provisions
Quarter-section apple pies and sequoia forests of halvah;
The animals are all animal-crackers and – as for all the birds –
They fly around fully cooked with carving knives in their beaks
Ready to serve you.
                          Will come at your call.
                                    Lightlith adun to man's muth…

A damned
            dull
                    place.
                            At the end: the death of the senses:
And sleep
            for these tired children…
                                    some long Saturnian sleep…
In the seed of the passion fruit under the convolvuli
Of hashish and hookah.
                            And who is it now shall keep
An unwavering eye on those horrible green birds?
(So asketh the Poet: Mr. William Butler Yeats.)

Not I, cries the magpie and I fly up
                            up

❊   ❊   ❊   ❊   ❊

And into the Eighth Heaven…

                    Cloudy here…
                              cloudy
As rock forms bulging out in a shadowy cave,
But bright like marble clouds…and shifting like clouds…
                                  almost
I can make out the forms of marmoreal heroes of the First Heaven –
In these stone skies
              sublimed…
                   And then gone.
                       And the light
Cloudy as trees in the distance…
                       or the morning fog in Lisbon…
Or the winter for over North Dakota, but warm, warm.
This is the heaven of unfixed forms, of pure potential –
The forms as of clouds: shape-shifting.
                        But now I think I can see
The Elk-Headed man in the climax forest where animal shapes
Fluent as smoke, race by in the ceremonial hunt:
The long night-running.
              The clouds shift.
                    And above them – stars!

And now I see at last what I'm seeing: a proscenium curtain
From an oldtime smalltown theater or boondock opera house!
It's covered with ads: *Dr. Payne: Dentist,* says one,
And, on the other corner, *Painless Parker: Extractions.*
& filling stations with gas: selling for ten cents a gallon;

& feed-and-seed stores, & dry-goods & ladies' millinery shoppes,
& grocers & greengrocers cheek-by-jowl, Old Uncle Tom Cobley and all!
And finally at the center of the gallimaufry a magnificent old
Nickols and Shepherd engine – a steam-threshing tractor!
From which comes *real smoke* rising to form those clouds…
And the clouds rising almost-but-not-quite up
To those Fixed Stars – painted above the proscenium arch…
They shine serenely on – one of them turning blue…

At the corners of the curtain (as at the round earth's corners) the four blue-blowers,
Trumpeting cherubim, blare the news of the four elements –
(O Samael, Azazel, Azael, Mahazael! Angels at last!) –
And a Fifth Angel is blasting from up in the cheap seats –
From Nigger Heaven aloft where all the colors blend.
Here is another theater of pure potential where small boys –
Their friends and parents, aunts, uncles, cousins and second
Cousins (and cats and dogs and the pig in the parlor and *le bœuf sur le toit*)
Are preparing a shower of shit to salute the villainous villain!

OUT OF IMPERFECT CONFUSION TO ARGUE A PURER CHAOS!

The theater curtain is canted off to the left – or I am –
Taking the shape of a warped diamond.
                                        The West glows yellow
Where the first of the cherubim blows – and his name is Louie Armstrong!
Guardian angel of the first of the Hopi worlds – TOKPELA!
And the angel of the Second World in the blue south – TOKPA –
Is Sidney Bechet!
            KASKURZA, the Third World, lies

In the red east where Bix blows his magical horn!
And now, from the black north where our present battered sick
And sad old Fourth World – TUWAQACHI – reels and rolls,
The angel – Bach or Jelly Roll Morton! – is playing a bottom blues…

On the curtain, the central engine purrs and groans; the smoke
Rises…
      And a city grows from the smoke: white buildings,
Spires of light, battlemented turrets and topless towers
Glow incandescent, aspiring, powered by interior suns…
Then…
     a little puff…
         a small cloud
            blooms
Over the city…
      neck like a young girl's…
            but grows –
Grows: like Fate, an enormous cock, or a woman's head…
And in her coiffeur the nine-million swans of Bohr and Einstein
Are mating in thunder and lightning…
         the City flashes…
            explodes…
Like a bundle of kitchen matches dropped into an open stove,
Like a Mexican fiesta
     Nagasaki
       fireworks
         Hiroshima…
Black skeletons of bright buildings…
        ash in the wind

Like gray snow…

       a host burning…

             nations of smoke…

And a single face leans

        down

            from the hell-high cloud:

Hair

    burning

        genitals

           on fire

              steam

                spouting

From under the fingernails the brain bubbling out of the ears
The eyes like live coals the heart already a cinder…

But the wind shifts…

        the clouds reform…

                it hasn't happened

Yet

    The All-World Burn-out.

           Yet.

              In this heaven where all

Is potential: the clouds reform and the world goes on.

                I rise,

(Lightly, out of the smokestack of the old Nichols and Shepherd,
And out and over the curtain and above the Fixed Stars
[Painted in DayGlo] just over the high proscenium arch)

Lofted, fainting and parched, borne up by a thermal draft
Of ebullient plumed seraphim into the Ninth Heaven…

❊   ❊   ❊   ❊   ❊

Blind.
    This is the heaven I'm not allowed to see…
Heaven of Transformation…
        SAQUASOHUH…
               the Fifth
World.
    Blindfold.
       But beside me someone…
            my guide or guard
Steers my progress.
       I feel, under my feet, the long
Grass and the short grass as of old prairie…
The dizzying musk of a summer noon: the olfactory rasp
Of sunflower and sage and the satiny scent of the wild rose.
And I hear the insects now: threading the heavy air
With their brilliant needles of colored sound while the birds of the day –
Field sparrow, meadowlark, robin, and all their friends and neighbors –
Are filling the dome of noon with the honey and crystal of song…

And perhaps there's another singing I hear – but I'm drunk and fainting –
In this golden rain of sound and scent – (For I drink the air:
Nectar of middle summer in the High Plains…).
          My senses
Are being invented again!

I stumble.
                              The blindfold slips…

And I see…

              – but *what?*

                      Green and gold…

                              – The fields of a farm!
– Must have been laid out by Grant Wood and Joan Miró!
Dakota abstract…

                      and the combines sing as if they were free!
(Or as if they'd at least been paid for) and the fields lie free to the sun.

Away to the north I make out the shapes of a climax forest
From under whose skirts, green and green-gold, nine rivers run:
The Maple, the Yalu, Clark's Fork, the Red of the North, the Volga,
The Mississippi, the Amazon, the Congo and the Cheyenne –
And all of them flowing pure and clean! – Wood nymphs and water nymphs –
Sport on the flowery banks and the rainbowed fish on the bottom
Flail their fins in the white sand and whisp their tails on the gravel,
Or trouble the shallows to curds – running for food or fun!
– And all of the newborn rivers a'race to the mother Deep,
To the salmon-shadowed, herring-haunted, pristine, Whale-singing sea!

But that's not all the song I hear, either!
                              Aren't those…

Lathes…or birds?

                      A lathe made of singing birds or a bird
Transformed into a lathe without loss of freedom or song?

The spirits are alive in the natural world – in wood and water
In the grass underfoot, in the names and colors of winds and directions –
Are they entering again the arts and the artifacts of men?

No answer from my guard or guide who adjusts the blindfold.
(And the singing is louder – though I still can't make out the words!)
"Your son will see and be where you can not," he says.
"Remember four things: body; and soul; spirit;
And the dirt from handling our world under our fingernails.
Now: baby's gone.
                    Goodbye.
                              Just fly up through that smokehole there."

                    ❋   ❋   ❋   ❋   ❋

And I feel myself – lighter than air rising…
                                        rising
                                              smoke
And spirit (brushed by the wings of smoke, feathers of seraphim)
Through the smokehole of hogan or teepee or Primum Mobile
Into…

          these are the *other* stars!
                              – the fires and flags
Of constellations we have not yet seen…
                              – and the Blue Star –
SAQUASOHUH – blazes toward me.
                    In this light,

Supernal, of that Great Star, my Shadow, freed, races
Many sleeps and leagues and parsecs into the luminous Void!
And along that shadowtrack I see a flag – reversed –
Stars for bars! – all ass-over-teakettle! – flag of the Poor!

And now the dance begins in that still unearthly light:
(*Ævum* [L.] or "*Æveternity*" – according to St. Thomas:
"The environment of angels")
                                in the Empyrean.
                                        And the Angels dance,
And the Demons – O
                    Samael!
                            Azazel!
                                Azael!
                                    Mahazael!
Fire
    Water
            Earth
                Air
                    – and the Fifth Element! –
Dancing!
            – As they did in the Ninth Heaven!
                                    – With bird, beast,
Water and flower and the flowering earth of the Republic of Freedom!
And they *shake* hands…
                    take hands…
                                the Angels set free…
                                            – the Demons:
                                                angelized! –

In the cantrip circle…

                 dancing left…

                         widdershins –

                                   against the clock:

Countertime!

               And at center: the Blue Star Kachina,

The little goddess!

               And my guide from the Ninth Heaven!

                                      But now

He is blindfolded –

          and now,

                   as they begin to sing

That song I've been hearing so long without ever getting the words

I know I will know his voice and the whole sense of the song:

And

    I…

        (perhaps it is I…)

                 hear…

                         – AUM! AUM!!

(The three syllables: of creation…preservation…destruction…

Waking…dream…dreamless sleep…and the silence of fulfillment…)

AUM! AUM! AUM!

               And the echo: AUN! AUN!

(Meaning: yet…nevertheless…just the same…still…although…although…)

AUM! AUM! **AUM!** And the contradiction comes

As always and ever it must: AUN! *AUN!* **AUN!**

AUM! AUN! AUM! AUN! AUM! AUN!

5.   And I wake in the rocking sled with the old familiar stars
Reeling over my head in the cold Dakota night –
And the Northern Lights are stringing a harp toward the far pole…

AUM! AUM!
        It is not the song I heard in dream;
It is Doctor Dog, the Eternal Puppy, from up at the farm.

AUN! AUN!
        The answer comes from the neighbor dog,
From farther up-coulee: the O'Daly-Neruda ranchito.
– And from somewhere out to the west a rooster is praying for sunrise
Like a muezzin left in the rain so long that his voice is rusty.

The wind rings its changes in the smithies of the inner ear…
Somewhere, through miles of starlight, a train is breathing its last;
And near at hand a glass abacus of a sleet-shirted tree
Adds up the breeze…
        AUM!
          AUN!
            And the harness bells
Sing; and the trace-chains chime; and Cal and my father talk;
And the dogs howl.
        AUM! AUN!
          It is *like* the song
I heard in my dream…

almost…

           but I still can't make out words…

In my mitten the last of the cookie my grandmother gave me at parting,
The little Persephone, crumbles but I lick the crumbs from my hand.
I try to go back to my dream…

           we have crossed the river.

                  I doze…

Drift…

    sleep without dream…

        and then we are home in the silence.

While the men are putting the horses away my mother and I
Bundle the little ones off to their beds, then bring the presents
Out of their secret places and spread them under the tree.
No yule tree at all, but a stunted Oak: brought back
From a merry six-months-before-Christmas Sandhills Juneberry hunt!
It is gay in the holiday gauds the children have made or found:
Strange shapes of river-washed wood and small stream-rounded stones
Shellacked and gleaming; the colors of sun-worked bits of glass
From farmstead junkyards salvaged and magpied away for a year.
Cold among them, the eyes of a long-dissected doll
Peer our from fallen feathers – the swank of the springtime birds,
And through that fallen light the skeletons of tiny fish
Now shine, now shadow, as if hiding their unscaled bony shame!
Fish, flesh, fowl, animal, vegetable, mineral –
All the intricate systems simplified…

           In the grand

Design of death…

resolved…
      And yet those gleams and glows
Have a kind of life like life itself…
     and…
       pleasing…
         to children…

All that is most alive is what has not yet been born…
Says the little angel who stands at the top of the tree.
An angel homemade out of raffia, straw, and native grass,
He strides off in all directions as the drafts blow in the room
Wearing a hat like a Zapatista with a crown that is painted blue:
Kachina, guerrilla, revolutionary soldier, he swings his rifle of straw.

Too tired to count how many presents I got, I see
My Christmas stocking hung from a chair. I touch…and –
Hark! The hand I lost in the afternoon is there!
I seize the runaway and climb the stair to the grandfather dark.

The snow-snakes are wearing away the corners of the worn house
Like the sand-snakes of the arid summer but the stars are still secure
Or seem so
    through the window –
       and one may be turning blue!
A few feathers of snow fall…
      and, in the coulee,
Under the rocky ice the holy water moves
Slow and secret south to the river…
       and the bells of Lisbon

Sing the last song of the night…
And the bells of Lisbon
(Portugal) sing: and the wind blows away the cathedrals
As the trucks of the armed workers roar away to the north
Where the Communist peasants are separating land from landlords
And lords from the land.
Or so they dream…
while on Rua do Karma
A snow of leaflets drifts through revolutionary song…

And now, in my upstairs room at six-fifteen South Eleventh,
In Moorhead, Minnesota, the snow in my paperweight
(And in all this weight of paper) is sifting cold and slow
Over the miniature farmhouse under its dome of glass
And paper…
where the boy sleeps…
(there, or on Rua do Karma,
Older…
or elsewhere…
struggling…
among the ancient disorders
Of the unmade world).
And now, in his sleep, the boy hears –
And he in Portugal –
and I
through the slowly lightening window
Hear the final chorus of the song we have longed to hear:

Light falls slant on the long south slopes,
            On the pheasant-covert willow, the hawk-nest dark and foxes' hollow
As the year grows old.
                  Who will escape the cold?

                  These will endure
The scour of snow and the breakneck ice
            Where the print-scar mousetracks blur in the evergreen light
And the night-hunting high birds whirl –
All engines of feather and fur:
                  These will endure.

                  But how shall our pride,
Manwoman'schild, in the bone-chilling black frost born,
            Where host or hide
Who is bound in his orbit between iron and gold
            Robbed of his starry fire with the cold
Sewed in his side –
                  How shall he abide?

                  Bear him his gift,
            To bless his work,
Who, farming the dark on the love-worn stony plot,
            The heaven-turning stormy rock of this sharecrop world
His only brother warms and harms;
            Who, without feathers or fur,
Faces the gunfire cold of the old warring
                              new
                        year –

Bless! Grant him gift and gear,
Against the night and riding of his need,
To seed the turning furrow of his light.

Explicit carmen.

– North Dakota–Portugal–Moorhead, Minnesota, 1984

CIRCLING BACK TO OURSELVES

"From here it is necessary to ship all bodies east." So McGrath, writing from Los Angeles in the fall of 1954, began his long poem about twentieth-century America. The line works like the poem it opens, containing layers of meanings. Most immediately, it is an epitaph for the American era of western expansion, as well as a recognition of the costs of that history. It is also a metaphor for our need to confront that history in order to initiate a new moment. The line holds a sharply ironic and sinister sense, echoing the fact of gold shipped east. It is as though to ship the bodies east – those casualties who had been used up and forgotten – is the first necessary act toward creating a consciousness for comprehending our past – and only then, potentially changing our future. The bodies are the evidences of America's darker and usually unrecognized history; those who paid for the fortunes of such people as Jay Gould, who from Wall Street, in attempting to corner the market on the nation's gold, almost single-handedly caused Black Friday of 1869. But there is more within this line the more we think about it. On the most fundamental and mythical level, it speaks to the connection between death and birth, the ancient biological cycle of the seasons, each day reborn out of the east. Sending the bodies east is not only a judgment against history, but also an act of revival through the cycles of nature, and by extension through history which holds the potential for rebirth from each of its decaying ages. The line is paradoxical as is so much of McGrath's poetry, centered in dialectics – returning

the bodies to the sources of history is more than a circular judgment, but a confrontation of our history required to free ourselves from the false myths of our past (false consciousness), and thereby allow new potentials in our future. Immediately with this opening line, the poem suggests the need for a rebirth, a necessary awakening of consciousness to invent a new history that will involve us as more than its objects, as more than bodies, but rather, as the poem later suggests, its authors. McGrath certainly intended the poem to accomplish this feat, since he thought of poetry as a vehicle for the creation of consciousness.

Letter, which speaks throughout of "circularity," 400 pages later suggests the possibility for such a rebirth through consciousness when it closes with a prayer and blessing for "Manwoman'schild." McGrath is thinking specifically of his own sleeping son as he writes in the predawn morning (while also remembering himself as child), but he means all children. The poem that begins with shipping bodies east toward the dawn (and the origins of history) ends with the coming of dawn at the close of the old year, the poet asking that the child be provided "gift and gear, / Against the night and riding of his need, / To seed the turning furrow of his light." It is Christmas, the season of gifts and renewal – and the poem itself might be regarded as one of those gifts. Certainly the word "gear" echoes the "Kachina, guerrilla, revolutionary soldier" mentioned three pages earlier, "the little angel who stands at the top of the tree." This angel-Kachina says to the then child poet: "All that is most alive is what has not yet been born…" (page 402), an expression of potential. In a metaphorical sense, this "Manwoman's-child" (all children) becomes the incarnation of what the Kachina symbolizes. In Hopi practice, though not invested with sacred power, a Kachina doll is a gift presented to a child, representing ancestral spirits; in political terms, ancestors are the "spirits" of history, the dead the poem has determined must be shipped east. The creation of the Kachina is the act of revealing and recapturing history (in a sense resurrecting the dead), allowing the past to become for us a gift, a helper, rather than a method of oppression. We can gain this ancestral help only through consciousness – or to use one of McGrath's metaphors, through awakening. The extended use in *Letter* of Hopi mythology° serves to help dismantle to bankrupt hierarchical mythology of Christianity and western class history while at the same time presenting a metaphor of a better future. His hope, then, for his sleeping son, for all children, for the sleeping world, is that we will awaken to and from history, into the potentials of a new world.

"Circularity," which forces us to confront the past and provides the potential of rebirth from it, is not only one of the central motifs of the poem, but as our example illustrates, also one of the poem's methods. The fact is, method and message merge in this work. This poem is not a flat linear narrative. The past, present, and future are shuffled among each other, until time itself becomes circular, just as the poet, remembering himself as a child climbing the stairs toward sleep, almost in the same instant speaks of his own sleeping son. Nor is circularity necessarily always the same thing – it can be useful or detrimental – or in a dialectical sense, both at once. It can simply recycle the same wrong consciousness, and so contribute to the enforcement of the status quo: "Circularity! That's half the curse of the times: / It is to stop the circulation of circulating / Libraries – that's the trouble" (page 48). Circularity is paradoxical in nature itself: "The stars are shifting in the permanent sky…" (page 74) – and also in politics: "Nightmare, nightmare, struggle, despair and dream…" (page 57). Out of this recurrent power of history, and its resulting despair, comes dream, in the poem meaning the power to imagine a different history, "The cantrip circle where wish is king of the woods" (page 94). A cantrip is a spell, a charm, an illusion, what McGrath labels "the second-order rebellion," rebellion of the first order, of course, being physical and actual, that is, the first circle where physical work and its struggles occur (cf. pages 18–19). The imagining of a different history applies to both the future and the past: the act of overturning and reinventing the consciousness of the past allows for fantasy to shape the future.

The idea of fantasy, in *Letter* always a social enterprise, as a necessary prerequisite to action, comes most directly through Caudwell and Freud (who influenced Caudwell), both sources with which McGrath was quite familiar. In Freud, fantasy is wish fulfillment of needs (most prominent in dreams), which the ego can make actual within the limitations of reality. In Caudwell, fantasy becomes

---

° McGrath's source for Hopi mythology was *The Book of the Hopi* by Frank Waters (cf. McGrath, Thomas. Interview with Reginald Gibbons and Terrence Des Pres. *TriQuarterly* 70 [Fall 1987]).

the organization of social emotions and desires, deriving from social needs, for the accomplishment within reality of actual benefits. McGrath sees the poem itself, the building of the Kachina, the cantrip circle, as methods for the creation of this social wish-dream. Near the poem's conclusion the poet speaks of "the cantrip circle…dancing left… widdershins – against the clock: Countertime! And at the center: the Blue Star Kachina" (page 399) – as if to reverse history with the power of fantasy and imagination. It is interesting to note that a counterclockwise circle, adjoined in tangent to a clockwise one, forms the symbol for infinity as it originated in India. It was later flattened into the Arabic sign that McGrath comically calls the "Lazy eight" and compares to children "adream in the heaven of unfixed forms" (page 370). In its origins the infinity symbol was also the sign of twin gods who were magicians and healers. Interestingly, in Hopi mythology twin deities were assigned seats at the opposing poles of the world axis to keep the planet rotating properly, from which they also sent out through the earth vibratory messages as beneficial guardians. According to Frank Waters, a counterclockwise swastika indicates the earth in Hopi mythology, balanced with a clockwise swastika that indicates the sun, another version of infinity as dialectical opposites. Regardless of whether McGrath consciously intended these connections, the poem does counterpose two directions of history, clockwise and counter-clockwise, in effect canceling time. It also connects infinity to dream and dream to magic, that is, imagination as socially engaged fantasy. This consciousness would ultimately leap beyond history (recall that the Kachina is in the center of the circle), and so the association

of dream with infinity is more than a curious coincidence but goes to our true connection with the universe, as McGrath asserts in a statement of his own function within the poem:

> And I am only a device of memory
> To call forth into this Present the flowering dead and
> the living
> To enter the labyrinth and blaze the trail for the
> enduring journey
> Toward the round dance and commune of light…
> to dive through the night of rock
> (In which the statues of heroes sleep) beyond history
> to Origin
> To build the Legend where all journeys are one
> where Identity
> Exists
> where speech becomes song
> *(page 136)*

Such a world is of the sort that children know, where everything that exists shares equally in existence – a world that is like the prepolitical and ahistorical time children naturally live in, with the difference that we would realize it as awakened adults. The poem refers to this world as the Fifth Season or the Fifth World, using as metaphor the Fifth World of Hopi mythology which, following the corrupt Fourth World of materialism, would be one of harmony initiated by the sign of the Blue Star Kachina, Saquasohuh. In some ways the use of Hopi mythology in the poem echoes, in other ways counters, Christian mythology. What is authentic in Western traditions, by this contrast, is relearned, the past reinvented. It is also consistent with the poem that the mythology of a subjugated people should usher in the next world. Hopi mythology has several other appealing benefits for the poem. It describes a culture that is not hierarchical, a social spirituality without the class structure reflected in the priest classes and dogma of Western religion. In this sense, its consciousness is essentially communal, a "spiritual" or social contrast to our individualistic capitalist world, which the poet equates to the materialist Fourth World described in Hopi mythology. Hopi culture also represents an older consciousness on the North American continent than the relatively contemporary dominant culture of capitalism, and unlike hierarchical and abstracted Christianity, it holds a direct mythical power of origins and ancestry.

The scope of this poem, then, goes far beyond being a critique of capitalism, not that such a critique should rationally require any apology unless we ignore the central character of the economic system. Even from the nation's inception the process President Eisenhower called "the military-industrial complex" was entrenched within the government's operations. Beginning with the Revolutionary War itself, the government was already funding the personal wealth of its military suppliers at the expense of its nation's interests, the most famous benefactor being Robert Morris. He became one of the richest men in the new nation by manipulating military supplies, even to the extent that his company withheld supplies in order to increase their cost to the government, while the troops themselves suffered or died of privation. Conveniently for Morris, he was chair of the government's Secret Committee which authorized military purchases. Previous to the war Colonel George Washington himself had already gained prime bottom land in excess of twenty thousand acres that was apparently intended as reward for the enlisted men of his First Virginia Regiment. The simple fact is that capitalism's oppression of

the working class is a manifestation of its rapacity for profits, a method which <u>necessarily</u> requires hierarchy. But capitalism is not the end – nor beginning – of the story of humankind. And if we go further into origins, as *Letter* does, we find that the fundamentals of nature, as the sciences of physics inform us, begin and end in the equality of all things:

> Maximum entropy
> End of circularity, everyone flat in the streets,
> Equal.
> That's when I saw for the first time
> Iron-jawed George, Jefferson with his flutes and farms
> And radical Madison – all of them deader than
>   mackerel.

> *(page 49)*

Entropy is literally the equal distribution of all energy and matter within any closed system. Through entropy or death, natural law insists upon the same ultimate event for everything, including apparently for the universe itself, and even more important, insists upon a universal oneness. In this law, whatever it may finally mean, we find our fundamental equality. In fact, the poem, in a Rabelaisian passage about World War II, makes death a cosmic event that the poet experiences:

> But no one comes down; only that corpse hung round
> My neck by the circling bomber – a stiff in the cloud-
>   high pastures
> Of the lacklight, strange, permanent, feckless,
>   enshrouding skies,
> Prowling:
> Fixed like the Hunter:
> Fixed like the Bear:
> In the cold house of the black starless North.

> *(page 104)*

The poem transforms this essentially negative law, the underlying equality to which all things are reduced, into positive "spiritual" or social equivalents that derive from the simple requirement that all life must struggle against it. A central motif is repeated throughout *Letter,* the idea, if not taken from Schiller himself, borrowed from Freud's quotation of Schiller: "hunger and love are what moves the world" (In *Civilization and Its Discontents,* from Schiller's *Die Weltweisen*).† McGrath repeats this idea in several versions throughout the poem, such as: "Love and hunger: all is done in these signs or never / Done. / Or done wrong" (page 204). From our fundamental equality, the fact of everyone governed by the same ultimate law, we can realize our same needs, our mutual dependence, our inherent communal oneness. This communal oneness is the expression of the negative equality of entropy or death converted into the positive, socially useful equality which, perhaps paradoxically, creates freedom; most immediately, freedom from class hierarchy and oppression, but also freedom to realize our essential nature within the universe. This essential nature is represented in the poem by the poet's experience of *satori.* Beyond reporting *satori* as a personal experience, itself interesting and allowing the poet to praise, McGrath uses the idea of it to show our interconnection and equality. Equality is certainly central to Buddhist enlightenment: an example is the comical story of an enlightened Buddhist who, propping his feet upon the lap of a statue of Buddha, is castigated by a passing monk for being irreverent. His response is simply the question: "Where is the world not holy that I might rest my feet?" It is class and hierarchy that contribute to our blindness of our true nature, our essential equality and larger connection to everything in the universe, a connection the poem argues is most clearly experienced as the infinity of *satori.* McGrath's *satori* experience is directly counterposed to the limiting rule of class history. Here again the poem's invocation of the dead appropriately reminds us of our mutual equality. The nature of the universe, its insistence upon underlying equality which on the one hand is expressed as the law of entropy and on the other hand as *satori,* places the seemly inviolable class history ultimately in violation of our own inherent relationship to the universe. McGrath's *satori* experience, its sense of the infinite, refers to our true nature in the universe: "the great open secret that we all know and forget / ...the wild, indifferent joy which is man's true estate" (page 123).

– *Dale Jacobson*

---

†More information on how our needs make us equal, aside from Marxist sources, might be found by consulting Mikhail Bakhtin. Aside from *Rabelais and His World,* I would also recommend *Problems of Dostoevsky's Poetics,* particularly chapter four. McGrath found the associations made by Terrence Des Pres of Bakhtin and his own work to be useful.

Thomas McGrath was born on a North Dakota farm in 1916. He attended the University of North Dakota, Louisiana State University, New College and was a Rhodes Scholar at Oxford University. He served in the Air Force in the Aleutian Islands during World War II, and was later blacklisted for his political convictions during the McCarthy era. He worked as a documentary film scriptwriter, and labor organizer, and taught at colleges and universities in Maine, California, New York, North Dakota, and Minnesota. He was founder and first editor of the poetry magazine *Crazy Horse* and was named to two Bush Foundation Fellowships, a Guggenheim Fellowship, a National Endowment for the Arts Senior Fellowship, and a Shelley Memorial Award.

His many books of poems include *Movie at the End of the World, Passages Toward the Dark, Echoes Inside the Labyrinth, Selected Poems 1938–1988,* and *Death Song.* He also wrote a novel and two children's books. His *Selected Poems 1938–1988* received the Lenore Marshall/*Nation* Prize and the Minnesota Book Award, and was nominated for the 1988 National Book Critics Circle Award in Poetry. Thomas McGrath died on September 20, 1990.

COLOPHON

This book is set in New Caledonia, designed for metal composition by the American William A. Dwiggins in 1939 after the Scotch faces of the nineteenth century. New Caledonia's inconspicuous style and narrow profile are suited to McGrath's wide-ranging voice and to the poem's very long lines. The interior page design is based on pentagonal geometery: five sides for the five worlds. The star dingbat is from the Adobe Woodtype Ornaments font. Set in the year of Hale-Bopp by Valerie Brewster, Scribe Typography. Printed on Glatfelter Author's (acid-free, 85% recycled, 10% post-consumer stock) at McNaughton & Gunn.